Androgynous Judaism

Masculine and Feminine in the Dual Torah

Androgynous Judaism

Masculine and Feminine in the Dual Torah

By

Jacob Neusner

Mercer University Press
Macon, Georgia

ISBN 0–86554–428–X

Androgynous Judaism
Masculine and Feminine in the Dual Torah

by Jacob Neusner

Copyright © 1993
Mercer University Press
Macon, Georgia

Printed in the United States of America.

The paper used in this publication meets the minimum requirements of American Standard for Information Sciences—Permanence of Paper for Printed Library materials, ANSI Z39.48–1984.

Library of Congress Cataloging-in-Publication Data

Neusner, Jacob, 1932–
    Androgynous Judaism : masculine and feminine in the dual Torah /
by Jacob Neusner.
    xiv + 202 pp. 6 x 9" (15 x 23 cm.)
    Includes bibliographical references and index.
    ISBN 0-86554-426-X
1. Sex in rabbinical literature. 2. Women in rabbinical literature. 3. Rabbinical literature—History and criticism. 4. Mishnah—Criticism, interpretation, etc. 5. Sex role—Religious aspects—Judaism. 6. Judaism—History—Talmudic period, 10–425.
I. Title.
BM496.9.S48N48   1993
222'.1083053—dc20   93–32291
                                                      CIP

Contents

Preface

This book shows that the Judaism of the dual Torah is a masculine formulation of an androgynous religious structure and system. Androgyneity is serial: now feminine, in the end of days, masculine. God wants holy Israel now to embody traits defined as feminine, woman to the nations' ravishing man, so that, in the world that is coming, Israel may find itself transformed into man—but man still with woman's virtues. Since the systemic statements themselves specify what they mean by feminine and masculine virtues, the present characterization accurately paraphrases the documents' own formulations of male and female virtue, and, consequently, any account of the feminine in the Judaism of the dual Torah in its formative age must represent this Judaism as profoundly androgynous in its fundamental structure and system.

But the androgyneity is particular to this Judaism and forms a distinctive expression of its systemic character; it would not be easily replicated in any other. Specifically, just as the account of creation in the written part of the Torah represents male and female in profound unity,[1] for its part, the oral part of the Torah also defines an androgynous Judaism. In that way, the androgyneity of the oral part of the Torah fulfills and completes the androgyneity of the Creation tale of the written part of the Torah by making the mythic both concrete and specific, extensive and dense, for the social order and the private, inner life as well. The unity of the Torah comes to expression in its portrayal of the profound complementarity and mutual dependency of the two sexes, each prior in its realm and exemplary in its virtue. The unity of the two parts of the Torah in a profound sense finds its corporal counterpart in the unity of

---

[1]See Phyllis Trible, "Depatriarchalizing in Biblical Interpretation," *Journal of the American Academy of Religion* 41 (1971): 30-48. I reviewed the theoretical literature of feminism, down to 1979, as pertinent to the study of the law of the Mishnah in my *A History of the Mishnaic Law of Women*, Vol. V., *The Mishnaic System of Women* (Leiden: E. J. Brill, 1980). I have found somewhat disheartening feminist writings on Judaism produced in the past decade or so, since, in the main, a certain predetermined program has impeded the analytical inquiry; I found writings such as Trible's more helpful in guiding me here. But that is not to ignore much good work as well, exemplified for the study of Judaism of the dual Torah by Meyer Gruber's *Motherhood of God. And Other Essays* South Florida Studies in the History of Judaism (Atlanta: Scholars Press, 1992).

man and woman. Not only so, but the androgyneity, formulated in serial terms for historical purposes as well, was made to stand, in the life of human relationships between the sexes, for the condition of Israel among the nations: feminine Israel, masculine nations—for now. That remarkable sense for the proportion, balance, and deep harmony of the feminine and the masculine, realized in the here and now of normative behavior and belief, action and attitude alike, accounts for the success of Judaism through the ages in governing that specific "Israel" that it aspired to define.

This is not to suggest for one minute that this androgynous Judaism spoke for Israel's women and men equally. That is not so. Androgynous Judaism was the formation of men; no women are recorded in the canonical writings as consequential authorities. The classical documents of the Judaism of the dual Torah, ca. 200–600 C.E. [=A.D.]—that is, the Judaism set forth by rabbinic literature and normative from antiquity to our own time—derive entirely from men. They moreover set forth a system that is for all practical purposes dominated by men. Part One of this book, with its account of the profoundly male bias of the *halakhah,* the normative law, validates that simple statement. But these are men who identify with the virtues they see in women, and who put forth a religious system that means to feminize Israel, endowing the enchanted nation with the virtues that the sages themselves classify as those of women.

So this Judaism's normative writings hold together in balanced proportion traits that are masculine in the system's own representation of the masculine along with those that are feminine as the system defines femininity. When the dual Torah introduces the latter, it highlights the participation of women in narratives meant to convey norms of sentiment, attitude, and emotion. Part Two makes that point. And—still more to the point—that Judaism assigns priority, at the systemic center, to values and virtues the canon itself classifies as feminine. Israel achieves its authentic relationship to God when Israel is feminine to God's masculine role; its proper virtue when it conforms to those traits of emotion and attitude that the system assigns to women. Part Three shows how this works.

Seen whole and in context, that Judaism has therefore to be classified as androgynous in a very simple sense: the Judaism of the dual Torah emerges as a masculine structure bearing a feminine system. No successful theory of the social order can ignore the distinctive perspective, concern, and aspiration, of one half of the society that is envisaged by such a theory, and no working structure and system can endure for long in which one or the other of the two sexes finds itself permanently submerged and treated as systemically marginal. This Judaism did not treat women in such a way, but, as we shall see, insisted that men adopt traits of attitude and emotion that the Judaism itself classified as feminine. And, I maintain, the best explanation for the remarkable success of the Judaism of the dual Torah derives from its effective androgyneity, that is, the system's demonstrated capacity over long centuries to persuade women to value the traits the system deems feminine and to require men to transform themselves into women by conforming to those same traits. Feminine Israel in the here and now, we shall see, makes itself worthy of the coming of the Messiah at the end of days, at which point Israel assumes its masculine identity (once again). It follows that Judaism is serially androgynous, and that defines the subtext of this book.

These observations concerning the androgyneity of the Judaism that became and now remains normative self-evidently contradict the prevailing characterization of "Judaism," ordinarily meaning, the Judaism of the dual Torah. For this Judaism ordinarily finds itself represented entirely as the formation of men, expressing their dominance and their values. Chapters One and Two leave no doubt that that representation corresponds to the practical rules of the law, or *halakhah*. And yet, other canonical documents portray as normative traits that those writings clearly classify as feminine. When, in Chapters Three and Four, however, we examine the documents' dogmas concerning theology, emotions, right attitude, intentionality, and sentiment—matters collectively assigned the name *aggadah*, or lore—we discover that at the systemic center are attitudes associated with women by the narratives and the exegesis of Scripture. The traits here called feminine are those associated by the writers of these compositions with women—and powerfully advocated as traits that must characterize all Israel.

Judaism therefore emerges—so Chapter Five maintains—as androgynous. The masculine comes to expression in one range of discourse, the feminine in another. When in legal texts "our sages of blessed memory" form legislation having to do with women, they treat women as abnormal, men as the norm; the legal system forms a wholly masculine statement on women. When in theological texts these same sages address issues of attitude, emotion, sentiment, imagination, and right intentionality, they portray virtues that they carefully and explicitly classify as feminine. And they assign the highest priority to these feminine virtues, asking Israel to see itself as a woman, God's bride, no less. Masculine and feminine, kept distinct as law and theology, respectively, indeed form a union. Then androgynous Judaism makes its systemic statement through the very fundamental message that it delivers on matters of gender and sex-role: the feminine heart in the masculine body of Judaism will be what defines the authentic character of eternal Israel.

The Judaism of the dual Torah correctly understood therefore is neither masculine nor feminine, but something else: (1) a perfect union of the two, (2) according to the masculine priority in setting the forms, the feminine has the status of the exemplary in determining the substance in all matters that count. Resting on the distinction between structure and system, that is the thesis of this book. Evidence and argument in behalf of this simple proposition, as is clear, unfolds in three main parts: first, in Part One, the demonstration of the masculine character of the structure, that is, the *halakhah;* second, in Part Two, the characterization by the documents of the Torah themselves—of the feminine quality of the working system; and, finally, in Part Three, the explanation of the remarkable success of this Judaism by appeal to its perfect union, in approved emotions and attitudes, of feminine traits in both public policy and private life.

When I refer to "masculine" or "feminine" traits, as is amply signaled in what has already been said, I mean traits that the writings themselves represent as feminine or as masculine. I do not mean traits that stereotypes, received from hither and yon, classify in such a way. When I maintain that the law views men as normal, women as abnormal, and legislates to embody that view in legal rules concerning women's status, it is because the Mishnah's laws time and again express that viewpoint, which I reasonably attribute to the masculine bias. When I allege that theological doctrines concerning the right relationship of Israel to God set forth feminine, as against masculine, traits, it is because *Song of Songs Rabbah* says exactly that. And when I classify as feminine the doctrine of approved emotions, the general theory of virtue, that the Judaism of the dual Torah sets forth from beginning to end, it is because the feminine, defined in *Song of Songs Rabbah,* dictates that classification and no other. Hence the classification-scheme that sustains my characterization of this Judaism as fundamentally androgynous derives from the rules of taxonomy set forth within the canon of the system itself.

If this book bears broader implications for the study of religion, these may be set forth in a single sentence. Characterizing religions as masculine or feminine may well delude, since so far as religions address the social order of the community that embodies them, they encompass both sexes, and they also must do so in a manner acceptable, plausible, or at least, tolerable, to each. There is no Israel made up only of men, and however deeply masculine the systemic bias demonstrably was—the exclusion of women from the liturgical life has only come to an end in our own time—the system of the dual Torah also proposed to turn men into women, defining women's virtues as the system itself did. That must suggest the notion of classifying a religion as masculine or as feminine, or God as masculine or as feminine, has to compete with an entirely different notion. It is that so far as a religious system addresses the social order and proposes to define it, that system must make a statement in balance between the sexes, making provision for the traits and aspirations of each. Other solutions besides that of the serial androgyneity adopted by our sages of blessed memory may suggest themselves, but, in context, this one proved durable and tough.

So to address my own day: if feminist Judaisms emerge, excluding men, they will not serve and cannot stand, any more than have rigidly masculine Judaisms in times past and in our own day proved plausible. God made Adam "in our image, after our likeness," and that is, in the Torah's own words, "Male and female." Our sages of blessed memory set forth an androgynous Torah because they fully grasped the androgynous character, in attitude, emotion, feeling, and aspiration, of God made manifest in the Torah. But how that is to play itself out, if in another than serial setting, remains to be discovered. It goes without saying that androgynous Judaism in no way lays claim to an egalitarian position on gender-relationships. That is because it does not regard the sexes as essentially the same; it recognizes differences, values and honors them, and undertakes to reenforce them. But at the same time, the androgyneity I claim to have discovered in the canonical writings insists that to be truly Israel, men must turn themselves into women, accepting their subordinate position, entering into their dependent situation. This they must do to realize in this world the virtues that God values, that same

God that is both man and woman by the criteria of our sages of blessed memory themselves, by the definition of the Torah of Sinai.

That strikes me as a judgment on gender that transcends the egalitarian. Accordingly, I mean here to challenge the competing, and, I think, wrong, readings of the Judaism of the dual Torah and to call into question the premise that any viable religious system can express one sex's aspirations to the exclusion or the subordination of the other sex and its aspirations. If here, in that Judaism that so much feminist literature despises, I can show profound, structural, normative androgyneity, then some may wish to reconsider not only the (mis)characterization of this Judaism, but the very notion of a gender-bias in a religious system of any standing and consequence.

But of special interest to me—all I care about, really—is Judaic feminism. We today celebrate the advent of women to the rabbinate and to scholarship on Judaism. Reform, Conservative, and Reconstructionist seminaries are fully egalitarian, and British Orthodoxy only just now has made provision for women's minyanim [quorums required for worship]. In the State of Israel, moreover, the institutions of the Judaism of the dual Torah, which predominate, encompass yeshivot [talmudic schools] for women. So every sector of Judaism, each within its premises and possibilities, has responded to the opportunities of the age. When women were first admitted to Hebrew Union College-Jewish Institute of Religion, in the earliest 1970s, I participated actively in recruiting women for that rabbinate. The second woman to go to that rabbinical school was a student of mine, and, over the next decade, I sent one or more women to that school as well. When the Conservative rabbinical school followed suit, I of course did what I could to recruit women for it.

Having good credentials—indeed, having been credited with the founding, in my *History of the Mishnaic Law of Women*, of women's studies in Judaism, an honor I do not claim in my own behalf—I have the right to participate in yet another way. While women have taken their rightful place in the rabbinate of some of the American Judaisms, as much as in the classical institutions of other of those Judaisms, they have yet to make a mark for themselves in scholarship on Judaism. And that is their fault. While numerous women hold professorships in the peripheral aspects of Jewish studies (the ethnic, the historical, the sociological, for example), very few women have accepted the more rigorous, but more consequential, disciplines of the classical disciplines of Judaic studies: study of the canonical literature and its history. Apart from one important scholar, Judith Hauptmann, I cannot point to a single contribution by a woman in the form of a book on any of the classical studies of Judaism, not on the Midrash- or Talmudic literature, not on the theology, not on the *halakhah*, not on any of the normative subjects of the Torah. When I went in search of women to participate in projects I was organizing (e.g., in the translation of rabbinic classics, dictionaries, encyclopaedias, and the like) or to contribute second or third books to monograph series under my editorship, I found only one weighty candidate, a seasoned, accomplished scholar of the Talmud, Professor Hauptmann.

True, we may point to some dissertations of promise, which I have been quick to nurture or to publish in series under my editorship. But with the single named exception, there is not a single important woman-scholar in any aspect of the study of Judaism in its normative statement, in the dual Torah. Until there is, women cannot claim to have taken their rightful place in the center of the life of the Torah. The promise of Jewish feminism has yet to be kept. If the trivialities and banalities, the light-weight and the ephemeral, the strident and the special pleading, the "Jewish woman" anthologies and the "Jewish woman" thematic compilations, which today masquerade as "Jewish scholarship," turn out to represent the whole of the feminist contribution to scholarship on Judaism, on the one side, and to study of the Torah, on the other, then the entire movement will have condemned itself to inconsequence.

No work of mine can omit reference to the exceptionally favorable circumstances in which I conduct my research. I wrote this book as part of my labor of research scholarship, expressed through both publication and teaching at the University of South Florida, which has afforded me an ideal situation in which to conduct a scholarly life. I express my thanks for not only the advantage of a Distinguished Research Professorship, which must be the best job in the world for a scholar, but also of a substantial research expense fund, ample research time, and some stimulating and cordial colleagues. In the prior chapters of my career, I never knew a university that prized professors' scholarship and publication and treated with respect those professors who actively and methodically pursue research.

I was fortunate to be able to consult Professor Judith Ochshorn, Department of Women's Studies at University of South Florida, whose important criticism of my original thinking pointed me in the direction that this book takes. She was the one who insisted I avoid stereotyping the masculine and the feminine, by proving that the documents themselves, and not a classification-scheme I bring to the documents, define matters in the terms and categories at hand. That fundamental point, which I owe to her, accounts for the entire theory set forth here. I am fortunate to work at a university that pursues Women's Studies in an intellectually rigorous manner.

But that only underscores the advantages of my present situation over any I ever have known. The University of South Florida, among all ten universities that comprise the Florida State University System as a whole, exemplify the high standards of professionalism that prevail in publicly-sponsored higher education in the USA and provide the model that privately-sponsored universities would do well to emulate. Here there are rules, achievement counts, and presidents, provosts, and deans honor and respect the university's principal mission: scholarship, scholarship alone —both in the classroom and in publication. Here at last I find integrity governing in the lives of people true to their vocation and their mission.

It always gives me special pleasure to present my ideas in the vessel designed for them by my wife. The tapestry on the cover responds, out of the matrix of our lives together, to a photograph of her late father's mother and father, who lived in Ostrolenka, Poland, and perished together somewhere in Poland during the German occupation, probably in 1942 or 1943. I visited the town and found apartment houses built over the old cemetery of the Jewish community. So this will have to be their families' —my children's ancestors'—*masevah* [memorial]. When, in 1938, my late father-in-law went to Ostrolenka from Paterson, NJ, with the means of bringing them home to the USA and safety, they chose to remain where they were, in the conviction that only in Poland could one live the Godly life of Judaism. But it was not to be.

Jacob Neusner
Distinguished Research Professor of Religious Studies
University of South Florida,Tampa

Introduction

The Feminine and the Masculine by This Torah's Own Word

In medium and message, the Judaism of the dual Torah is androgynous. First comes the medium. The Judaism of the dual Torah sets forth its propositions in two distinct media. Each bears distinctive traits that the documents of the Torah themselves classify as masculine and feminine, respectively. These distinct media of discourse are called by the Hebrew names *halakhah*, meaning normative law, and *aggadah*, conveniently translated as lore, but more broadly covering theological matters of conviction, belief, attitude, sentiment, and correct emotion. Law or *halakhah* sets forth normative rules of conduct and conviction, dictating the governing laws of practical affairs. Lore or *aggadah* forms the realm of the evocative and the empathetic. Through narrative, exegesis, and sagacious sayings and observations the *aggadah* comes to expression, and through *aggadah* the system sets forth its propositions that concern right relationship and right attitude beyond the measure of the law: its general theory of who and what is Israel and how Israel is to know and love God. It will quickly become clear that the *halakhah* is wholly the realm of the masculine, form and substance alike, with masculine defined very simply: male dominance.

Our survey of important documents of *aggadah*, narratives in one of the Talmuds, exegesis of scripture in a compilation of such exegeses, will show us that, where the system exposes its feminine side, it does so in *aggadah* and not in *halakhah*. The *aggadah* portrays the feminine, with the feminine defined equally simply: traits associated with women or classified as feminine in the writings themselves. The challenge of the theology of this Judaism, from one age to the next, always asks, how the *halakhah* and the *aggadah* on any given dimension of human existence coincide to make a single statement, and in Chapter Five we shall consider one such proposal to meet that challenge.

The entire message of this Judaism requires both media to make a single statement. For, as already suggested in the Preface, no religious system can long endure without a balanced, consensual statement that both sexes affirm and advance. But though the system set forth in the canonical writings makes its one statement through both media, commonly saying the same thing through each, it utilizes each medium for the delivery of its own distinctive message. The *halakhic* medium makes the masculine statement, the *aggadic,* the feminine one.[1] Only in the union of the two does the systemic statement emerge whole, complete, and final.

The entirety of the statement of the Judaism of the dual Torah then comes to expression in the uniform voice of the two parts of the Torah speaking in unison. As, in the Ten Commandments, "Remember the Sabbath day to keep it holy" and "Keep the Sabbath day" came forth in a single voice, so in the dual Torah, we hear only harmony in the duet of the sexes, formulated in the dual message at hand. But, as we shall see, when we reach the systemic center, the point at which we are told what matters most of all, the feminine takes priority in every way that counts. The soprano outshines the baritone. And that explains why the *aggadah*'s portion of the dual Torah's statement takes priority. Women now figure where they formerly were excluded. Virtues defined as feminine and associated with women set the norm for all Israel, and Israel itself attains its authentic definition when it adopts feminine attitudes, emotions, and relationships. Women are never asked to turn themselves into men, but men are asked to adopt virtues explicitly characterized as feminine. That point is critical: not our stereotyped definitions of the

---

[1]When the *aggadic* and *halakhic* dimensions of this Judaism part company, as they have in our own times, the message becomes distorted and the two sexes lose sight of the iron rule of interdependence and fundamental complementarity, balance, proportion, and parity. I leave it for experts in modern and contemporary classical Judaic *halakhah* and *aggadah* to identify the points of separation in what was, in the documents portrayed here, a balanced and proportionate relationship between the sexes as equals, with women deciding what counted in the long run and made most difference to God. And, we remind ourselves, not a line in the documents at hand can be read without knowledge of what it means for the writers to maintain that they record the Torah revealed by God to Israel through Moses at Sinai.

masculine and feminine categories, but the documents' own definitions of virtues they deem distinctively masculine, as against those they define as particularly feminine, govern. Stereotypes they are—but theirs, not ours! And that fact validates the entire analysis of the androgynous character of their Judaic system.

What requires emphasis at the very outset is how we know the classification of attitudes or rules as masculine or as feminine to begin with. The answer, already tacit, is simple: the system itself tells us. We do not merely adopt existing stereotypes that circulate in general in treating as feminine virtues the traits of humility and forbearance, passivity and conciliation, self-abnegation and self-denial, accommodation rather than rebellion. The documents we shall examine explicitly classify such virtues as feminine. Israel when it is authentic, the way God wants it to be, is represented as feminine, therefore accepting and enduring. Israel is to place its entire trust in God, the way the document's good wife trusts in total dependence upon her husband. Eternal Israel's vocation in the here and now is to relate to God as wife to husband. Israelite men must cultivate the sentiments and emotions of women, learn from women how properly to feel and respond. They at the same time define the social order and govern. So the division of attitudes into feminine and masculine classifications depends not on a taxonomy external to the sources—how things allegedly are in general or how they are imagined to be!—but solely on the sources' own characterization of matters. And, it goes without saying, how things really were in the social world of the Jews' everyday life we simply do not know.

It follows that the Judaism of the dual Torah exhibits a profoundly, wholly androgynous character. The *halakhah* or law, in these pages represented by the Mishnah, sets forth masculine perspectives. Part One proves that fact beyond any doubt. The *aggadah* or lore—represented by narrative and exegetical passages of the Talmud of the Land of Israel and *Song of Songs Rabbah*—conveys feminine values. That is the picture that emerges in Part Two. But the feminine proves the definitive, since it is attitudes and relationships portrayed here as feminine that characterize the right way of thinking and acting; the highest aspiration of the system, the formation of *zekhut*—what I call "responsive grace"—finds fulfillment in feminine self-sacrifice, not masculine aggression. This takes priority over

study of the Torah, a male monopoly.[2] So we deal with the union of the
male and the female, with the masculine defining the form and structure,
the feminine, the substance and working of the system. The union of the
two—the masculine, the feminine, as classified in the writings themselves
—then comes about in a simple way. The law defines the structure, the
lore, the system. The one describes how things are, the other, how they
are meant to function; the one sets forth the structure, standing firm, the
other, the system, enduring through time and change.

The upshot for the interpretation of gender roles, as portrayed in the
classical writings themselves, is not to be missed. While the Judaism of
the dual Torah has, with sound reason, been classified as a patriarchal
religious system, that proves only a partial truth. In fact, before us is a
religious system, assuredly the work of men, that holds in the balance
and assigns critical roles to both masculine and feminine traits, but that,
in the center and heart of matters, affirms the feminine as determinative.
That is to say, without *halakhah* and *aggadah,* law and lore, the masculine and the feminine, in union and in balance and in proportion, there
is no Judaism so far as the canon of the dual Torah is concerned. But, as
between the two, *aggadah* instructs concerning the ultimate matters of
importance, the systemic center, the points of ultimate determinacy—and
remission. *Aggadah* speaks of systemic reversals, where the priorities of
the halakhah are ignored, and other priorities privileged. That is to say,
the *aggadah* speaks of what the law cannot coerce but most highly

---

[2]It is worth observing that metaphors for "Israel" in the Mishnah emphasize the
hierarchically classified community formed of priests, Levites, and Israelites, women
enjoying caste status only through that of their father's or husbands. But the metaphors
for that same "Israel" in the Talmud of the Land of Israel and the associated Midrash-
compilations, *Genesis Rabbah* and *Leviticus Rabbah*, invoke the definitions deriving from
genealogy and coming to expression in the family. "Israel" is now represented as the
extended family of Abraham and Sarah, Isaac and Rebecca, Jacob and Leah and Rachel.
The reason I do not devote a chapter to spelling out that observation is that I have not
observed in the canonical writings any indication that the "kingdom of priests and the
holy people," that is, the hierarchical caste system of the Mishnah's transitive Israel, is
classified as distinctively masculine, or that the genealogical metaphor involves feminine
traits or virtues. Others may pursue that matter, but so far as I can now tell, the criterion
I have set forth here, classification as to gender by the documents themselves, would not
be met in such a taxonomy. I have spelled out the succession of metaphors in my
Judaism and its Social Metaphors. Israel in the History of Jewish Thought. (New York:
Cambridge University Press, 1988).

Mishnah

values. And the priority accorded to *aggadah* comes to expression in a simple fact: the Torah and Israel in *aggadah* are represented as feminine, and the system's highest priorities for attitudes, emotions, and actions of ultimate grace are accorded to what the system itself portrays as feminine, and not masculine, or feminine as well as masculine. Let me now review the main arguments of the book and explain how the evidence sustains those arguments.

Part One: The Masculine. If we wish to know how the *halakhah* defines the masculine and the feminine, we start with the Mishnah, a philosophical law code of ca. 200 C.E., and that is for two compelling reasons. The most important is that the Mishnah is explicit on the subject. For women define one of the Mishnah's six formative and generative categories, taking a fundamental and important position in the entire systemic structure. In fact, as I shall explain, the Mishnah's system-builders found it necessary to introduce in a prominent position the subject of women because it was solely through that subject, as through the other five constitutive topics of their document, that they found it possible to make a principal part of the systemic statement that they proposed to set forth.

Second, the Mishnah is the right starting point not only because of the prominence accorded to women, but also for a quite formal reason. It is the Mishnah's own priority in the Judaic legal system: beyond the scriptural law codes, the first and most important code; and paramount over the scriptural law codes, absorbing into its topical structure and system whatever of scripture's law the system as a whole would make its own. We therein select the normative and official statement of formative Judaism. For the entire legal system of the Judaism of the dual Torah rests upon the Mishnah, on the one side, and scripture, on the other.

But as between the two documents, the Mishnah is the more important. Since the Mishnah defines the categorical structure of the law, all future legal development would take the form of amplification and exegesis of the Mishnah's laws as set forth within the Mishnah's principles of legal organization. The Mishnah's laws of course would be brought into relationship, and shown to cohere, with those of scripture; but the law, as distinct from laws, would emerge out of the Mishnah's program. Two further facts validate selecting the Mishnah as the author-itative representation of the system's legal structure. First, important components of the Mishnah's legal system take up topics to which scripture is indifferent. Second, the Mishnah dictated the selection of the passages of scripture that would come to the fore and assigned secondary status to other passages of scripture. The law of this Judaism, set forth in the Mishnah, a philosophical law code of ca. 200 C.E., is masculine, reflecting a male perspective, treating women as abnormal, men as normal. The account of the social order, carefully classified by castes, set forth in the Mishnah, sets forth a hierarchy in which men take priority. It follows that the principal structures of this Judaism, set forth in law, express a theory of male dominance.

Part Two: The Feminine. But in the exegetical literature of the dual Torah, the Talmuds for the Mishnah (ca. 400 and 600 C.E. for the Land of Israel and Babylonia, respectively) and the definitive reading of a vividly controversial work of scripture in which gender figures prominently, the Song of Songs, set forth in the Midrash *Song of Songs Rabbah* (of approximately the same period as the Talmud of Babylonia), take a different view. Carrying forward the exegesis of the Mishnah in its own terms, the Talmuds at the same time define a value-system that imposes a system of feminine virtues on the masculine structure of the law. This is in three ways.

First, while the Mishnah and the Talmuds concur that the single paramount act is study of the Torah, at the same time the Talmuds recognize another virtue that exceeds study of the Torah in its power.

Second, while the law identifies attitude and intentionality as critical criteria of differentiation, the Mishnah and the Talmuds alike define as the most cherished attitudes, the most to be emulated emotions, those ordinarily assigned the status of feminine.

And, third, in reading the Song of Songs, the sages know the two this-worldly foci of the holy—Israel and the Torah—as feminine in relationship to the supernatural and all-powerful God.

Part Three: Androgyne Judaism. If Israel hopes to see the Messiah, Israel will have to assume traits and virtues explicitly classified as feminine. The very same attitudes and actions—those of resignation, reconciliation, renunciation—that evoke Heaven's response in the form of *zekhut,* a matter explained at great length in Part Two, are the ones that in virtue and other emotions Israel must evince to win God's reconciliation and forgiveness. So the right relationship between Israel and God is the relationship of woman to man, wife to husband as portrayed in the *halakhah*. And that, as a matter of acknowledged, social-historical fact, also describes the relationship of Israel to the nations even now. That is why Israel must transform itself into a feminine nation, at least for now. The *aggadah*'s framing of matters therefore coincides with the experience of the world that Israel every day encounters. What Israel must do, then, is renounce, resign, reconcile, give up, make do—and be glad for the attitude of self-abnegation. This feminine Israel, making virtue of necessity in a very literal sense, will accomplish through the regeneration of the heart, of the emotional life, in such a way that men learn how to feel like women, relate to one another and to the world beyond the way women are portrayed as relating to one another and the world, which is to say, the way Israel relates to God.

The androgyneity of Judaism thus comes to expression in a quite remarkable way. The formative documents of Judaism put forward a structure that is portrayed in wholly masculine terms, and at the same time one that is described as to its determinative and governing priorities as systemically feminine. On the one hand, women are excluded from the activities of the sage, whether discipleship and Torah-study or communal authority and leadership, so it follows that this portrait of the Judaic structure and system stands for male authors and authorships. The documents we examine, all of them normative and definitive for Judaism from their own day to ours, therefore put forth a different account of the relationship of masculine and feminine, and of masculine. But, on the other hand, women's virtues, women's attitudes, women's modes of negotiation and conciliation, rather than men's virtues of aggression and assertion—all classified out of the documents we shall examine—define the future. To state matters as they will emerge, what Israel must be, not what Israel must do, decides the future, and being, not doing, defines feminine, as against masculine, existence—once more: as these documents portray gender-traits.

What is at stake in these observations hardly requires much amplification. While commonly characterized, and with sound reason, as a male, or patriarchal, religion, this Judaism in fact will be shown in this book to hold in a tight and balanced union virtues conventionally classified as male with those deemed female. In point of fact, this Judaism will be demonstrated to assign priority, at the systemic centers—whether those concerning public behavior or personal attitude, whether those involving this-worldly and human or other-worldly and divine values and virtues—to the traits ordinarily assigned the status of the feminine, as against the masculine. So Judaism in its formative writings comes from male intellectuals who explicitly defined a male religious structure that functioned as a female system. In this way they defined a religious system responsive to the deepest and most characteristic qualities of both halves of eternal Israel, God's people, the women and the men.

Since the classification of some values or virtues as masculine, others as feminine, is at the foundations of this work, the precise reasoning behind the taxic structure set forth here requires a clear definition.

First and most important, I identify as feminine the traits that sages themselves characterize as feminine, which is to say, traits associated with women in stories sages tell, and as masculine the traits that the same sages set forth in the wholly-male setting. That accounts for my insistence upon the feminine classification to which the complex of actions, attitudes, and emotions associated with the word *zekhut* pertain, covering Chapter Three in particular.

Second and concomitantly, I identify as masculine the traits that predominate in stories or sayings in which men alone participate, or in which self-evidently-male attitudes (men take priority, men are normal, women are subordinate, women are abnormal) define the givens. That explains why my account of the place of women in the legal structure and system of the Mishnah takes for granted that that system speaks for men about women and in no way allows for a feminine viewpoint on matters. That accounts for the classification of what is masculine, and stands behind the interpretation of the data set forth in Chapters One and Two.

Third, where the documents themselves treat as feminine one group of symbols or activities, and as masculine another, there I reproduce the classification-system native to the writings themselves. That justifies my presentation of the relationship between the genders laid out in *Song of Songs Rabbah,* which (I am confident readers will quickly recognize) simply paraphrases precisely the perspective of the (male) writers themselves. This explains Chapter Four and, consequently, also Chapter Five.

It follows, obviously, I do not propose to suggest that, intrinsically, genetically, or "by nature alone," some traits belong to men, others to women. Nor can anybody imagine that all cultures classify as male or female the same traits in the same way that this Judaism does, since that is manifestly untrue. To recapitulate what is central to all that follows: in reading the doctrine of emotions as fundamentally feminine in its indicative traits, I simply follow what the documents maintain is feminine and spell out as virtues of women. In then alleging that principal writings of formative Judaism insist that Israel feminize itself, I paraphrase—where I do not cite verbatim—what those writings themselves maintain.

No study pertinent to feminism can pretend to ignore contemporary considerations, and this one certainly does not do so. This book sets forth the hypothesis that the Judaism of the dual Torah can be understood as a whole and working system only when its perfect union of the masculine and the feminine is fully grasped. Nor is this Judaism correctly interpreted if the priority it accords to feminine virtues is not recognized. The masculine—the law—speaks of the obligatory, the other,—the lore—the votive; the former dictates norms, the latter encourages acts of grace. The masculine in the foreground, the feminine at the heart and soul, the structure set forth a male order for society, but the system placed its highest value on female attitudes that are to govern the way in which the social order functioned. What that fact means is simple. The surface is studded with symptoms of male dominance, a male perspective, a male definition of the norm and the normal. Certainly, in all matters of power and preferment and the politics of prominence, males predominate; females scarcely appear at all. But the same sages who design a male social structure also designate the female traits—traits I shall show they themselves value and also associate with women—as those to be preferred. Judaism in its formative writings comprises a masculine structure sustaining a feminine system.

What makes that fact relevant even now demands articulation. My thesis is that the Judaism of the dual Torah today, as in times past, depends for its continued vitality upon sustaining its long-term balance, maintaining the parity between the sexes in its own idiom and by its own means. As successful a religious system as history has ever known, this Judaism sustained itself in trying times from its first full presentation, in the Talmud of Babylonia, to the present day, and today defines the norm as well. And that invites the further hypothesis set forth here. Because of its remarkable power to join in proportion the male and the female, the system found a stable balance to accommodate the distinct attitudes and values of both genders and to derive strength and sustenance from each. But in the end, this Judaism must be classified as feminine, because at the points of stress, within the systemic center, in the moments of systemic remission, it gave priority to the female virtues over the male ones.

That decision, which designed a theory of the social order in accord with masculine perspectives but described a social system that functioned in line with feminine values, as a matter of hypothesis accounts for the stability of the Judaism of the dual Torah in the long history of Israel, the eternal people of God. The union of God, Torah, and Israel formed a marriage—to be sure one full of strife, but an enduring and, on all parties' parts, an unbreakable one. As I shall argue at the conclusion of Chapter Five, it was the fair definition and precise distribution of the categories of masculine and feminine, held in balance and accorded each its rightful place, that in the end account for that fact. I do not pretend to know, in the here and now, how that balance is to be maintained, or even whether it has been upset. I only set forth as a matter of hypothesis that holding the whole together forms the sole guide to the long future.

If I had to set forth in a single passage what I believe is at stake in androgyne Judaism, it is the system's account of God's most profound preference, which is for those traits that the system knows as feminine but wishes to nurture in men's hearts and minds as well. This comes to expression in the simple statement, God favors the pursued over the pursuer.

1.   A. "God seeks what has been driven away" (Qoh 3:15).

B. R. Huna in the name of R. Joseph said, "It is always the case that 'God seeks what has been driven away' [favoring the victim].

C. "You find when a righteous man pursues a righteous man, 'God seeks what has been driven away.'

D. "When a wicked man pursues a wicked man, 'God seeks what has been driven away.'

E. "All the more so when a wicked man pursues a righteous man, 'God seeks what has been driven away.'

F. "[The same principle applies] even when you come around to a case in which a righteous man pursues a wicked man, 'God seeks what has been driven away.' "

2.   A. R. Yosé b. R. Yudan in the name of R. Yosé b. R. Nehorai says, "It is always the case that the Holy One, blessed be he, demands an accounting for the blood of those who have been pursued from the hand of the pursuer.

B. "Abel was pursued by Cain, and God sought [an accounting for] the pursued: 'And the Lord looked [favorably] upon Abel and his meal offering' [Gen 4:4].

C. "Noah was pursued by his generation, and God sought [an accounting for] the pursued: 'You and all your household shall come into the ark' [Gen 7:1]. And it says, 'For this is like the days of Noah to me, as I swore [that the waters of Noah should no more go over the earth]' [Isa 54:9].

D. "Abraham was pursued by Nimrod, 'and God seeks what has been driven away': 'You are the Lord, the God who chose Abram and brought him out of Ur' [Neh 9:7].

E. "Isaac was pursued by Ishmael, 'and God seeks what has been driven away': 'For through Isaac will seed be called for you' [Gen 21:12].

F. "Jacob was pursued by Esau, 'and God seeks what has been driven away': 'For the Lord has chosen Jacob, Israel for his prized possession' [Ps 135:4].

G. "Moses was pursued by Pharaoh, 'and God seeks what has been driven away': 'Had not Moses His chosen stood in the breach before Him' [Ps 106:23].

H. "David was pursued by Saul, 'and God seeks what has been driven away': 'And he chose David, his servant' [Ps 78:70].

I. "Israel was pursued by the nations, 'and God seeks what has been driven away': 'And you has the Lord chosen to be a people to him' [Deut 14:2].

J. "And the rule applies also to the matter of offerings. A bull is pursued by a lion, a sheep is pursued by a wolf, a goat is pursued by a leopard.

K. "Therefore the Holy One, blessed be he, has said, 'Do not make offerings before me from those animals that pursue, but from those that are pursued: "When a bull, a sheep, or a goat is born" ' " (Lev 22:27).

Leviticus Rabbah **XXVII:V**

The pursuer imposes, demands, insists; the pursued negotiates, yields, pleads. Since, both parts of the Torah state explicitly, in gender relationships, man is the pursuer (seeking his rib back), woman the pursued, the pertinence of this powerful passage to the pages of this book is self-evident. That right relationship is the one that is not coerced, not manipulated, not one defined by a dominant party upon a subordinated one. It is a relationship of mutuality, negotiation, response to what is freely given through what cannot be demanded but only volunteered. Israel should relate to God in accord with these virtues.

The structure of Israel's political economy as portrayed by androgynous Judaism rests upon divine response to acts of will consisting of submission, on one's own, to the will of Heaven; these acts endowed Israel with a lien and entitlement upon Heaven. What we cannot by our own will impose, we can by the act of renunciation of our own will evoke. What we cannot accomplish through coercion, we can achieve through submission. God will do for us what we cannot do for ourselves —when we do for God what God cannot make us do. This means, in a wholly concrete and tangible sense, love God with all the heart, the soul, the might we have. God then stands above the rules of the created world, because God will respond not to what we do in conformity to the rules alone, but also to what we do beyond the requirement of the rules. God is above the rules, and we can gain a response from God when, on some one, unique occasion, we too do more than obey—but love, spontaneously and all at once, with the whole of our being.

That is the conception of God that—as Chapter Three, the climax of the exposition of this book, will show us—*zekhut,* as a conception of power in Heaven and power in humanity, contains. In the relationship between God and humanity expressed in the conception of *zekhut,* we reach the understanding of what the Torah means when it tells us that we are in God's image and after God's likeness: we are then, "in our image," the very mirror-image of God. God's will forms the mirror-image of ours: when we are humble, God responds; when we demand, God withdraws. We must exhibit the very virtues that the oral Torah imputes to women, if we hope through atonement to become once more at one with God.

Part One

The Masculine

Chapter One

Women in the System of the Mishnah

Since a principal premise of this work maintains that the *halakhah* sets forth an essentially male structure, how better to validate that premise than examine the manner in which the law in the main beams of its structure accommodates—defines and treats—the category of women? We want to know where, when, and why the topic of women arises, and what importance the systemic documents accord to that topic, defining the statement they wish to make through what they say about women in particular. For if we have to describe the category, the feminine, as the *halakhah* defines and disposes of that category, there can be no better candidate for the examination of the definition of the category of the feminine than the system's treatment of women in the setting of the generative law code itself, the Mishnah.

The first document of the Judaism of the dual Torah after Scripture and a document entirely devoted to matters of *halakhah*, the Mishnah defined all that followed. It set forth a coherent, closed system, providing in its own pages, in rhetoric and in rule alike, all that is needed to understand its message. Since all the law of its Judaism flowed from its laws (where possible, to be sure, having been brought into relationship with the laws of scripture), the Mishnah is the sole starting point for an analysis of the *halakhah*'s perspective on the feminine.

That choice is justified by a second, equally compelling and simple fact. Women form a principal, indeed, a generative category for the *halakhah,* beginning with the Mishnah. The Mishnah is divided into six large topical units, and one of the six is Women, inclusive of family rules. It follows that there, in the details of the laws themselves, we follow the legal system's basic and governing attitude toward women in general. Our interest is not in listing all relevant entries in which women figure, but in characterizing the legal system's very definition of what is at stake when the subject of women comes to the fore. That formulation of matters permits us to speak of not merely discrete rules concerning women, but the very definition of what we mean when we speak of the feminine. It follows that, at stake is not a check-list of discrete rulings, but a systematic account of the very definition and position of women in general, the theory that individual rulings express in concrete ways.[1]

The Mishnah's System

To grasp in proper context and proportion how women figure in the system of the Mishnah,[2] we have to consider the document in its own

---

[1]This chapter summarizes the results of my systemic analysis presented in *A History of the Mishnaic Law of Women*, Vol. V, *The Mishnaic System of Women* (Leiden: E. J. Brill, 1980). The individual tractates are set forth in an analytical translation, both in the Mishnah's statement and the Tosefta's amplification, in my *A History of the Mishnaic Law of Women*, vol. I, *Yebamot. Translation and Explanation*; vol. II, *Ketubot. Translation and Explanation*; vol. III, *Nedarim, Nazir. Translation and Explanation*; vol. IV, *Sotah, Gittin, Qiddushin. Translation and Explanation* (Leiden: E. J. Brill, 1979-1980).

The commentaries of the two Talmuds on those Mishnah tractates are translated into English in the following: *The Talmud of Babylonia. An American Translation*, Brown Judaic Studies (Chico, then Atlanta: Scholars Press, 1984-1993): vol. XIII.A, *Tractate Yebamot. Chapters One through Three*; vol. XIII.B, *Tractate Yebamot. Chapters Four through Six*; vol. XIII.C, *Tractate Yebamot. Chapters Seven through Nine*; vol. XIII.D, *Tractate Yebamot. Chapters Ten through Sixteen*; vol. XIV.A, *Tractate Ketubot. Chapters One through Three*; vol. XIV.B, *Tractate Ketubot. Chapters Four through Seven*; vol. XIV.C, *Tractate Ketubot. Chapters Eight through Thirteen*; vol. XV.A, *Tractate Nedarim. Chapters One through Four*; vol. XV.B, *Tractate Nedarim. Chapters Five through Eleven*; vol. XVII, *Tractate Sotah*; vol. XVIII.A, *Tractate Gittin. Chapters One through Three*; vol. XVIII.B, *Tractate Gittin. Chapters Four and Five*; vol. XVIII.C, *Tractate Gittin. Chapters Six through Nine*; vol. XIX.A, *Tractate Qiddushin. Chapter One*; vol. XIX.B, *Tractate Qiddushin. Chapters Two through Four*; and *The Talmud of the Land of Israel. A Preliminary Translation and Explanation, IX-XII, XIV-XV, XVII-XXXV* (Chicago: The University of Chicago Press, 1982-1993): vol. XXI, *Yebamot* (1986); vol. XXII, *Ketubot* (1985); vol. XXIII *Nedarim* (1985); vol. XXIV *Nazir* (1985); vol. XXV, *Gittin* (1985); vol. XXVI, *Qiddushin* (1984).

The presentation in this and the following chapters rests on the translations and commentaries of these works.

[2]My introduction to the Mishnah, along with all other documents of the dual Torah of late antiquity, is set forth in my *Anchor Reference Library Introduction to Rabbinic Literature* (New York: Doubleday, 1994) and to the historical formation of Judaism in the complementary volume, *Anchor Reference Library: Judaism. An Historical Introduction*

terms and take account of the vast structure that the document sets forth. For we deal with a coherent and cogent formulation, not a mere scrapbook of rulings or a collection of statutes. Still, to characterize the Mishnah as a whole, only a few observations are required. The Mishnah, produced at about 200 C.E. under the sponsorship of Judah, Patriarch (*nasi*) or ethnic ruler of the Jews of the Land of Israel, organizes its materials by topics of both a theoretical and practical character. Its topical structure breaks down into topical subdivisions and comprises sixty-two tractates:

1. **Agriculture** (*Zera'im*): *Berakhot* (Blessings); *Pe'ah* (the corner of the field); *Demai* (doubtfully tithed produce); *Kil'ayim* (mixed seeds); *Shebi'it* (the seventh year); *Terumot* (heave offering or priestly rations); *Ma'aserot* (tithes); *Ma'aser Sheni* (second tithe); *Hallah* (dough offering); *'Orlah* (produce of trees in the first three years after planting, which is prohibited); and *Bikkurim* (first fruits).

2. **Appointed Times** (*Mo'ed*): *Shabbat* (the Sabbath); *'Erubin* (the fictive fusion meal or or boundary); *Pesahim* (Passover); *Sheqalim* (the Temple tax); *Yoma* (the Day of Atonement); *Sukkah* (the festival of Tabernacles); *Besah* (the preparation of food on the festivals and Sabbath); *Rosh Hashshanah* (the New Year); *Ta'anit* (fast days); *Megillah* (Purim); *Mo'ed Qatan* (the intermediate days of the festivals of Passover and Tabernacles); *Hagigah* (the festal offering).

3. **Women** (*Nashim*): *Yebamot* (the levirate widow); *Ketubot* (the marriage contract); *Nedarim* (vows); *Nazir* (the special vow of the Nazirite); *Sotah* (the wife accused of adultery); *Gittin* (writs of divorce); *Qiddushin* (betrothal).

4. **Damages** or civil law (*Neziqin*): *Baba Qamma, Baba Mesi'a, Baba Batra* (civil law, covering damages and torts, then correct conduct of business, labor, and real estate transactions); *Sanhedrin* (institutions of government; criminal penalties); *Makkot* (flogging); *Shabu'ot* (oaths); *'Eduyyot* (a collection arranged on other than topical lines); *Horayot* (rules governing improper conduct of civil authorities);

5. **Holy Things** (*Qodoshim*): *Zebahim* (every day animal offerings); *Menahot* (meal offerings); *Hullin* (animals slaughtered for secular purposes); *Bekhorot* (firstlings); *'Arakhin* (vows of valuation); *Temurah*

(New York: Doubleday, 1995). Both are edited by Professor David Noel Freedman.

(vows of exchange of a beast for an already consecrated beast); *Keritot* (penalty of extirpation or premature death); *Me'ilah* (sacrilege); *Tamid* (the daily whole offering); *Middot* (the layout of the temple building); *Qinnim* (how to deal with bird offerings designated for a given purpose and then mixed up);

6. **Purity** (*Toharot*): *Kelim* (susceptibility of utensils to uncleanness); *Ohalot* (transmission of corpse-uncleanness in the tent of a corpse); *Nega'im* (the uncleanness described at Lev 13-14); *Parah* (the preparation of purification-water); *Tohorot* (problems of doubt in connection with matters of cleanness); *Miqva'ot* (immersion-pools); *Niddah* (menstrual uncleanness); *Makhshirin* (rendering susceptible to uncleanness produce that is dry and so not susceptible); *Zabim* (the uncleanness covered at Lev 15); *Tebul-Yom* (the uncleanness of one who has immersed on that self-same day and awaits sunset for completion of the purification rites); *Yadayim* (the uncleanness of hands); *'Uqsin* (the uncleanness transmitted through what is connected to unclean produce).

In volume, the sixth division covers approximately a quarter of the entire document. Topics of interest to the priesthood and the Temple, such as priestly fees, conduct of the cult on holy days, conduct of the cult on ordinary days and management and upkeep of the Temple, and the rules of cultic cleanness, predominate in the first, second, fifth, and sixth divisions, in volume well over two-thirds of the whole. Rules governing the social order form the bulk of the third and fourth. Of the sixty-two tractates, only *'Eduyyot* is organized along other than topical lines; its compilers collected sayings on diverse subjects as these were attributed to particular authorities.[3]

The stress of the Mishnah throughout on the priestly caste and the Temple cult point to the document's principal concern, which centered upon sanctification, understood as the correct arrangement of all things, each in its proper category, each called by its rightful name, just as at the

---

[3]The Mishnah as printed today always includes *'Abot* (sayings of the sages), but that tractate reached closure about a generation later than the Mishnah, ca. 250 C.E. While it serves as its initial apologetic, it does not conform to the formal, rhetorical, or logical traits characteristic of the Mishnah overall and stands quite alone in the entire canon of this Judaism. Hence while printed editions of the Mishnah, including mine, number sixty-three tractates, there are only sixty-two to be taken into account as part of a single documentary statement.

creation as portrayed in the Priestly document, and just as with the cult itself as set forth in Leviticus. Further, the thousands of rules and cases (with sages' disputes thereon) that comprise the document upon close reading turn out to express in concrete language abstract principles of hierarchical classification. These define the document's method and mark it as a work of a philosophical character. Not only so, but a variety of specific, recurrent concerns (for example, the relationship of being to becoming, actual to potential, the principles of economics, the politics) correspond point by point to comparable ones in Graeco-Roman philosophy, particularly Aristotle's tradition. This stress on proper order and right rule and the formulation of a philosophy, politics, and economics, within the principles of natural history set forth by Aristotle, explain why the Mishnah makes a statement to be classified as philosophy, that is, concerning the order of the natural world in its correspondence with the supernatural world.

The Philosophy of the Mishnah

The system of philosophy expressed through concrete and detailed law presented by the Mishnah, consists of a coherent logic and topic, a cogent world-view and comprehensive way of living. It is a world-view that speaks of transcendent things, a way of life in response to the supernatural meaning of what is done, a heightened and deepened perception of the sanctification of Israel in deed and in deliberation. Sanctification thus means two things: first, distinguishing Israel in all its dimensions from the world in all its ways; second, establishing the stability, order, regularity, predictability, and reliability of Israel in the world of nature and supernature in particular at moments and in contexts of danger. Danger means instability, disorder, irregularity, uncertainty, and betrayal. Each topic of the system as a whole takes up a critical and indispensable moment or context of social being. Through what is said in regard to each of the Mishnah's principal topics, what the system expressed through normative rules as a whole wishes to declare is fully expressed. Yet if the parts severally and jointly give the message of the whole, the whole cannot exist without all of the parts, so well joined and carefully crafted are they all. The details become clear in our survey of the document's topical program, in which the topic of women plays a prominent role.

To understand the complete system set forth by the Mishnah, we rapidly review the divisions as they were finally spelled out, excluding the Division of Women, to which we shall devote the shank of this chapter.

The Division of Agriculture

The Division of Agriculture treats two topics: first, producing crops in accord with the scriptural rules on the subject; second, paying the required offerings and tithes to the priests, Levites, and poor. The principal point of the Division is that the Land is holy, because God has a claim both on it and upon what it produces. God's claim must be honored by setting aside a portion of the produce for those for whom God has designated it. God's ownership must be acknowledged by observing the rules God has laid down for use of the Land. In the temporal context in which the Mishnah was produced, some generations after the disastrous defeat by the Romans of Bar Kokhba and the permanent closure of Jerusalem to Jews' access, the stress of the division brought assurance that those aspects of the sanctification of Israel—land of Israel, Israel itself and its social order, the holy cycle of time—that survived also remained holy and subject to the rules of Heaven.

The Division of Appointed Times

The Division of Appointed Times carried forward the same emphasis upon sanctification, now of the high points of the lunar-solar calendar of Israel. The second division forms a system in which the advent of a holy day, like the Sabbath of creation, sanctifies the life of the Israelite village through imposing on the village rules on the model of those of the Temple. The purpose of the system, therefore, is to bring into alignment the moment of sanctification of the village and the life of the home with the moment of sanctification of the Temple on those same occasions of appointed times. The underlying and generative logic of the system comes to expression in a concrete way here. We recall the rule of like and opposite, comparison and contrast. What is not like something follows the rule opposite to that pertaining to that something. Here, therefore, since the village is the mirror image of the Temple, the upshot is dictated by the analogical-contrastive logic of the system as a whole.

If things are done in one way in the Temple, they will be done in the opposite way in the village. Together the village and the Temple on the occasion of the holy day therefore form a single continuum, a completed creation, thus awaiting sanctification. The village is made like the Temple in that on appointed times one may not freely cross the lines distinguishing the village from the rest of the world, just as one may not freely cross the lines distinguishing the Temple from the world. But the village is a mirror image of the Temple. The boundary lines prevent free entry into the Temple, so they restrict free egress from the village. On the holy day what one may do in the Temple is precisely what one may not do in the village.

So the advent of the holy day affects the village by bringing it into sacred symmetry in such wise as to effect a system of opposites; each is holy, in a way precisely the opposite of the other. Because of the underlying conception of perfection attained through the union of opposites, the village is not represented as conforming to the model of the cult, but of constituting its antithesis. The world thus regains perfection when on the holy day heaven and earth are united, the whole completed and done: the heaven, the earth, and all their hosts. This moment of perfection renders the events of ordinary time, of "history," essentially irrelevant. For what really matters in time is that moment in which sacred time intervenes and effects the perfection formed of the union of heaven and earth, of Temple, in the model of the former, and Israel, its complement. It is not a return to a perfect time but a recovery of perfect being, a fulfillment of creation, which explains the essentially ahistorical character of the Mishnah's Division on Appointed Times. Sanctification constitutes an ontological category and is effected by the creator.

This explains why the division in its rich detail is composed of two quite distinct sets of materials. First, it addresses what one does in the sacred space of the Temple on the occasion of sacred time, as distinct from what one does in that same sacred space on ordinary, undifferentiated days, which is a subject worked out in Holy Things. Second, the Division defines how for the occasion of the holy day one creates a corresponding space in one's own circumstance, and what one does, within that space, during sacred time. The division as a whole holds together through a shared, generative metaphor. It is, as I said, the comparison, in the context of sacred time, of the spatial life of the Temple to the spatial life of the village, with activities and restrictions to be specified for each, upon the common occasion of the Sabbath or festival. The Mishnah's purpose therefore is to correlate the sanctity of the Temple, as defined by the holy day, with the restrictions of space and of action that make the life of the village different and holy, as defined by the holy day.

The Division of Damages

The Division of Damages comprises two subsystems, which fit together in a logical way. One part presents rules for the normal conduct of civil society. These cover commerce, trade, real estate, and other matters of everyday intercourse, as well as mishaps, such as damages by chattels and persons, fraud, overcharge, interest, and the like, in that same context of everyday social life. The other part describes the institutions governing the normal conduct of civil society, that is, courts of administration, and the penalties at the disposal of the government for the enforcement of the law. The two subjects form a single tight and systematic dissertation on the nature of Israelite society and its economic, social, and political relationships, as the Mishnah envisages them. The main point of the first of the two parts of the Division is that the task of society is to maintain perfect stasis, to preserve the prevailing situation, and to secure the stability of all relationships. To this end, in the interchanges of buying and selling, giving and taking, borrowing and lending, it is important that there be an essential equality of interchange. No party in the end should have more than what he had at the outset, and none should be the victim of a sizable shift in fortune and circumstance. All parties' rights to, and in, this stable and unchanging economy of society are to be preserved. When the condition of a person is violated, so far as possible the law will secure the restoration of the antecedent status.

The goal of the system of civil law is the recovery of the prevailing order and balance, the preservation of the established wholeness of the social economy. This idea is powerfully expressed in the organization of the three tractates that comprise the civil law, which treat first abnormal and then normal transactions. The framers deal with damages done by chattels and by human beings, thefts and other sorts of malfeasance against the property of others. The civil law in both aspects pays closest attention to how the property and person of the injured party so far as possible are restored to their prior condition, that is, a state of normality.

So attention to torts focuses upon penalties paid by the malefactor to the victim, rather than upon penalties inflicted by the court on the malefactor for what he has done. When speaking of damages, the Mishnah thus takes as its principal concern the restoration of the fortune of victims of assault or robbery. Then the framers take up the complementary and corresponding set of topics, the regulation of normal transactions. When we rapidly survey the kinds of transactions of special interest, we see from the topics selected for discussion what we have already uncovered in the deepest structure of organization and articulation of the basic theme.

The other half of this same unit of three tractates presents laws governing normal and routine transactions, many of them of the same sort as those dealt with in the first half. Bailments, for example, occur in both wings of the triple tractate, first, bailments subjected to misappropriation, or accusation thereof, by the bailiff, then, bailments transacted under normal circumstances. Under the rubric of routine transactions are those of workers and householders, that is, the purchase and sale of labor; rentals and bailments; real estate transactions; and inheritances and estates. Of the lot, the one involving real estate transactions is the most fully articulated and covers the widest range of problems and topics. The three tractates of the civil law all together thus provide a complete account of the orderly governance of balanced transactions and unchanging civil relationships within Israelite society under ordinary conditions.

The character and interests of the Division of Damages present probative evidence of the larger program of the philosophers of the Mishnah. Their intention is to create nothing less than a full-scale Israelite government, subject to the administration of sages. This government is fully supplied with a constitution and bylaws. It makes provision for a court system and procedures, as well as a full set of laws governing civil society and criminal justice. This government, moreover, mediates between its own community and the outside ("pagan") world. Through its system of laws, it expresses its judgment of the others and at the same time defines, protects, and defends its own society and social frontiers. It even makes provision for procedures of remission, to expiate its own errors. The (then non-existent) Israelite government imagined by the second-century philosophers centers upon the (then non-existent) Temple, and the (then forbidden) city, Jerusalem. For the Temple is one principal focus. There the highest court is in session; there the high priest reigns.

The penalties for law infringement are of three kinds, one of which involves sacrifice in the Temple. (The others are compensation, physical punishment, and death.) The basic conception of punishment, moreover, is that unintentional infringement of the rules of society, whether "religious" or otherwise, is not penalized but rather expiated through an offering in the Temple. If a member of the people of Israel intentionally infringes against the law, to be sure, that one must be removed from society and is put to death. And if there is a claim of one member of the people against another, that must be righted, so that the prior, prevailing status may be restored. So offerings in the Temple are given up to appease heaven and restore a whole bond between heaven and Israel, specifically on those occasions when without malice or ill will an Israelite has disturbed the relationship. Israelite civil society without a Temple is not stable or normal, and not to be imagined. And the Mishnah is above all an act of imagination in defiance of reality.

The plan for the government involves a clear-cut philosophy of society, a philosophy that defines the purpose of the government and ensures that its task is not merely to perpetuate its own power. What the Israelite government, within the Mishnaic fantasy, is supposed to do is to preserve that state of perfection that, within the same fantasy, the society to begin everywhere attains and expresses. This is in at least five aspects.

First of all, one of the ongoing principles of the law, expressed in one tractate after another, is that people are to follow and maintain the prevailing practice of their locale. Second, the purpose of civil penalties, as we have noted, is to restore the injured party to his prior condition, so far as this is possible, rather than merely to penalize the aggressor. Third, there is the conception of true value, meaning that a given object has an intrinsic worth, which, in the course of a transaction, must be paid. In this way, the seller does not leave the transaction any richer than when he entered it, or the buyer any poorer (parallel to penalties for damages). Fourth, there can be no usury—a biblical prohibition adopted and vastly enriched in the Mishnaic thought—for money ("coins") is what it is. Any pretense that it has become more than what it was violates, in its way, the conception of true value. Fifth, when real estate is divided, it must be done with full attention to the rights of all concerned, so that, once more, one party does not gain at the expense of the other. In these and many other aspects, the law expresses its obsession with the perfect stasis of Israelite society. Its paramount purpose is in preserving and ensuring that that perfection of the division of this world is kept inviolate or restored to its true status when violated.

The Division of Holy Things

The Division of Holy Things presents a system of sacrifice and sanctuary. The division centers upon the everyday and rules always applicable to the cult: the daily whole offering, the sin offering and guilt-offering that one may bring any time under ordinary circumstances; the right sequence of diverse offerings; the way in which the rites of the whole-, sin-, and guilt-offerings are carried out; what sorts of animals are acceptable; the accompanying cereal offerings; the support and provision of animals for the cult and of meat for the priesthood; the support and material maintenance of the cult and its building. We have a system before us: the system of the cult of the Jerusalem Temple, seen as an ordinary and everyday affair, a continuing and routine operation. That is why special rules for the cult, both in respect to the altar and in regard to the maintenance of the buildings, personnel, and even the hold city, will be elsewhere—in Appointed Times and Agriculture. But from the perspective of Holy Things, those divisions intersect by supplying special rules and raising extraordinary (Agriculture: land-bound; Appointed Times: time-bound) considerations for that theme that Holy Things claims to set forth in its most general and unexceptional way: the cult as something permanent and everyday.

The Division of Purities

The Division of Purities presents a very simple system of three principal parts: sources of uncleanness, objects and substances susceptible to uncleanness, and modes of purification from uncleanness. So it tells the story of what makes a given sort of object unclean and what makes it clean. Viewed as a whole, the Division of Purities treats the interplay of persons, food, and liquids. Dry inanimate objects or food are not suscep-tible to uncleanness. What is wet is susceptible. So liquids activate the system. What is unclean, moreover, emerges from uncleanness through the operation of liquids, specifically, through immersion in fit water of requisite volume and in natural condition. Liquids thus deactivate the system. Thus, water in its natural condition is what concludes the process by removing uncleanness. Water in its unnatural condition, that is, deliberately affected by human agency, is what imparts susceptibility to uncleanness to begin with. The uncleanness of persons, furthermore, is signified by body liquids or flux in the case of the menstruating woman and the *zab* (the person suffering from the form of uncleanness described at Lev 15:1ff.). Corpse uncleanness is conceived to be a kind of effluent, a viscous gas that flows like liquid. Utensils for their part receive uncleanness when they form receptacles able to contain liquid.

In sum, we have a system in which the invisible flow of fluid-like substances or powers serve to put food, drink, and receptacles into the status of uncleanness and to remove those things from that status. Whether or not we call the system "metaphysical," it certainly has no material base but is conditioned upon highly abstract notions. Thus in material terms, the effect of liquid is upon food, drink, utensils, and man. The consequence has to do with who may eat and drink what food and liquid and with what food and drink may be consumed in which pots and pans. These loci are specified by tractates on utensils and on food and drink.

The human being is ambivalent. Persons fall in the middle, between sources and loci of uncleanness, because they are both. They serve as sources of uncleanness. They also become unclean. The *zab* suffering the uncleanness described in Leviticus 15, the menstruating woman, the woman after childbirth, and the person afflicted with the skin ailment described in Leviticus 13 and 14—all are sources of uncleanness. But being unclean, they fall within the system's loci, its program of consequences. So they make other things unclean and are subject to penalties because they are unclean. Unambiguous sources of uncleanness never also constitute loci affected by uncleanness. They always are unclean and never can become clean: the corpse, the dead creeping thing, and things like them. Inanimate sources of uncleanness and inanimate objects are affected by uncleanness. Systemically unique, man and liquids have the capacity to inaugurate the processes of uncleanness (as sources) and also are subject to those same processes (as objects of uncleanness).

Omitted Divisions

When we listen to the silences of the system of the Mishnah, as much as to its points of stress, we hear a single message, one never articulated but everywhere present: what is the meaning of what has happened to Israel, and what is Israel to do next? It is a message of a system that answered a single encompassing question, and the question formed a stunning counterpart to that of the sixth century B.C.E. The Pentateuchal system addressed one reading of the events of the sixth century, highlighted by the destruction of the Jerusalem Temple in 586 B.C.E. At stake was how Israel as defined by that system related to its land, represented by its Temple, and the message may be simply stated: what appears to be the given is in fact a gift, subject to stipulations. The precipitating event for the Mishnaic system was the destruction of the Jerusalem Temple in 70 C.E.; the question turned obsession with the defeat of Bar Kokhba and the closure of Jerusalem to Jews. The urgent issue taken up by the Mishnah was, specifically, what, in the aftermath of the destruction of the holy place and holy cult, remained of the sanctity of the holy caste, the priesthood, the holy land, and, above all, the holy people and its holy way of life? The answer was that sanctity persists, indelibly, in Israel, the people, in its way of life, in its land, in its priesthood, in its food, in its mode of sustaining life, in its manner of procreating and so sustaining the nation.

The Mishnah's system therefore focused upon the holiness of the life of Israel, the people, a holiness that had formerly centered on the Temple. The logically consequent question was, what is the meaning of sanctity, and how shall Israel attain, or give evidence of, sanctification. The answer to the question derived from the original creation, the end of the Temple directing attention to the beginning of the natural world that the Temple had (and would again) embodied. For the meaning of sanctity, the framers therefore turned to that first act of sanctification, the one in creation. It came about when, all things in array, in place, each with its proper name, God blessed and sanctified the seventh day on the eve of the first Sabbath. Creation was made ready for the blessing and the sanctification when all things were very good, that is to say, in their rightful order, called by their rightful name. An orderly nature was a sanctified and blessed nature, so dictated scripture in the name of the supernatural. So to receive the blessing and to be made holy, all things in nature and society were to be set in right array. Given the condition of Israel, the people, in its land, in the aftermath of the catastrophic war against Rome led by Bar Kokhba in 132–135 C.E., putting things in order was no easy task. But that is why, after all, the question pressed, the answer proving inexorable and obvious. The condition of society corresponded to the critical question that obsessed the system-builders.

Women in the System of the Mishnah

This protracted and general description brings us to the Division of Women, to be seen in the context of the Mishnah's system as a whole. Now we can understand in correct perspective the treatment of the topic, women, because we shall be able to account, within the system's own logic, for the prominence accorded to that topic and, further, identify the message that is set forth through what is said about that topic. What we shall see is that the masculine viewpoint prevails, beginning to end, and that it makes its appearance in no subtle or subterranean way but right on the surface of matters. In the *halakhah* as set forth by the Mishnah, women matter in systemic context when, and only when, they relate to men, and men are assumed to form the structure and guarantee the stability of the entire society.

The Division of Women

Five of the seven tractates of this division are devoted to the formation and dissolution of the marital bond. Of them, three treat what is done by man here on earth, that is, formation of a marital bond through betrothal and marriage contract and dissolution through divorce and its consequences: *Qiddushin,*[4] *Ketubot,*[5] and *Gittin.*[6] One of them is devoted to what by woman is done here on earth: *Sotah.*[7] And *Yebamot,*[8] greatest of the

---

[4] Betrothals.

[5] Marriage contracts and the settlement thereof; the transfer of property in connection with the transfer of a woman from the father's to the husband's domain.

[6] Writs of divorce.

[7] The wife suspected of adultery and the rite of drinking the bitter water described in

seven in size and in formal and substantive brilliance, deals with the corresponding heavenly intervention into the formation and end of a marriage: the effect of death upon the marital bond and the dissolution, through death, of that bond. The other two tractates, *Nedarim*[9] and *Nazir*,[10] draw into one the two realms of reality, Heaven and earth, as they work out the effects of vows taken by women and subject to the confirmation or abrogation of the father or husband. These vows make a deep impact upon the marital life of the woman who has taken such a vow. So, in all, the division and its system delineate the natural and supernatural character of the woman's role in the social economy framed by man: the beginning, end, and middle of that relationship.

The Mishnaic system of women thus focuses upon the two crucial stages in the transfer of women and of property from one domain to another: (1) the leaving of the father's house to the husband's through marriage, and (2) the leaving of the husband's house at the marriage's dissolution through divorce or through the husband's death or the wife's infidelity. There is yet a third point of interest, though it is much less important than these first two stages: (3) the duration of the marriage. But the handful of rules on that subject hardly matches the enormous and dense corpus of laws on betrothal, marriage contracts, divorce, levirate marriage and the dissolution thereof, and the wife accused of adultery, with fundamental consequences for the continuation or the dissolution of the marriage. Finally, included within the division and at a few points relevant to women in particular are rules of vows in general and of the special vow to be a Nazir, the former included because, in the scriptural treatment of the theme, the rights of the father or husband to annul the vows of a daughter or wife form the central problematic, and the latter included for no very clear reason except that it is a species of which the vow is the genus.

To the message and the purpose of the Mishnaic system of women, woman is essential and central. But she is not critical. She sets the stage for the processes of the sacred. It is she who can be made sacred to man. It is she who ceases to stand within a man's sacred circle. But God,

---

Num 5.

[8]Levirate marriages, in accord with the rule of Deut 25:10-15.

[9]Vows.

[10]The vow of the Nazirite, as in Num 6.

through supernature, and man, through the documentary expression of his will and intention, possess the active power of sanctification. Like the Holy Land of Mishnah's division of Agriculture, the Holy Temple of the division of Sacrifices, and the potentially holy realm of the clean of the division of Purities, women for the division of Women define a principal component of the Mishnah's orderly conception of reality. Women form a chief component of the six-part realm of the sacred. It is, as I said, their position in the social economy of the Israelite reality, natural and supernatural, that is the subject of the division and its tractates.

But the whole—this six-part realm—is always important in *relationship* to man on earth and God in Heaven. Sanctification is effected through process and relationship. The center of logical tension is critical relationship. The problematic of the subject is generated *at* the critical points of the relationship. The relationship, that is, *the process,* is what makes holy or marks as profane. God and man shape and effect that process. Earth, woman, cult, and the cult-like realm of the clean— these foci of the sacred form that inert matter made holy or marked as profane by the will and deed of God and of man, who is like God. This, I conceive, is the problematic so phrased as to elicit the desired response in our division. *The system shapes the problematic that defines how the topic will be explored and made consequential.* The Mishnah's is a system of sanctification through the word of God and through that which corresponds to God's word on earth, which is the will of man. If, as I have said, the division yields no propositions of encompassing and fundamental importance but merely legal facts about documents and relationships signified through documents, it still says a great deal both as a system and also in behalf of Mishnah's system as a whole.

Let us now consider the seven tractates and rapidly survey their principal topics.

Yebamot

The levirate connection is null in a case of consanguinity; *halisah* (Deut 25:10ff.—the rite of removing the shoe) but no levirate marriage; a normal levirate connection, worked out through *halisah* or consummation of the marriage; marriage into the priesthood and the right to eat heave-offering; severing the marital bond; marital ties subject to doubt; the rite of *halisah*; the right of refusal; infirm marital bonds; the deaf-mute, the minor male; severing the marital bond through death of the husband; the woman's testimony; identifying a corpse.

Ketubot

> The material rights of the parties to the marital union; the wife, the father, the husband; conflicting claims; fines paid to the father in the case of rape or seduction; the father's material rights; the husband's material rights; rules for the duration of the marriage; the wife's duties to the husband; the husband's marital rights and duties; the dowry; property rights of the wife while she is married; settlement of the marriage contract in the event of the husband's death; multiple claims on an estate; the support of the widow.

Nedarim

> The language of vows: euphemisms; language of no effect or of limited effect; the binding effects of vows, not to derive benefit in general, not to eat some specific kind of food in particular, and not to use certain objects; temporal application of vows; the absolution of vows; grounds for absolution; annulling the vows of a daughter and of a wife; the husband's power to annul the wife's vows; vows of a woman who is not subject to abrogation.

Nazir

> Becoming a Nazir with special reference to the vow: the language of the vow, stipulations, the duration of the vow; annulling the Nazirite vow; the offerings required of the Nazir; designation and disposition; prohibitions on the Nazir; the grape, contracting corpse-uncleanness, cutting the hair.

Soṭah

> Invoking the ordeal of the bitter water, narrative of the ordeal and its conduct; rules of the ordeal: exemptions and applicability, testimony; rites conducted in Hebrew: the anointed for battle and the draft exemptions, the rite of the heifer and the neglected corpse.

Giṭṭin

> Delivering a writ of divorce; preparing a writ of divorce; two irrelevant constructions: (I) confirming the prevailing supposition; (II) fifteen rulings made for the good order of society; the law of agency in writs of divorce; receiving the writ, appointing an agent to prepare and deliver a writ of divorce; stipulations in writs of divorce; invalid and impaired writs of divorce; improper delivery, improper preparation, improper stipulations, improper witnesses; grounds for divorce.

Qiddushin
> Rules of acquisition of a woman in betrothal; procedures of betrothal;
> agency, the token of betrothal, stipulations; impaired betrothals;
> stipulations; doubts in matters of betrothal; appropriate candidates for
> betrothal; castes and outcastes; the status of the offspring of impaired
> marriages; castes and marriage among castes; miscellanies and homilies.

We see in this detailed account of the division's repertoire of themes that
we have an encompassing account of the formation, duration, and
dissolution of marriages. The topic is worked out in a fairly systematic
and orderly way. The Mishnaic system of women clearly does not
pretend to deal with every topic pertinent to women. Indeed, it is what
we do not find, as much as what we do, that permits us to claim we have
a system. For when we can point to exclusions, we realize decisions have
been made, within the potentialities of the *theme* of women, on what
belongs and what does not belong to a distinctive *system* of women.

Now what are we to make of these data? Taken one by one, they
have been read to yield a generalization of stifling generality: men are on
top, women on the bottom. That is both true and irrelevant. Not only so,
but, when we have examined a much broader range of evidence than the
halakhic, we shall see the opposite fact: women—as portrayed by men!—
define the values, men merely the concrete norms that convey and
preserve those values. Efforts at thematic description and interpretation
of data such as those before us are inadequate not merely because they
rest upon false epistemological foundations, wrenching out of context and
depriving of all specific meaning the facts of the themes subject to
description and interpretation. They are inadequate because the result produces exercises in confusion, triteness, and banality. Thematic approach
to the data of our seven tractates, among a vast profusion of facts about
"women in ancient Judaism," illustrates this proposition.

A single example suffices to show that collecting and arranging rules
concerning women, without a theory of systemic analysis, yields banalities and platitudes—and, in accord with the argument of this book,
misleading ones at that! Leonard Swidler provides a stunningly apt
illustration of the helplessness of thematic description in the face of the
diverse data required by its program. His treatment of the subject proves
simply witless, for in the end he can only set up two categories for
interpretation, and they produce no interpretation at all. These are first,
positive, and second, negative, sayings. He culls innumerable, diverse

rabbinic sayings in favor of women and diverse sayings against them. He then concludes:

> On the basis of the evidence of both the positive and negative rabbinic statements about women thus far analyzed . . . it would be correct to conclude that quantitatively and qualitatively the negative attitude vastly outweighs the positive. It can be said, therefore, that the attitude of the ancient rabbis toward women was a continuation of the negative attitude toward women that evolved from the return from the Exile through the later Wisdom, apocryphal, and pseudepigraphical literature. In fact, it was in a way an intensification of it, in that the rabbis, through their great influence on the masses of Judaism, projected it most forcefully into the every day life of the observant Jew.[11]

It follows that, for Swidler, masses of material have been suitably pigeonholed and utilized; by his judgment, some are favorable, some unfavorable. In the balance, the overall effect is negative. What we learn from this judgment, how we better understand the data he has assembled, and the means by which we may interpret in a richer and fuller way than before the larger constructions out of which the data are drawn are questions he does not answer. He cannot. Hunting and gathering, collecting and arranging facts—these are necessary to all scholarship, but insufficient to learning of consequence.

There is yet one question I do not see answered. If we know what he claims we know, then what else do we know? If it is so that "the negative attitude vastly outweighs the positive," then what do we learn that we want to know? That is, if we exclude acutely contemporary aspirations for reform, then—so what? It does not appear to a fair number of scholars that their task includes the making of such judgments in this context. And, beyond these considerations of method, there also is the commanding fact that, as we shall see, Swidler is simply wrong in his characterization of the whole. In fact, as Chapters Three through Five will show us, this particular Judaism, assuredly the formation of men and the expression of an entirely male viewpoint, forms its systemic center, the message of its remissions and systemic reversals, around women's

---

[11]*Women in Judaism: The Status of Women in Formative Judaism* (Metuchen: Scarecrow Press, 1976) 82.

virtues, deemed to belong to women as much as to men by the very force
of the presentation thereof.

Women in Other Judaic Systems

Before proceeding to an account of women in the system of the Mishnah,
we do well to consider for purposes of comparison and contrast a more
systematic account of the matter than Swidler has given us. Specifically,
documentary characterizations of women in other Judaic systems and
their laws have been set forth. Accordingly, we now compare the data
before us, deriving from a document of one Judaic religious system, with
treatment of women in other Judaic systems altogether. We begin with
the observations of Abel Isaksson. While he does not show that there was
an Essenic system of women (indeed, he shows there was none), he does
make the effort to relate unsystematized facts about women in the Essene
writings to the larger integrated system of the Essenes. His main point is
that the details of the Essene writings take on meaning only within their
own system and cannot be properly interpreted when they stand apart
from that system:

> In spite of their literal interpretation of the Pentateuch, the Qumran
> people came to maintain a view of marriage and a practice of marriage
> which differed greatly from the O.T. view and the view expressed in the
> rabbinical literature. This fact has proved to be entirely due to the
> basically eschatological ideology of the Qumran community. They
> considered themselves to be engaged in a war in the eschatological
> period against the children of darkness. They therefore live in
> accordance with the laws relating to the holy war, even as regards
> marriage. The young man has a right to take a wife and live with her
> for a period of five years. After this period, the laws relating to the holy
> war stipulate that he is to refrain entirely from sexual cohabitation with
> his wife. Should his wife die during this five-year period, the man has
> nevertheless done his duty in propagating his race. He may not take
> another wife. Anyone who does so shows that he is not capable of
> living in accordance with the laws of the holy war but is addicted to
> fornication. The husband does not need to divorce his wife when he
> reaches the age of 25 but it is likely that such divorces occurred,
> sometimes perhaps on the plea that the husband wished to avoid all
> suspicion that he had sexual intercourse with his wife even after the age

of 25, when under the laws of the holy war he was no longer allowed to have it. The man who had reached the age of 25 was to live in sexual abstinence, in order to be able to do his part in the holy war against the children of darkness.

The men of Qumran were not monks governed by ascetic rules and refraining from marriage in order to combat the lust of the flesh or from aversion to women. They were soldiers mustered and sanctified to fight in the eschatological war against the children of darkness. The laws of this war allowed them to be married for a period in their youth and to live with their wives and beget children. But these laws also required them to live for the greater part of their lives in sexual abstinence. Every detail in the Qumran community's view of marriage and every detail in which its marriage *halakhah* differs from those of other contemporary Jewish groups has proved to have originated in the basically eschatological ideology which dominated the life of the whole sect. This also means that the Qumran community's view of marriage must not be interpreted as an isolated detail in its ethical system. *Its moral principles on the subject of marriage are indissolubly linked with its eschatology.*[12]

Isaksson properly italicizes his concluding sentence. It would be difficult to improve upon his approach. We now very rapidly review other candidates, in the period in which Mishnah's system comes into being, for comparison, whether of minor details or of whole systems. The work will not detail us for very long.

The one point of comparison between the Mishnah's and other Judaic systems is readily missed: it is the very prominence accorded by the Mishnah, but by no other Judaic legal system, to the subject of women; they form a principal building block, a major component in the topical structure of the law itself. And that is unique among the Judaisms of the time and place. So far as I am able to see, the Israelite world produced no other document on women analogous to Mishnah's. The topical structure of the Mishnah, its inclusions and omissions, appears quite distinctive in its context. Of the Israelite world we may be certain: among extant materials there is no system involving women as a principal component, although all constructions we do have in hand include facts

---

[12]Abel Isaksson, *Marriage and Ministry in the New Temple. A Study with Special Reference to Mt. 19:13-22 and I Cor. 11:3-16* (Lund, 1965) 64-65.

about, and references to, women; but that, of course, is a very different thing. Obviously, the treatment of women, the role accorded to them in society, the place enjoyed by them in the imaginative and religious life of the diverse groups of late antiquity—all of these aspects of life required, and certainly received, attention.

But how the facts about these matters fit into the larger context of which they were a part and how these larger contexts may be described and so made available for comparison and systemic analysis I do not know. When, therefore, we state, as we must, that Mishnah is the only system of women known to us in late antiquity, the appropriate qualifications have been made. Let us now survey other Israelite writings of approximately the same time as Mishnah comes into being.

The Zadokite Document (CD) presents laws but "not a comprehensive handbook of halakhah [law]." Rather we have "a series of *halakhic* statements, roughly arranged by subjects."[13] It follows that we cannot ask for the traits of CD's system as a whole, since we do not have access to the whole. We do have complete pericopes devoted to the oath, the order of the judges, purification with water, the Sabbath, the camp overseer, the meeting of all camps, preparing the requirements of the community, a woman's oath, and freewill gifts. The rule of the woman's oath (XVI, 10-13) simply observes that since the husband can annul the oath of the wife, he should not annul it unless he knows whether it ought to be carried out or annulled. If it is such as to lead to transgression of the covenant, let him annul it and not carry it out. Likewise is the rule for her father. It goes without saying that, so far as the presuppositions of Mishnah-tractate on vows, *Nedarim*, go, a vow contrary to what is written in the Torah is null to begin with and therefore will not require the husband's abrogation. An oath contrary to what is written in the Torah also is not binding. This hardly constitutes an ample "doctrine," let alone a system, of women or corpus of women's law. It is further forbidden to have sexual relations in Jerusalem (XII, 43), for reasons having to do with the theory of the character of the city, along the lines of Leviticus 15:18.

The relevant evidence in the *Temple Scroll* is summarized by Professor Baruch A. Levine as follows:

---

[13]Chaim Rabin, *The Zadokite Documents* (Oxford: Clarendon Press, 1958) x. Further references in this paragraph are to pp. 76 and 58-59.

(1) Col. 65:7-66:12 of the Scroll present a version of Deut 2:13-23:1. There are lacunae in the Scroll, which can be reliably restored since, in other respects, the Scroll's version is faithful to the biblical original. The only variations are dialectical and orthographic.

(2) Col. 66:12-17 take up the cue of Deut 23:1, which is a statement on incest, prohibiting marriage with the wife of one's father, and link to what preceded a version of the incest code of Lev 18 (cf. Lev 20). The Scroll, as preserved, breaks off before this code is completed. Originally, it undoubtedly took up a part of the missing last column, col. 67. The listed incestuous unions are as follows: (a) the wife of one's brother, including a half-brother, either by one's father or mother, (b) one's sister, including one's half-sister, either by one's father or mother, (c) the sister of one's father or the sister of one's mother (aunts), and (d) one's niece, the daughter of one's brother or one's sister.

The significant addition here is, of course, the prohibition of marriage with nieces, not mentioned in Leviticus or elsewhere in scripture (cf. *Zadokite Document* V:f.).

(3) Col. 57:15-19 of the Scroll introduce into the code of conduct for Israelite kings two provisions, deriving from Deut 17:17: (a) the king must be monogamous, and (b) the king is not only forbidden to marry gentile women, but must marry a woman from his father's household, or family (cf. *Zadokite Document* IV:20f. and Ezek 36:16).

The prohibition of marriage with nieces, and the question of monogamy are discussed in Baruch A. Levine, "The *Temple Scroll:* Aspects of its Historical Provenance and Literary Character," *BASOR,* no. 232.

(4) Col. 53:14-54:5 contain the Scroll's version of Num. 30:3f. on the matter of vows *(nedarim)* and the respective roles of father and husband regarding vows pronounced by women. Except for the conversion of 3rd person references to God into 1st person references ("to Me," instead of "to the Lord,") the Scroll's version is essentially faithful to the biblical original.

(5) Col. 63:10-15 of the Scroll present a version of the law governing marriage with captive women, Deut. 21:10f. The statements regarding marriage are biblical, but the Scroll adds a stricture, which actually concerns purity, more than marriage, itself. The Scroll forbids

the captive wife from partaking of *shelamim* offerings or what it calls *tohorah,* "pure, sanctified food" for seven years.[14]

On the basis of this evidence, it is not possible to maintain that the *Temple Scroll* presents anything like a system of women. Apart from a couple of scriptural rules, the *Temple Scroll* and Mishnah's systemic construction have nothing in common. Two of the points at which the theme of women is important to the *Temple Scroll* and on which the author has something to say other than to cite scripture—Levine's Numbers 2 and 5—are not treated at all by Mishnah's division of Women. The third— Levine's Number 2—is shared, both in theme and detail, in *Yebamot.* For *Yebamot,* however, the list of incestuous unions forms a part of the factual substructure of the tractate. It scarcely forms a focus of inquiry or defines a critical problematic. So there is one point of intersection at the factual level, and none at that of generative conceptions, between Mishnah's division of Women and the *Temple Scroll's* allusions to women. Of greater consequence, the latter document in no way treats the theme of women systematically—for example, within the program of scripture's available allusions—nor does the theme play a major role in the *Temple Scroll's* system. What Mishnah and the *Temple Scroll* share is simply scripture or, more accurately, a couple of facts supplied to both by scripture.

If our problem were the position of women in general, then germane to our account would be the prominence assigned to women in all four Gospels. The women of Jesus' day and country seem to have had great liberty of movement and action.[15] But there is no doctrine of women in the Gospels, nor can we find in the occasional remarks in Paul's letters even a remote equivalent to the Mishnaic system of women. The Gospels' picture of women as a prominent and independent group in society is confirmed by the trove of legal documents belonging to a Jewish woman of the early second century C.E. Among the Cave of Letters of the Bar Kokhba finds is the marriage-contract of a woman,

---

[14]Personal letter.

[15]James Donaldson, *Woman: Her Position and Influence in Ancient Greece and Rome and Among the Early Christians* (New York: longmans, Green, 1907) 149. We of course do not mean to ignore the enormous literature on this subject; I refer to this item to show the general tenor of opinion.

among other legal documents pertaining to her affairs.[16] The account of the affairs of this woman, Babata, leaves no doubt of her legal capacities. She received all the properties of her husband during his own lifetime and took possession of them when he died. She remarried and inherited another large property. She undertook and effected numerous important litigations and in general supervised what was hers. Any picture of the Israelite woman of the second century as chattel and a dumb animal hardly accords with the actualities revealed in the legal documents of Babata. The upshot is that the picture drawn by the Mishnah's laws and the picture of the status of women we derive from other documents that pertain to the same place and time hardly coincide. But ours is not a problem of determining historical facts but religious conceptions set forth in systems of the social order.

For that purpose, a more useful approach to the interpretation of women in the system of the Mishnah derives from Michelle Zimbalist Rosaldo, who observes:

> A woman's status will be lowest in those societies where there is a firm differentiation between domestic and public spheres of activity and where women are isolated from one another and placed under a single man's authority, in the home.[17]

It would appear at first glance that the present system accords to the woman a low status, indeed, for it conforms in its basic social and familial datum to Rosaldo's definition. Women not only are assigned tasks limited to the home, but they also are given few tasks in common and, outside of the home, are perceived merely to gossip in the moonlight.

But this is somewhat misleading. We observe, for one thing, that even while married, women may become property owners of substance, as their fathers leave them land. True, the husband enjoys the usufruct so long as the marriage continues. But the woman is ultimate owner. That means the husband has every material reason to want to preserve those

---

[16]Yigael Yadin, *Bar Kokhba. The Rediscovery of the Legendary Hero of the Second Jewish Revolt against Rome* (London: Weidenfeld and Nicccolson, 1971) 222-53.

[17]In Michaelle Zimbalist and Louise Lamphere, eds., *Women, Culture, and Society* (Stanford: Stanford University Press, 1974) 36.

conditions that will secure and perpetuate the marriage. Moreover, the Mishnah makes provision for a husband's relinquishing his rights over his wife's property, even as a condition of marriage. This means that the world outside the linguistic frame of the Mishnah looked much different from that inside, as the case of Babata suggests. Of greater importance than practical affairs, the Mishnah within its theoretical frame does accord the woman rights of property. It does secure the marriage, through the marriage contract and its settlement upon the occasion of divorce or death of the husband, so that in no way is the wife utterly and completely dependent upon the husband. That does not mean the woman enjoys a position, in her realm, equivalent to that of the man, in his. But it does mean that a woman's status in this system is not utterly lacking a measure of autonomy, dignity, and control of her own affairs. The measure, to be sure, is not overflowing.

The Mishnah as a Patriarchal Document

The Mishnah is produced within, and can only imagine, a patriarchal society. Its legislation on women to begin with expresses the values of that society. This is self-evident in that the critical points of the system— beginning, end of marriage—define what is important about woman. What requires close attention and regulation is important because the relationship of woman to man constitutes the criterion of significance. Women's relationships to other women never come under discussion, except as a realm from which a woman may not be wholly cut off at her husband's whim. But if there were activities used by women "as a basis for female solidarity and worth," the Mishnah does not legislate about them. Since it is what the Mishnah deems important that the Mishnah chooses for its careful scrutiny, the point is obvious. The Mishnah does not imagine that men live apart from women or that women exist outside of relationship with, and therefore control of, men.

The Mishnah is a man's document and imagines a man's world. Women have rights, protected by man and Heaven alike. But these rights pertain, specifically, to the relationship of women to men (and Heaven), and specified among them is none of consequence outside of male society. The reason, I think it is clear, is that relationship is derivative and dependent upon that to which relationship is formed. Man is at the center. That fact will make all the more striking the contrary perspective set forth in other documents in the canon of the Judaism of the dual Torah, also produced by men, also expressive of a male viewpoint—by definition.

But, to remain entirely within the framework of the *halakhah*, which is where men have their say and set forth the norms of social behavior, we may ask, how does what the *halakhah* says about women fit in with what the *halakhah* has to say about each and every other topic to which the Mishnah assigns systemic importance? In fact, when we can explain what the system wishes to say concerning women, we uncover the systemic message as a whole, for the critical issue of the meaning of the Mishnah's system of women brings us to the center of the Mishnah's meaning, which the system of women, like all other Mishnaic systems, expresses in language particular to its topic. What the Mishnah wishes to state it states systemically, as a whole. The parts and the details take on meaning only as part of that whole. When we understand why the Mishnah chooses the six topics it chooses, and not some other set of six—or five, or nine or sixty-three—topics shall we make sense of what the Mishnah says about, and through, each of those topics. To that inquiry, women mean no more, and no less, than albatrosses, rocks, trees, or study of Torah, on which we have neither tractates nor divisions, or torts, purities, or agricultural offerings to priests, on which we have both. It is the simple fact that, to say what the system-builders wished to convey, they selected women (as much as Purities or Holy Things or Damages) because through that particular topic they were uniquely able to deliver an important component of the systemic message as a whole, there, and not through the topic of rocks, trees, or Torah-study for that matter.

The first and most important point is that the Mishnah's meaning is defined not only by, but also in behalf of, the Mishnah's authorities. All we have in hand is a statement of how they imagine things should be. As I said, whole divisions (for instance, Holy Things and Purities) dwell upon matters that, at the moment at which the systems came into being and were worked out, simply did not exist. Others speak of matters that, at the time of discourse, lay wholly outside the practical power and authority of the participants to the discussion, for example, the organization of a government spelled out in *Sanhedrin*. Still others take for granted that only a small number of people will keep the law properly, as in the case of the larger part of Agricultural Rules. So the Mishnah speaks for its authorities and tells us what is on their minds, that alone. Only in later times would the Israelite world come to approximate, and even to conform to, Mishnah's vision of reality. But the meaning of which we presently speak is in the minds of a handful of men.

From these men's perspective, second, women are abnormal; men are normal.[18] I am inclined to think that the reason they choose to work out a division on Women flows from that fact. And, when we recall that the only other systems of women worthy of the name come to us under priestly auspices, in the Priestly Code (Lev 1-15) and in the Holiness Code (Lev 17ff.), we can hardly be surprised at the selection of women, for the men before us create the Mishnah as a scribal-priestly document. Women in the priestly perspective of the holy life are excluded from the centers of holiness. They cannot enter the sensitive domain of the cult, cannot perform the cultic service, and cannot participate even in the cultic liturgy. Likewise, in time to come, when Rabbinic Judaism comes to full expression so that study of Torah comes to be seen as a cultic act, the Rabbi as equivalent to the priest, and the community of Israel assembled for study of Torah as equivalent to the Holy Temple, it would be perfectly "natural" to continue the exclusion of women. The Dual Torah's is a Judaic system in which people who are neither priests nor scribes take up the method of the priests and the message of the scribes. To all of this, women form an anomaly and a threat, just as the priests concluded in Ezra's time when they produced Leviticus. That is why, as in other matters of anomaly or threat, the Mishnah must devote a rather considerable measure of attention to forming a system of women—a system of law to regulate the irregular.

Woman as Anomaly

We shall now dwell on this matter of woman as anomaly because here we identify the core and key to the world-view laid out for us in the division of Women. The treatment and selection of women constitute the exegetical fulcrum for the Mishnaic system as a whole. To repeat my

---

[18]The notion of the woman as anomalous, which I first read in Simone de Beauvoir, *The Second Sex* (1953) will now come to the fore as the hermeneutical fulcrum for the interpretation of the Mishnah's system of Women and, as I shall argue, of Mishnah's system as a whole.

main proposition: when we make sense of Mishnah's choice of the theme, Women, and what it wishes to say about that theme, we shall find ourselves at the heart of the Mishnaic system of reality-building. To begin with, if we are going to be able to make sense of Mishnah's choices, its inclusions and exclusions in its discourse on women, it must, I think, be because of the basic conception of woman. They are abnormal and excluded, something out of the ordinary. That is why they form a focus on sanctification: restoration of the extraordinary to the ordinary and the normal.

Let me spell this out. The Mishnah cannot declare a dead creeping thing clean. The Mishnah cannot make women into men. It can provide for the purification of what is made unclean. It can provide for a world in which it is normal for woman to be subject to man—father or husband—and a system that regularizes the transfer of women from the hand of the father to that of the husband. The regulation of the transfer of women is Mishnah's way of effecting the sanctification of what, for the moment, disturbs and disorders the orderly world. The work of sanctification *becomes* necessary in particular at the point of danger and disorder. An order of women must be devoted, therefore, to just these things, so as to preserve the normal modes of creation ("how these things really are") so that maleness, that is, normality, may encompass all, even and especially at the critical point of transfer.

In this sense, the process outlined in the division of Purities for the restoration of normality, meaning cleanness, to what is abnormal, meaning uncleanness, is suggestive. What the Mishnah proposes is to restore the equilibrium disturbed by the encounter with the disruptive, disorganizing, and abnormal sources of uncleanness specified in the Priestly writings. So the division of Purities centers attention on the point of abnormality and its restoration to normality: sources of uncleanness, foci on uncleanness, modes of purification.[19] Now, when we reflect on the view of women contained in the Mishnah, we observe a parallel interest in the point of abnormality and the restoration to normality of women: the moment at which a woman changes hands. So Rosaldo states:

---

[19]This fact is spelled out at great length in my *Purities*, XXII (Leiden: E. J. Brill, 1977).

The fact that men, in contrast to women, can be said to be associated
with culture reflects another aspect of cultural definitions of the female.
Recent studies of symbolic culture have suggested that whatever violates
a society's sense of order will be seen as threatening, nasty, disorderly,
or wrong. . . . The idea of "order" depends, logically, on "disorder" as
its opposite. . . . Now I would suggest that women in many societies
will be seen as something "anomalous." Insofar as men, in their
institutionalized relations of kinships, politics, and so on, define the
public order, women are their opposite. Where men are classified in
terms of ranked, institutional positions, women are simply women and
their activities, interests, and differences receive only idiosyncratic note.
Where male activities are justified and rationalized by a fine societal
classification, by a system of norms acknowledging their different
pursuits, women are classified together, and their particular goals are
ignored. From the point of view of the larger social system, they are
seen as deviants or manipulators; because systems of social
classification rarely make room for their interests, they are not publicly
understood. But women defy the ideal of the male order. They may be
defined as virgins, yet be necessary to the group's regeneration. They
may be excluded from authority, yet exercise all sorts of informal
power. Their status may be derived from their male relations, yet they
outlive their husbands and fathers. And insofar as the presence of
women does introduce such contradictions, women will be seen as
anomalous and defined as dangerous, dirty, and polluting, as something
to be set apart.[20]

Rosaldo further states: "Women in conventional roles are not threatening.
A woman who is a wife and a mother is benign." Now, as we have
observed, it is the point at which a woman is perceived as threatening
—when she has the capacity to become a wife and a mother but is not
yet in a position of realizing it, or when she ceases to be a wife—that her
status requires the regulation, ordering, and protection of the Mishnah's
elaborate and reverent intellectual attention.

About woman as wife the Mishnah has little to say; about woman as
mother, I cannot think of ten relevant lines in the Mishnah's division of
Women! For these are not the topics to which the Mishnah will devote
itself. The three systemically anomalous tractates from this perspective

---

[20] *Women, Culture, and Society,* 31-32.

are not so far out of line. *Sotah*, of course, attends to the wife who is not a good wife. *Nedarim*, bearing *Nazir* in its wake, treats those moments specified by scripture as especially important in the daughter's relationship to the father or the wife's to the husband. These are moments at which the father or the husband may intervene in the relationship of daughter or wife to God. In the present context, that relationship is unruly and dangerous, exactly like the relationship of daughter leaving father or of wife leaving husband, that is, at the critical moment of betrothal and consummation of the marriage, with attendant property settlement; or divorce or husband's death, at the critical moment of the dissolution of the marriage, with attendant property settlement.

The Mishnah's system addresses and means to create an ordered and well-regulated world. The Mishnah states that which is the order and regulation for such a world. The division of Purities spells out the balance and wholeness of the system of cleanness, defining what is a source of uncleanness, a focus affected by uncleanness, and a mode of effecting cleanness or restoring the balance and the wholeness of the system in stasis. It is the most complete statement of that wholeness and regulation that are at every point besought and realized. The division of Holy Things addresses a different sort of message, speaking, as the division of Purities does not, to a real world. But it is the message that is unreal, for in 200 C.E. there is no cult. Holy Things provides a map for a world that is both no more and not yet, for a Temple that was and will be. The stasis attained therein, it must follow, is to portray how things truly are, at a moment at which they are not that way at all.

By contrast to Purities, which conceives of a sequence of states in a reality out there and tells the regulations for each of those states, Holy Things speaks of how things are in mind, at a moment at which mind is all there is. When we come to the division of Women, therefore, we find ourselves confronted by a familiar problem, expressed through (merely) unfamiliar facts. The familiar problem is an anomalous fact. An anomaly is, for this system, a situation requiring human interventions so that affairs may be brought into stasis, that is, made to conform with the heavenly projections of the created world. That quest for stasis, order and regulation, which constitute wholeness and completeness, in the division of Women takes up yet another circumstance of uncertainty. This it confronts at its most uncertain. The system subjects the anomaly of woman to the capacity for ordering and regulating, which is the gift and skill of priests and scribes.

The anomaly of woman therefore is addressed at its most anomalous, that is, disorderly and dangerous, moment, the point at which women move from one setting and status to another. The very essence of the anomaly, woman's sexuality, is scarcely mentioned. But it always is just beneath the surface. For what defines the woman's status—what is rarely made explicit in the division of Women—is not whether or not she may have sexual relations, but with whom she may have them and with what consequence. It is assumed that, from long before the advent of puberty, a girl may be married and in any event is a candidate for sexuality. From puberty onward she will be married. But what is selected for intense and continuing concern is with whom she may legitimately do so, and with what economic and social effect. There is no sexual deed without public consequence; and only rarely will a sexual deed not yield economic results, in the aspect of the transfer of property from one hand to another. So, as I said, what is anomalous is the woman's sexuality, which is treated in a way wholly different from man's. And the goal and purpose of the Mishnah's division of Women are to bring under control and force into stasis all of the wild and unruly potentialities of sexuality, with their dreadful threat of uncontrolled shifts in personal status and material possession alike.

The Mishnah invokes Heaven's interest in this most critical moment for individual and society alike. Its conception is that what is rightly done on earth is confirmed in Heaven. A married woman who has sexual relations with any man but her husband has not merely committed a crime on earth. She has sinned against Heaven. It follows that when a married woman receives a writ of divorce and so is free to enter into relationships with any man of her choosing, the perceptions of that woman are affected in Heaven just as much as are those of man on earth. What was beforehand a crime and a sin afterward is holy, not subject to punishment at all. The woman may contract a new marriage on earth that Heaven, for its part, will oversee and sanctify. What is stated in these simple propositions is that those crucial and critical turnings at which a woman changes hands produce concern and response in Heaven above as much as on earth below. And the reason, as I suggested at the beginning, is that Heaven is invoked specifically at those times, and in those circumstances, in which the Mishnah confronts a situation of anomaly or disorder and proposes to effect suitable regulation and besought order.

It is to a situation that is so fraught with danger as to threaten the order and regularity of the stable, sacred society in its perfection and at its point of stasis that the Mishnah will devote its principal cognitive and legislative efforts. For that situation, the Mishnah will invoke Heaven and express its most vivid concern for sanctification. What breaks established routine or what is broken out of established routine is what is subject to the fully articulated and extensive reflections of a whole division of the Mishnah, or, in Hebrew, a *seder,* an order, of the whole. The Mishnah, as usual, provides its own most reliable exegesis in calling each one of its six principal divisions a *seder,* an order. The anomaly of woman is worked out—that is, held in stasis—by assigning her to man's domain. It follows that the stasis is disturbed at the point when she changes hands. Then Mishnah's instincts for regulating and thereby restoring the balance and order of the world are aroused. So from the recognition of the anomalous character of women, we find ourselves moving toward the most profound and fundamental affirmations of the Mishnah about the works of sanctification: the foci and the means. Women are sanctified through the deeds of men. So, too, are earth and time, the fruit of the herd and of the field, the bed,[21] chair, table, and hearth—but, in the nature of things, women most of all.

So much for matters in theory. Let us turn to some concrete cases of how a women's situation is treated, which will show us the correct context in which to describe the halakhic stance: women in the Mishnah's legal system of hierarchical classification.

---

[21]I do not make reference to the menstrual taboo because Mishnah's *system* of Women does not deal with it. Menstrual laws are a subdivision, or tractate, of the system of Purities. That fact has to be interpreted in its own terms, and, while interesting, plays no role in the argument of this book. It strikes me as a problem that requires investigation in its own context, and since the Mishnah's framers define that context outside of the Division of Women but in the Division of Purities, the topic demands its own setting. Nothing written on the subject, so far as the Mishnah's rules figure, strikes me as having addressed the systemic question at all, but I have nothing better to contribute at this time.

Chapter Two

Women and Caste in Mishnaic Law

The Mishnaic law of women defines the position of women in the social economy of Israel's supernatural and natural reality. That position acquires definition in relationship to men, who give form to the Israelite social economy. It is effected through both supernatural and natural, this-worldly, action. What man and woman do on earth provokes a response in Heaven, and the correspondences are perfect. So the position of women is defined and secured in Heaven and here on earth, and that position, always and invariably relative to men, is what comes into consideration. The principal point of interest on Mishnah's part is the time at which a women changes hands. That is, she becomes, and ceases to be, holy to a particular man, enters and leaves the marital union. These are the dangerous and disorderly points in the relationship of woman to man, therefore, as I said, also to society. These generalizations now require concrete illustration.

From this general picture of the systemic message that the Mishnah's law sets forth through its treatment of the topic of women, we now turn to a concrete account of how various laws treat that topic. For, just as we should not want to lose sight of the system as a whole, so too we do not wish to ignore the details that all together go to compose the systemic statement. Since the household forms the building block of the Mishnah's theory of the social order and also, as a matter of simple fact, the sole realm in which women are imagined to function, the way in which women are portrayed within the household defines the focus of our study. For the other realms of social action, politics, the Temple, the world of Torah-study, to name three, entirely exclude women. A mark of the *halakhah's* expectation of an *aggadic* realm of complementarity and conclusion is to be discerned at just this point. For women do form one half of the entire social order; they have a heavy stake in social action, politics, and the Temple; they too stand at Sinai and receive the Torah.

If the *halakhah* does not legislate concerning them in those circumstances, it cannot be because no *halakhah* applies. It is, rather, because in those realms of activity and imagination, normative rules do not pertain to begin with, but formulations of value, sentiment, and attitude, take over. When it comes to normative rules of *halakhah*, by contrast, it is only in the household that the Mishnah legislates for women in particular. So far as the *halakhah* is concerned, *it* is only there that women play any active, sentient, and differentiated role, e.g., as other than furniture or oxen.[1] And once more, we remind ourselves, the Judaism of the dual Torah never conceives of women as comparable to furniture or oxen, except in the limited realm of the *halakhah;* in the world measured by the *aggadah,* by contrast, women define highly sentient, indeed critical actors in Israel's life. They impose the shape of their particular attitudes, the structure of their distinctive perspective, upon the world of Israel viewed all together and all at once. The laws we shall now examine do not suggest so, nor could these laws explain why that should be so. But in Chapters Three and Four we shall find ample evidence to balance the severely-masculine character (again, masculine by the canon's own criteria) of what we are about to examine. The *halakhah* read without the *aggadah* seriously distorts the facts of Israel's social order as defined by the dual Torah. But, to begin with, the *halakhah* still has to be examined in its own terms. That is what we now shall do.

I. Women in the Household

The social vision of the Judaism of the Mishnah says the same thing about everything. Accordingly, knowing the urgent question and the self-evidently valid answer of the system, we can predict what the system has to say about any topic it chooses to treat. The social vision of the Mishnah's Judaism encompasses issues of gender, social structure and construction, wealth and transactions in property, the organization of the castes of society. In all these matters the system seeks the principles of

---

[1]For a detailed account of this problem, see Judith Romney Wegner, *Chattel or Person? The Status of Women in the Mishnah* (New York: Oxford University Press, 1988).

order and proper classification, identifying as problems the occasions for disorder and improper disposition of persons or resources. The fact that we can find our document saying one thing about many things tells us that the document stands for a well-considered view of the whole, and, when we come to the theological and philosophical program of the same writing, that consistent viewpoint will guide us to what matters and what is to be said about what matters.

As Chapter One has shown us, the principal focus of a social vision framed by men, such as that of the Mishnah, not only encompasses, but focuses upon, woman, who is perceived as the indicative abnormality in a world to which men are normal. But to place into perspective the Mishnah's vision of woman, we have to locate woman within the larger structure defined by the household. That is for two reasons. First of all, as a matter of definition, woman forms the other half of the whole that is the householder. Second, since, as we have already seen, the household forms the building block of the social construction envisioned by the Mishnah's framers, it is in that setting that every other component of the social world of the system must situate itself.

In the conception at hand, which sees Israel as made up, on earth, of households and villages, the economic unit also framed the social one, and the two together composed, in conglomerates, the political one, hence a political economy (*polis, oikos*), initiated within an economic definition formed out of the elements of production. That explains why women cannot be addressed outside of the framework of the economic unit of production defined by the household. For, throughout, the Mishnah makes a single cogent statement that the organizing unit of society and politics finds its definition in the irreducible unit of economic production. The Mishnah conceives no other economic unit of production than the household, though it recognizes that such existed; its authorship perceived no other social unit of organization than the household and the conglomeration of households, though that limited vision omitted all reference to substantial parts of the population perceived to be present e.g., craftsmen, the unemployed, the landless, and the like. But what about woman in particular?

The framers of the Mishnah, for example, do not imagine a household headed by a woman; a divorced woman is assumed to return to her father's household. The framers make no provision for the economic activity of isolated individuals, out of synchronic relationship with a household or a village made up of householders. Accordingly, craftsmen and day laborers or other workers, skilled and otherwise, enter the world of social and economic transactions only in relationship to the householder. The upshot, therefore, is that the social world is made up of households, and, since households may be made up of many families, e.g., husbands, wives, children, all of them dependents upon the householder, households in no way are to be confused with the family. The indicator of the family is kinship, that of the household, "propinquity or residence." And yet, even residence is not always a criterion for membership in the household unit, since the craftsmen and day laborers are not assumed to live in the household-compound at all. Accordingly, the household forms an economic unit, with secondary criteria deriving from that primary fact.

II. Women at the Interstices: Mishnah-tractate *Yebamot* Chapter Ten (*m. Yebam.* 10:1-5)

As we realize in general terms, it is when the status of the woman is uncertain that she forms a systemic crisis. Precisely how, at such a circumstance, she is dealt with is now to be addressed. For our sample of the Mishnah's treatment of interstitial women, we take up consideration of the disposition of matters of doubt in marital ties. We do not know whether she is now married, the husband's whereabouts being unknown. She remarries. If she does so with permission of the court, one set of penalties is incurred, if without, another; and the former proves far the more drastic. In *m. Yebamot* 10:1-5, we have to consider the results of an erroneous union. Let us consider the composition of the sustained passage.

M. *Yebamot* 10:1 is the keystone of the first unit. There we discover that a woman's husband has gone abroad and been reported dead. The woman remarries. Then the husband turns out not to have died. At first glance, the consequences are unambiguous. The woman is put away by both men and receives financial compensation from neither. These penalties are so worked out as to treat the woman as an adulterer. But there are some complications. First, several second century authorities protest that, in certain property-matters, the woman does have a valid claim. Second, *m. Yebamot* 10:1S makes explicit that these rules are invoked if the woman marries *with* a court's permission. In this case, she has deliberately violated the sanctity of her first marriage. But, if she does not have permission to remarry, she may return to the first husband, and the second marriage is null. *m. Yebamot* 10:2 contradicts this view, by saying that if the woman remarried with a court's permission, she nonetheless is put away; but she owes no sin-offering. If she did not have a court's permission, she also is put away, but now she does owe an offering. The harmonization of these rules at *m. Yebamot* 10:1S and *m. Yebamot* 10:2A need not detain us.

At *m. Yebamot* 10:3-4 we have a series of cases in which a man or a woman enters into a marriage and finds out it was not valid. For instance, if a man goes abroad with his son his wife is told that the man has died, and then the son also died, she is exempt from levirate marriage. If she finds out that she was not exempt—the son having died first—she turns out to have to be divorced from the second husband. Children by that husband are *mamzers* [bastards]. The principle here is that the children of unions formed in violation of a negative commandment are *mamzers*. Sages hold that violation of levirate rules— negative commandments—does not produce *mamzers*. There are several other cases in which marriage has taken place because of incorrect information, with the result that the woman must go forth and the children are *mamzers*. At *m. Yebamot* 10:4 we have a man who marries his wife's sister, falsely assuming his wife has died. Such a marriage is null and of no effect. If a man is told that his wife has died and he marries her sister and discovers that at the time of the remarriage the wife had not died, but she subsequently did die, then children born before the actual death are deemed *mamzers,* those afterward, not. *M. Yebamot* 10:5 concludes this construction with a sequence of marriages that presents a rather simple conundrum for solution.

1.   A. The woman whose husband went overseas,
     B. and whom they came and told, "Your husband has died,"
     C. and who remarried,
     D. and whose husband afterward returned,
     E. (1) goes forth from this one [the second husband] and from that one [the first].
     F. And (2) she requires a writ of divorce from this one and from that.

G. And she has no claim of (3) [payment of her] marriage-contract, (4) of usufruct, (5) of alimony, or (6) of indemnification, either on this one or on that.

H. (7) If she had collected anything [of G] from this one or from that, she must return it.

I. (8) And the offspring is deemed a *mamzer*, whether born of the one marriage or the other.

J. And (9) neither one of the [if he is a priest] becomes unclean for her [if she should die and require burial].

K. And neither one of them has the right either (10) to what she finds or (11) to the fruit of her labor, or (12) to annul her vows.

L. [If] (13) she was an Israelite girl, she is rendered invalid for marriage into the priesthood; a Levite, from eating tithe; and a priest-girl, from eating heave-offering.

M. And the heirs of either one of the husbands do not inherit her *ketubah* [=marriage-settlement].

N. And if they died, a brother of this one and a brother of that perform the rite of *halisah* but do not enter into levirate marriage.

O. R. Yosé says, "Her marriage-contract is [a lien] on the property of her first husband."

P. R Eleazar says, "The first husband has a right to what she finds and to the fruit of her labor and to annul her vows."

Q. R. Simeon says, "Having sexual relations with her or performing a rite of *halisah* with her on the part of the brother of the first husband exempts her co-wife [from levirate connection].

R. "And offspring from him is not a *mamzer*."

S. But if she should remarry without permission, [since the remarriage was an inadvertent transgression and null], she is permitted to return to him.

m. **Yebamot 10:1**

This is formally and substantively a slightly complicated pericope. What makes it formally difficult is the succession of unformulated disputes, that is, **O** contradicts **G3**, **P** rejects **K**, **Q-R** differ from **I**—three points at which named authorities would have stated matters in their own way. Furthermore, **S** presupposes a contrary statement, e.g., at **C** ("who remarried *with permission*"). The omission is noteworthy because *m. Yebamot* 10:2 sets up precisely the contrast expected at *m. Yebamot* 10:1 (and, it goes without saying, routinely read into *m. Yebamot* 10:1). It would appear that the formulation of **A-D** as protasis, and **E-N** as a long apodosis, is distinct from the additional opinions, **O-R**, and what must be deemed an exegetical gloss of fundamental importance is as **S**.

Let us turn to the problems of substance. If we read our case, **A-D**, without **S**'s qualification, then we have a clear-cut case of deliberate remarriage in error. The husband has not died; the second marriage is null. There are, as I count them, thirteen specific consequences of that fact, all of them based on the conception that the deliberate remarriage was valid and the woman is penalized on its account. The woman is prohibited to remain wed to either man (**E**). She must be properly divorced by each (**F**). She has no material claim on either man (**G-H**). That is, she loses her payment of a marriage-contract. The husband does not have to compensate her for the usufruct of *melog*-property. He does not have to provide support for her. He does not have to compensate her for the wear and tear on property belonging to her. If the woman has collected any of the items of **G**, she must restore the goods. If she produced offspring with the second, the child is a *mamzer;* if she went back to the first man and produced offspring with him, that child is a *mamzer* also (**I**). Neither one is deemed her husband as regards burial (**J**) or any other aspect of marriage (**K**). **L** is clear as stated.

The marriage-contract is not inherited by the heirs, **M**. The reference is to male heirs of the woman, who ordinarily would have a claim on the payment of the marriage-contract. If the woman and the two men die, the male children do not inherit the payment. **N** is consistent with **F**. Just as the second man must give a writ of divorce, so his surviving brother must perform the rite of *halisah*. Yosé, as we saw, differs from **G3**. The first husband does owe the marriage-contract. Eleazar concurs with Yosé's general conception, but at **K** Simeon turns to **N** and regards the brother of the first husband as levir in all regards; therefore the second man's brother need not perform the rite of *halisah*. **R** differs from **I(8)**. Offspring from the first husband are valid. It follows that, in the specified details, authorities for **O-R** will not concur that the first husband's relationship has been totally severed by the unfortunate mistake of his wife.

S is a separate conception. It interprets the most fundamental supposition of the whole. It holds that we invoke these thirteen penalties specifically when the woman went to court and got permission to remarry. They suppose she has done so deliberately. But if she did not go to court and simply assumed the husband dead, her action is in error. The second marriage never was valid, as it would have been had she enjoyed a court's protection. It follows that, in the conception of S, we invoke none of the penalties and the woman simply reverts to her original status.

> **1.** A. [If] she was remarried at the instruction of a court,
>
>   B. She is to go forth,
>
>   C. but she is exempt from the requirement of bringing an offering.
>
>   D. [If] she did not remarry at the instruction of a court, she goes forth,
>
>   E. and she is liable to the requirement of bringing an offering.
>
>   F. The authority of the court is strong enough to exempt
>
>   G. [If] the court instructed her to remarry, and she went and entered an unsuitable union,
>
>   H. she is liable for the requirement of bringing an offering.
>
>   I. For the court permitted her only to marry [properly].
>
> m. Yebamot 10:2

M. Yebamot 10:2 augments *m. Yebamot* 10:1**A-D**, on which the pericope depends for context and meaning. **A-C** are balanced against **D-E**, then **F** comments on the whole. **G-I** form an integral, additional gloss. The point is that if the court approved her remarriage, she does not owe a sin-offering, but otherwise she does. **G-I** then clarify the obvious: if she married as a widow to a high priest or a divorcee to an ordinary priest, the court's instruction has not been carried out and its leniency no longer pertains. The real question is whether *m. Yebamot* 10:1**S** and *m. Yebamot* 10:2**A-B** are in accord with one another. If we understand *m. Yebamot* 10:1**S** allows the woman to return to the first husband, and *m. Yebamot* 10:2**B** has her leave both men.

> **I.**
>
> **3.** A. The woman whose husband and son went overseas,
>
>   B. and whom they came and told, "Your husband died, and then your son died,"
>
>   C. and who remarried,
>
>   D. and whom they afterward told, "Matters were reversed"—

E. goes forth [from the second marriage].

F. And earlier and later offspring are in the status of *mamzer*.

II.

G. [If] they told her, "your son died and afterward your husband died," and she entered in levirate marriage, and afterward they told her, "Matters were reversed,"

H. she goes forth [from the levirate marriage].

I. And the earlier and later offspring are in the status of a *mamzer*.

III.

J. [If] they told her, "your husband died," and she married, and afterward they told her, "He was alive, but then he died,"

K. she goes forth [from the second marriage].

L. And the earlier offspring is a *mamzer,* but the later is not a *mamzer*.

IV.

M. [If] they told her, "Your husband died," and she became betrothed, and afterward her husband came home,

N. she is permitted to return to him.

O. Even though the second man gave her a writ of divorce, he has not rendered her invalid from marrying into the priesthood.

P. This did R. Eleazar b. Matya expound, *"And a woman divorced from her husband* (Lev 21:7)—and not from a man who is not her husband."

V.

4.   A. He whose wife went overseas, and whom they came and told, "Your wife has died,"

B. and who married her sister,

C. and whose wife thereafter came back—

D. she is permitted to come back to him.

E. He is permitted to marry the kinswomen of the second and the second woman is permitted to marry his kinsmen.

F. And if the first died, he is permitted to marry the second woman.

VI.

G. [If] they said to him, "She was alive, but then she died"—

H. the former offspring is a *mamzer* [born before the wife died], and the latter is not a *mamzer*.

I. R. Yosé says, "Anyone who invalidates [his wife] for [marriage] with others invalidates her for marriage for himself, and whoever does not invalidate his wife for marriage with others does not invalidate her for himself."

m. Yebamot 10:3–4

At *m. Yebamot* 10:3 we have three parallel cases (**A-L**). The opening unit is in the expected apocopation, and the rest in declarative sentences, as indicated. The important point throughout is the status of the offspring. The woman has a child *before* she hears that matters are not as she had supposed, then she has one *after* she receives the report. In the first case, the woman assumes, **A-C**, that since her husband did not die childless, she may remarry without levirate rites. If, **D**, matters are reversed, then her remarriage is null. The second marriage now is invalid. All offspring produced in the second marriage are in the status of a *mamzer* (in 'Aqiba's view [*m. Yebamot* 4:13]), since the woman has remarried without the rite of *halisah*. The same rule applies in the contrary situation of **G-I**, in which the woman discovers that she has married her brother-in-law, but not in a levirate connection, and this is prohibited. In the third case, the earlier offspring are produced before the husband died, the later ones, after his death. There is no reason for the latter to be deemed a *mamzer*. The application of *earlier . . . later . . .* at **F** and **I** is meaning-less, but at **L** is not (compare *b. Yeb.* 92a). **M-P** are distinct from the foregoing, although the basic problem is parallel. The betrothal is null and produces no effect, even though a writ of divorce is given.

M. Yebamot 10:4 gives us two cases parallel to *m. Yebamot* 10:3**G-I**, **J-L**. In the former case, we have marriage to the woman's sister, which turns out out be illegal. The marriage is treated, **E**, as entirely null, (I assume, along the lines of *m. Yebamot* 101A). In the final case, we have a problem of offspring, flowing from the foregoing situation. The rule is the same as at *m. Yebamot* 10:3**J-L**. An offspring produced while the wife was alive is a *mamzer,* but one produced after her death is not.

The interpretation of Yosé's saying, **I**, is not self-evident, since there is no clear connection to the context established at **A-H**. *B. Yebamot* 95b [=Babylonian Talmud tractate *Yebamot* p. 95, b = the reverse side of the page] wishes to read **I** in the setting of **A-D**. Then we have a man's wife and his brother-in-law who have gone abroad. The man believed they had died. He married his wife's sister, who had been married to his brother. The two then came home. May he then go back to his wife? Yes, he may. And, it follows, the brother-in-law also may return to marriage with his original wife. Thus since the man's wife is permitted to him, so is the brother-in-law's. This view is rejected, since the necessary language should be, "Whoever does not invalidate for himself does *not* invalidate for others." In another view, commentators have a man's wife go abroad with the husband of his wife's sister (his sister-in-law). They are reported dead. The man marries his wife's sister. The wife and brother-in-law come home. Since the man prohibits the sister of his wife from remarrying her husband—in line with *m. Yebamot* 10:1—he also prohibits his own wife from returning to him. If, on the other hand, his wife's sister has been unmarried or had married without permission and so may return to her husband, he does not prohibit his wife from return to him. But the other proposed interpretations of Yosé's saying require that we read into it considerations and conditions by no means contained at *m. Yebamot* 10:4A-H, so we had best concede we cannot interpret the saying solely within the limits of information provided by the Mishnah itself.Then, for this passage, we cannot explain the text at all. It happens.

5. A. (1) [If] they said to him, "Your wife has died,"

B. (2) and he married her sister b, the same father,

C. (3)[and they reported that] she died and he married her sister from the same mother,

D. (4)[and they reported that] she died and he married her sister from the same father,

E. (5) [And they reported that] she died, and he married her sister from the same mother—

F. and it turns out that all of them are alive—

G. he is permitted [to continue in marriage] with the first, the third, and the fifth,

H. and they exempt their co-wives.

I. But he is prohibited [to continue in marriage] with the second and the fourth,

J. and sexual relations [of the levir] with one of them does not exempt her co-wife.

K. And if he had intercourse with the second after the [actual] death of the first, he is permitted [to remain married to] to second and the fourth,

L. and they exempt their co-wives.

M. And he is prohibited [to remain married to] the third and the fifth.

N. And sexual relations with one of them does not exempt her co-wife.

m. Yebamot **10:5**

The sequence inaugurated at *m. Yebamot* 10:1 concludes with a conundrum. It is frequently the case in large-scale expositions of themes and problems that, at the end, the authorship will put in place a series of problems that require us to apply the general principles we already have been given and have mastered. This system is a mark of the careful composition of these expositions and reminds us of how thoughtfully the Mishnah's final authorship has presented its program. Now we have the problem.

A man learns that his wife has died. He then marries her sister by the same father but by a different mother. They then say the second wife has died. He marries the sister of the second wife by the same mother, but by a different father. His third wife thus is unrelated to the first. Then he is told that the third wife has died, so he marries her sister by the same father but a different mother. The fourth wife is unrelated to the first and second wives. Now his fourth wife is reported dead. He marries her sister by the same mother. The fifth wife is unrelated to the first, second, and third wives. All five wives turn out to be alive. The first, third, and fifth wives are unrelated to one another. The second wife is the sister of the first, and the fourth is the sister of the third. If the man died without offspring, and the first, third, or fifth wife should marry the levir, the other co-wives are exempt. The second and forth wives do not come before the levir, and sexual relations with them do not exempt the co-wives. At **K** we revise the case somewhat. The first wife really has died. Then the second and forth wives are valid, and the third and fifth are not, so the rest follows.

So much for the ordering of the disorderly case at hand. The abstraction, the system's acute interest in women is provoked when a woman's status proves interstitial or ambiguous, now takes on concrete meaning. At the same time, the law's complete indifference to matters of sentiment and emotion—how the woman will have felt, having gotten court permission to remarry, then finding herself and her offspring heavily penalized for obeying the court, for instance—requires one of two interpretations. Either the law completely ignores how people feel, or the law takes for granted mediating and mitigating factors and structures. The second proposition is made the more plausible by what follows in Chapters Three through Five.

III. Women, Marriage, and Caste Structure: Mishnah-tractate *Qiddushin* Chapter Four (*m. Qidd.* 4:1-14)

A second reason for the prominence accorded to woman in the system of the Mishnah now comes to the fore. It is that the caste system takes on concrete consequence principally when it comes to marriage: who may marry whom? And once marriage enters in, then women, of course, assume the principal position, since their wishes are taken into account, and they cannot, as a matter of law, be forced to marry someone they do not wish to have. But they also cannot choose anyone whom they do want. So the systemic goal—the orderly, hierarchical classification of all things in a single structure—is attained, therefore brought to full expression, with special respect to women in particular.

A well-ordered society, in which the economic is neatly organized in symmetrical units of production, with all things in place, in which women find their place within the structure of the well-composed unit of production, cannot ignore other castes and classes of persons, apart from women and the householders to whom they are correlated. For society attends to more than the material and familiar relationships that give form and meaning to its life. The well-composed society also relates to one another the differentiated entities of which it is composed. Now when we speak of the relationship of such entities, formed, for instance, by persons of various points of origin or hereditary standing, we also invoke the conception of hierarchization. This is not only so in the abstract, it is especially the case in the concrete setting of the Mishnah's social vision. Good order means all things are in the right place, and placing things requires ordering them: this above that, that below the other. Thus, we turn to the Mishnah's mode of hierarchization, which is to say, the caste-system that the Mishnah's framers utilize as part of their large-scale ordering of the society in stasis that they propose to envision.

The caste-system finds its expression in the speciation of the population by the criterion of marriage. Who may marry whom, and who may not marry whom, and how are the various marital categories identified? The answers to these questions form the basis for the caste-system that the Mishnah posits. The details to the answers, of course, derive from the adventitious facts of history; e.g., peoples whom the Israelites order in a hierarchy of relationship, classes within Israelite society identified by the sacerdotal origin and order, and the like. All these castes, each bearing its particular and specific indicators, then are held together by the common criterion of marriage.

The main point of the Mishnah's chapter on this subject, which we now consider, is that there are diverse groups who may not intermarry by reason of genealogical impairment or inherited caste-imperfection. *m. Qiddushin* 4:1 lists ten castes, in three divisions. Castes within a given division may intermarry, but castes excluded from said division may not. After some glosses at *m. Qiddushin* 4:2, *m. Qiddushin* 4:3 goes over the same issue and asks which castes may intermarry with which others. *M. Qiddushin* 4:4-5 deals with the investigation of the genealogy of women who present themselves as candidates for marriage. *M. Qiddushin* 4:6-7, finally, work out how daughters of impaired castes may marry those of unimpaired ones, with two distinct, yet intersecting, pericopes on this problem.

The matter of doubts in regard to betrothals is worked out with specific reference to the receipt of testimony, *m. Qiddushin* 4:8, 10-11, and cases of confusion. As to the former, a father is not believed to testify to the unimpaired status of his son (*m. Qidd.* 4:8). If there is a possibility that both a woman and her agent have accepted tokens of betrothal, we go by the one who has done so first. If we do not know who has done so first, both men have to give a writ of divorce. If, finally, a man goes abroad, he is believed to testify about the status of his wife and children when the wife and children are present. If the wife dies, he has to prove that the children's genealogy is unimpaired. The chapter and tractate end by paying attention to a different sort of caste-consideration, namely, the caste formed by professions that have particular relationships with women, a kind of secondary development of the conception of caste as indicated by marital status. These judgments are joined with homiletical materials about a woman's not being alone with men and *vice versa,* and about an unmarried man's not being allowed to teach children; and this matter leads to a long series of sayings about various vocations.

1. A. Ten castes came up from Babylonia: (1) priests, (2) Levites, (3) Israelites, (4) impaired priests, (5) converts, and (6) freed slaves, (7) *mamzers,* (8) *Netins,* (9) "silenced ones" *[shetuqi]* and (10) foundlings.

B. Priests, Levites, and Israelites are permitted to marry among one another.

C. Levites, Israelites, impaired priests, converts, and freed slaves are permitted to marry among one another.

2. A. And what are "silenced ones"?

B. Any who knows the identity of his mother but does not know the identity of his father.

C. And foundlings?

D. Any who was discovered in the market and knows neither his father nor his mother.

E. Abba Saul did call a "silenced one" *[shetuqi]* "one who is to be examined" *[beduqi].*

3. A. All those who are forbidden from entering into the congregation are permitted to marry one another.

B. R. Judah prohibits.

C. R. Eliezer says, "Those who are of certain status are permitted to intermarry with others who are of certain status."

D. Those who are of certain status and those who are of doubtful status, those who are of doubtful status and those who are of certain status, those who are of doubtful status and those who are of doubtful status—

E. "it is prohibited."

F. And who are those who are of doubtful status?

G. The "silenced ones," the foundling, and the Samaritan.

m. *Qiddushin* 4:1–3

Even though *m. Qiddushin* 4:3 is formally distinct from *m. Qiddushin* 4:1 and 2, I treat all three together because of the common theme; those distinct castes that may, or may not, cross lines and intermarry. The point of the excellent formal construction of *m. Qiddushin* 4:1, with its announced topic, **A**, and its triplet of rulings thereafter, **B**, **C**, and **D**, is to distinguish between the castes listed at **A**. The point that is made by **B** concerns whom priests may marry. **C-D** then are significant in omitting from **C** *mamzers* and below. *M. Qiddushin* 4:2 glosses *m. Qiddushin* 4:1, as is obvious. *M. Qiddushin* 4:3 takes up the issue of *m. Qiddushin* 4:1C: *mamzer, Netin* [=descendants of Gibeonites serving as temple slaves], "silenced one," foundling. Now we are not sure of the genealogy of the last two sorts.

All four sorts may not enter the congregation. A maintains that all four may intermarry, just as *m. Qiddushin* 4:1D already has told us. Judah rejects this view. Eliezer contributes a mediating opinion, permitting *mamzers* and *Netins* to intermarry, and prohibiting "silenced ones" and foundlings from intermarrying. It comes out that in his view a *mamzer* and *Netin* may intermarry; a *mamzer* and a *Netin* may not marry a "silenced on" or a foundling; and the same thing is said a second time; and a "silenced one" cannot marry another "silenced one" or a foundling. The intrusion of Samaritan at *m. Qiddushin* 4:3G is exceedingly odd, since, as we observe, the Samaritan has never been part of the antecedent discussion.

4. A. He who marries a priest-girl has to investigate her [genealogy] for four [generations, *via* the] mothers, who are eight:

B. (1) her mother, and (2) the mother of her mother, and (3) the mother of the father of her mother, and (4) her mother, and (5) the mother of her father, and (6) her mother, and (7) the mother of the father of her father, and (8) her mother.

C. And in the case of a Levite-girl and and Israelite-girl, they add on to them yet another [generation for genealogical inquiry].

5. A. They do not carry a genealogical inquiry backward from [proof that one's priestly ancestor has served] at the altar,

B. nor from [proof that one's Levitical ancestor has served] on the platform,

C. and from [proof that one's learned ancestor has served] in the Sanhedrin

D. And all those whose fathers are known to have held office as public officials or as charity-collectors they—marry them into the priesthood, and it is not necessary to conduct an inquiry.

E. R. Yosé says, "Also: He who was signed as a witness in the ancient archives in Sepphoris."

F. R. Hanina b. Antigonos says, "Also: Whoever was recorded in the king's army."

M. Qiddushin **4:4–5**

The one who marries the girl has to make sure that the girl is suitable for marriage to him. This is done by investigating the genealogies of two mothers on the mother's side and two on the father's side: her mother, the mother of her father's mother, her father's mother, and the mother of her father's father. Each of these yields four more as is spelled out. In the case of a marriage to a Levite-girl they all a mother on either side, e.g., the mother of the mother of her mother, and so on. *M. Qiddushin* 4:5**A-C** limit the foregoing, in the assumption that, from the specified points backward, the family title already has been carefully searched. The rest, **D, E, and F,** form a little appendix.

6. A. The daughter of a male of impaired priestly stock is invalid for marriage into the priesthood for all time.

B. An Israelite who married a woman of impaired priestly stock—his daughter is valid for marriage into the priesthood.

C. A man of impaired priestly stock who married an Israelite-girl—his daughter is invalid for marriage into the priesthood.

D. R. Judah says, "The daughter of a male proselyte is equivalent to the daughter of a male of impaired priestly stock."

7. A. R. Eliezer b. Jacob says, "An Israelite who married a female proselyte—his daughter is suitable for marriage into the priesthood.

B. "And a proselyte who married an Israelite-girl—his daughter is valid for marriage into the priesthood.

C. "But a male-proselyte who married a female-proselyte—his daughter is invalid for marriage into the priesthood.

D. "All the same are proselytes and freed slaves, even down
to ten generations—[the daughters cannot marry into the
priesthood]

E. "unless the mother is an Israelite."

F. R. Yosé says, "Also: A proselyte who married a female
proselyte: his daughter is valid for marriage into the priesthood."

m. Qiddushin 4:6–7

The contrast between *m. Qiddushin* 4:6A and *m. Qiddushin* 4:6B
stresses that a male of impaired priestly stock cannot produce a daughter
who may marry into the priesthood even several generations later. But a
female of impaired stock who marries an ordinary Israelite produces a
daughter who may marry into the priesthood. So the impairment passes
on through the male line without limit. In that case, **C** simply repeats
what **A** has already said. Judah's point, **D**, is to treat the daughter of the
male proselyte with an Israelite woman as unable to produce a daughter
able to marry into the priesthood; here too the impairment passes on
through the male line, just as a **A**. In all, therefore, the real pairs are *m.
Qiddushin* 4:6B, **C**, and **A**, **D**, but the whole of *m. Qiddushin* 4:6 must
be deemed a unitary construction of impressive precision.

Once more, then, *m. Qiddushin* gives us distinct pericopes, which, in
point of fact, yield significant differences of opinion, just as at *m.
Qiddushin* 4:1,3. For *m. Qiddushin* 4:7 presents Eliezer b. Jacob's view,
which is explicitly contrary to Judah's at *m. Qiddushin* 4:6D. Judah holds
that the daughter of a male proselyte carries forward the father's
impairment, in such wise that her daughter, even if produced with an
Israelite husband, cannot marry into the priesthood. Eliezer b. Jacob
rejects this view (*m. Qiddushin* 4:7B). He also maintains that a female-
proselyte produces a daughter eligible for marriage into the priesthood.
The sole point at which a proselyte suffers limitations in this regard, *m.
Qiddushin* 4:7C, is when a male-proselyte marries a female-proselyte.
D-E then generalize on the foregoing. Yosé, finally, rejects this view and
takes up the most lenient position of all, as against both Judah and
Eliezer b. Jacob. A couple who converted to Judaism produce a daughter
who may marry into the priesthood.

8. A. He who says, "This, my son, is a *mamzer*," is not
believed.

B. And even if both parties say concerning the foetus in the mother's womb, "It is a *mamzer*," they are not believed.

C. R. Judah says, "They are believed."

m. Qiddushin 4:8

The dispute is clear as stated; along the lines of *M. Qiddushin* 3:8, the father cannot discredit his offspring, A.

9. A. He who gave the power to his agent to accept tokens of betrothal for his daughter, but then he himself went and betrothed her—

I.

B. if his came first, his act of betrothal is valid.

II.

C. And if those of his agent came first, his act of betrothal is valid.

III.

D. And if it is not known [which came first], both parties give a writ of divorce.

E. But if they wanted, one of them gives a writ of divorce, and one consummates the marriage.

F. And so: A woman who gave the power to her agent to accept tokens of betrothal in her behalf, and then she herself went and accepted tokens of betrothal in her own behalf—

I.

G. if hers came first, her act of betrothal is valid.

II.

H. And if those of her agent came first, his act of betrothal is valid.

III.

I. And if it is not known [which of them came first], both parties give a writ of divorce.

J. But if they wanted, one of them gives a writ of divorce and one of them consummates the marriage.

m. Qiddushin 4:9

M. Qiddushin is clear in each of its balanced statements, A–E, F–J.

I.

10. A. He who went along with his wife overseas, and he and his wife and children came home,

B. and he said, "The woman who went abroad with me, lo, this is she, and these are her children"—

C. he does not have to bring proof concerning the woman or the children.

II.

D. [If he said,] "She died, and these are her children,"

E. he does bring proof about the children.

F. But he does not bring proof about the woman.

III.

11. A. [If he said], "I married a woman overseas. Lo, this is she, and these are her children,"

B. he brings proof concerning the woman, but he does not have to bring proof concerning the children

IV.

C. ". . . she died, and these are her children,"

D. he has to bring proof concerning the woman and the children

m. Qiddushin **4:10–11**

The issue of proof is to demonstrate the genealogical soundness of the wife and children. In the first case, the woman is confirmed as valid, and, further, we take for granted *m. Qiddushin* 4:10A–C, 4:11B, that the woman would protest if the children were not hers. If the man can prove that the children belong to the deceased woman, then they are accepted as suitable for marriage without further proof. If, *m. Qiddushin* 4:11A–B, the man can prove that the woman is genealogically sound, he need not prove the same concerning the children of that marriage. If, C–D, we have a case in which the overseas wife has died, the man has to show both that the woman was genealogically sound, and also that the children were her children.

12. A. A man should not remain alone with two women, but a woman may remain alone with two men.

B. R. Simeon says, "Also: One may stay alone with two women, when his wife is with him.

C. "And he sleeps with them in the same inn,

D. "Because his wife keeps watch over him."

E. A man may stay alone with his mother or with his daughter.

F. And he sleeps with them with flesh touching.

G. But if they [the son who is with the mother, the daughter with the father] grew up, this one sleeps in her garment, and that one sleeps in his garment.

13. A. An unmarried man may not teach scribes.

B. Nor may a woman teach scribes.

C. R. Eliezer says, "Also: He who has no wife may not teach scribes."

14. A. R. Judah says, "An unmarried man may not herd cattle.

B. "And two unmarried men may not sleep in the same cloak."

C. And sages permit it.

D. Whoever has business with women should not be alone with women.

E. And a man should not teach his son a trade which he has to practice among women.

F. R. Meir says, "A man should always teach his son a clean and easy trade. And let him pray to him to whom belong riches and possessions.

G. "For there is no trade which does not involve poverty or wealth.

H. "For poverty does not come from one's trade, nor does wealth come from one's trade.

I. "But all is in accord with a man's merit."

J. R. Simeon b. Eleazar says, "Have you ever seen a wild beast or a bird who has a trade? Yet they get along without difficulty. And were they not created only to serve me? And I was created to serve my Master. So is it not logical that I should get along without difficulty? But I have done evil and ruined my living."

L. Abba Gurion of Saidon says in the name of Abba Gurya, "A man should not teach his son to be an ass-driver, a camel-driver, a barber, a sailor, a herdsman, or a shopkeeper. For their trade is the trade of thieves."

M. R. Judah says in his name, "Most ass-drivers are evil, most camel-drivers are decent, most sailors are saintly, the best among physicians is going to Gehenna, and the best of butchers is a partner of Amalek."

N. R. Nehorai says, "I should lay aside every trade in the world and teach my son only Torah.

O. "For a man eats its fruits in this world, and the principal remains for the world to come.

P. "But other trades are not that way.

Q. "When a man gets sick or old or has pains and cannot do his job, lo, he dies of starvation.

R. "But with Torah it is not that way.

S. "But it keeps him from all evil when he is young, and it gives him a future and a hope when he is old.

T. "Concerning his youth, what does it say" *They who wait upon the Lord shall renew their strength* (Isa 40:31). And concerning his old age what does it say? *They shall still bring forth fruit in old age* (Ps 92:14).

U. "And so it was with regard to the patriarch Abraham, may he rest in peace, *And Abraham was old and well along in years, and the Lord blessed Abraham in all things* (Gen 24:1)

V. "We find that the patriarch Abraham kept the entire Torah even before it was revealed, since it says, *Since Abraham obeyed my voice and kept my charge, my commandments, my statutes, and my laws* (Gen 26:5)."

m. *Qiddushin* 4:12–14

M. Qiddushin 4:13 refers to teachers of young children. They should not be brought into close association with the mothers (**A**) or fathers (**B**) of the children. The formal and substantive traits of what follows require no comment. Now to the general picture of the social vision of the Mishnah that has emerged in Chapters Three and Four.

VI. The Social Vision of the Mishnah

It is through *halakhah,* such as we have now examined in some detail, that the Mishnah set forth its doctrine of women, a necessary and critical component of its larger structure of the social order. But the feminine can be defined only in relationship to the masculine and vice versa, so any picture of women in the *halakhah* of the Mishnah must encompass the Mishnah's view of men as well. And here, there is only one man who matters, and that is, the householder. So to complete our account of the feminine, we turn to the portrait of the masculine: man and his social traits in the halakhic structure of the Mishnah.

In everyday transactions, as the framers of the Mishnah sorted them out, the authorship of the document set forth a social vision we find effected in every detail. They proposed to effect the vision of a steady-state economy, engaged in always-equal exchanges of fixed wealth and intrinsic value. Essentially, the Mishnah's authorship aimed at the fair adjudication of conflict, worked out in such a way that no party gained, none lost, in any transaction. The task of Israelite society, as they saw it, was to maintain perfect stasis, to preserve the prevailing situation, to secure the stability of not only relationships but status and standing. To this end, in the interchanges of buying and selling, giving and taking, borrowing and lending, transactions of the market and exchanges with artisans and craftsmen and laborers, it is important to preserve the essential equality, not merely equity, of exchange. Fairness alone does not suffice. *Status quo ante* forms the criterion of the true market, reflecting as it does the exchange of value for value, in perfect balance. That is the way that, in reference to the market, the systemic point of urgency, the steady-state of the polity, therefore also of the economy, is stated. The upshot of their economics is simple. No party in the end may have more than what he had at the outset, and none may emerge as the victim of a sizable shift in fortune and circumstance. All parties' rights to and in the stable and unchanging political economy are preserved. When, therefore, the condition of a person is violated, the law will secure the restoration of the antecedent status.

Critical to the social system of the Mishnah is its principal social entity, the village, imagined as a society that never changes in any important way, comprising households, and the model, from household to village to "all Israel," comprehensively describes whatever of "Israel" the authorship at hand has chosen to describe. We have therefore to identify as systemically indicative the centrality of political economy—"community, self-sufficiency, and justice"—within the system of the Mishnah. It is no surprise, either, that the point of originality of the political economy of the Mishnah's system is its focus upon the society organized in relationship to the control of the means of production—the farm, for the household is always the agricultural unit.

In line with what I just said, I cannot point to any other systemic statement among the Judaisms of antiquity, to any other Judaism, that, in the pattern of the Mishnah, takes as its point of departure the definition of an "Israel" as a political economy, that is, as an aggregation of villages made up of households. We realize, in the context of social thought of ancient times, that this systemic focus upon political economy also identifies the Mishnah's authorship with the prevailing conventions of a long ago age and a far-away land, namely, Greece in the time of

Aristotle. For thinkers represented by Aristotle took for granted that society was formed of self-sufficient villages, made up of self-sufficient farms: households run by householders. But, we know, in general, nothing can have been further from the facts of the world of "Israel"; that is, the Jews in the land of Israel, made up as it was of not only villages but cities, not only small but larger holders, and, most of all, of people who held no land at all and never would.

In the context of a world of pervasive diversity, the Mishnah's authorship set forth a fantastic conception of a simple world of little blocks formed into big ones: households into villages, no empty spaces, but also, no vast cities. In the conception of the authorship of the Mishnah, community, or village (*polis*) is made up of households, and the household (*bayit/oikos*) constituted the building block of both society or community and also economy. It follows that the household forms the fundamental, irreducible, and of course, representative unit of the economy, the means of production, the locus and the unit of production. We should not confuse the household with class-status, e.g., thinking of the householder as identical with the wealthy. The opposite is suggested on every page of the Mishnah, in which householders vie with craftsmen for ownership of the leavings of the loom and the chips left behind by the adze.

The household, rather, forms an economic and a social classification, defined by function, specifically, economic function. A poor household was a household, and (in theory, the Mishnah's authorship knows none such in practice) a rich landholding that did not function as a center for a social and economic unit (e.g., a rural industrial farm) was not a household. The household constituted the center of the productive economic activities we now handle through the market. Within the household, all local, as distinct from cultic, economic (therefore social) activities and functions were held together. For the unit of production comprised also the unit of social organization, and, of greater import still, the building block of all larger social (now also political) units, with special reference to the village.

In its identification of the householder as the building block of society, to the neglect of the vast panoply of "others"—"non-householders" (including, after all, that half of the whole of the Israelite society comprising women)—the Mishnah's authorship reduced the dimensions of society to only a single component in it: the male land-owner engaged in agriculture. But that is the sole option open to a system that, for reasons of its own, wished to identify productivity with agriculture, individuality in God's image with ownership of land, and social standing and status, consequently, with ownership and control of the land that constituted the sole systemically-consequential means of production. Now if we were to list all of the persons and professions who enjoy no role in the system, or who are treated as ancillary to the system, we have to encompass not only workers—the entire landless working class!—but also craftsmen and artisans, teachers and physicians, clerks and officials, traders and merchants, the whole of the commercial establishment, not to mention women as a caste. Such an economics, disengaged from so large a sector of the economy of which it claimed, even if only in theory, to speak, can hardly be called an economics at all. And yet, as we have seen and shall realize still more keenly in the coming chapters, that economics bore an enormous burden of the systemic message and statement of the Judaism set forth by the authorship of the Mishnah.

Fair and just to all parties, the authorship of the Mishnah nonetheless speaks in particular for the Israelite landholding, proprietary male. The Mishnah's problems are the problems of the householder; its perspectives are his. Its sense of what is just and fair expresses his sense of the givenness and cosmic rightness of the present condition of society. These are men of substance and of means, however modest, aching for a stable and predictable world in which to tend their crops and herds, feed their families and dependents, keep to the natural rhythms of the seasons and lunar cycles, and, in all, live out their lives within strong and secure boundaries on earth and in heaven. This is why the sense of landed place and its limits, the sharp line drawn between village and world, on the one side, Israelite and gentile, on the second, and temple and world, on the third, evoke metaphysical correspondences. Householder, which is Israel, in the village, and temple, and beyond, form a correspondence. Only when we understand the systemic principle concerning God in relationship to Israel in its land shall we come to the fundamental and generative conception that reaches concrete expression in the here and now of the householder as the centerpiece of society.

In this regard, therefore, the Mishnah's social vision finds within its encompassing conception of who forms the *polis* and who merely occupies space within the polis its definition of the realm to which "economics" applies. In the Mishnah's social vision the householder is systemically the active force, and all other components of the actual economy (as distinct from the economics) prove systemically inert. As such, of course, the Mishnah's social vision ignores most of the actuality of the Jewish people in the Land of Israel in the first and second centuries. But then what of the economically active members of the *polis*, the one who had capital and knew how to use it? If they wished to enter that elevated "Israel" that formed the social center and substance of the Mishnah's Israel, they had to purchase land. The Mishnah's social vision thus describes a steady-state society.

Now wonder that the framers of the Mishnah conceived of the economy as one of self-sufficiency, made up as it was (in their minds, at least) of mostly self-sufficient households joined in essentially self-sufficient villages. They further carry forward the odd conception of the Priestly authorship of Leviticus that the ownership of the land is supposed to be stable, indeed inalienable from the family, if not from the individual, as at Leviticus 27, so that, if a family alienates inherited property, it reverts to that family's ownership after a span of time. The conception of steady-state economy therefore dominated, so that, as a matter of fact, in utter stasis, no one would rise above his natural or inherent standing, and no one would fall either. And that is the economy they portray and claim to regulate through their legislation. In such an economy, the market did not form the medium of rationing but in fact had no role to play, except one: to insure equal exchange in all transactions, so that the market formed an arena for transactions of equal value and worth among households each possessed of a steady-state worth. That is why in the market as much as in the holding of land, no one emerged richer or poorer than he was when he came to market, but all remained precisely as rich or as poor as they were at the commencement of a transaction.

To place the social vision of the Mishnah's authorship into context, we have now to ask the final question. For whom and to whom, then, does the Mishnah speak? This draws us back to the entire thematic program of the document, reviewed in Chapter Two. The answers to those questions allow us access to the social vision of the document.

The Priest

In so far as the Mishnah is a document about the holiness of Israel in its Land, it expresses that conception of sanctification and theory of its modes which will have been shaped among those to whom the Temple and its technology of joining heaven and holy Land through the sacred place defined the core of being, I mean, the caste of the priests.

The Scribe

In so far as the Mishnah takes up the way in which transactions are conducted among ordinary folk and takes the position that it is through documents with a supernatural consequence that transactions are embodied and expressed (surely the position of the relevant tractates on both Women and Damages), the Mishnah expresses what is self-evident to scribes.

Just as to the priest, there is a correspondence between the table of the Lord in the Temple and the locus of the divinity in the heavens, so, to the scribe, there is a correspondence between the documentary expression of the human will on earth, in writs of all sorts, in the orderly provision of courts for the predictable and just disposition of exchanges of persons and property, and heaven's judgment of these same matters. When a woman becomes sanctified to a particular man on earth, through the appropriate document governing the transfer of her person and property, in heaven as well, the woman is deemed truly sanctified to that man. A violation of the writ therefore is not merely a crime. It is a sin. That is why the Temple rite involving the wife accused of adultery is integral to the system of the Division of Women.

So there are these two social groups, not categorically symmetrical with one another, the priestly caste and the scribal profession, for whom in its topical program the Mishnah makes self-evident statements. We know, moreover, that in time to come, the scribal profession would become a focus of sanctification, too. The scribe would be transformed into the *rabbi*, locus of the holy through what he knew, just as the priest had been, and would remain, locus of the holy through what he could claim for genealogy. The tractates of special interest to scribes-become-rabbis and to their governance of Israelite society, those of Women and

Damages, together with certain others particularly relevant to utopian Israel beyond the system of the Land—those tractates would grow and grow. Others would remain essentially as they were with the closure of the Mishnah. So we must notice that the Mishnah, for its part, speaks for the program of topics important to the priests. It takes up the persona of the scribes, speaking through their voice and in their manner.

Now what we do not find, which becomes astonishing in the light of these observations, is sustained and serious attention to the matter of the caste of the priests and of the profession of the scribes. True, scattered through the tractates are exercises, occasionally sustained and important exercises, on the genealogy of the priestly caste, upon their marital obligations and duties, as well as on the things priests do and do not do in the cult, in collecting and eating their sanctified food, and in other topics of keen interest to priests. Indeed, it would be no exaggeration to say that the Mishnah's system seen whole is not a great deal more than a handbook of how the priestly caste wished to design its life in Israel and the world. And yet in the fundamental structure of the document, its organization into divisions and tractates, there is no place for a Division of the Priesthood, no room even for a complete tractate on the rules of the priesthood, except, as we have seen, for the pervasive way of life of the priestly caste, which is everywhere. This absence of sustained attention to the priesthood is striking, when we compare the way in which the priestly code at Leviticus 1-15 spells out its concerns: the priesthood, the cult, the matter of cultic cleanness. Since we do have divisions for the cult (the fifth) and for cleanness (the sixth) at Holy Things and Purities, we are struck that we do not have this third division: the priesthood.

We must, moreover, be equally surprised that, for a document so rich in the importance lent to petty matters of how a writ is folded and where the witnesses sign, so obsessed with the making of long lists and the organization of all knowledge into neat piles of symmetrically arranged words, the scribes who know how to make lists and match words nowhere come to the fore. They speak through the document. But they stand behind the curtains. They write the script, arrange the sets, design the costumes, situate the players in their place on the stage, raise the curtain—and play no role at all. We have no division or tractate on such matters as how a person becomes a scribe, how a scribe conducts his work, who forms the center of the scribal profession and how authority is gained therein, the rights and place of the scribe in the system of governance through courts, the organization and conduct of schools or circles of masters and disciples through which the scribal arts are taught and perpetuated. This absence of even minimal information on the way in which the scribal profession takes shape and does its work is stunning when we realize that, within a brief generation, the Mishnah as a whole would fall into the hands of scribes, to be called rabbis, both in the Land of Israel and in Babylonia. These rabbis would make of the Mishnah exactly what they wished. Construed from the perspective of the makers of the Mishnah, the priests and the scribes who provide contents and form, substance and style, therefore, the Mishnah turns out to omit all reference to actors, when laying out the world which is their play.

The Householder

The metaphor of the theater for the economy of Israel, the household of holy Land and people, space and time, cult and home, leads to yet another perspective. When we look out upon the vast drama portrayed by the Mishnah, lacking as it does an account of the one who wrote the book, and the one about whom the book was written, we notice yet one more missing component. In the fundamental and generative structure of the Mishnah, that is, at the foundations of Judaism, we find no account of that other necessary constituent: the audience. *To whom* the document speaks is never specified. What group ("class") generates the Mishnah's problems is not at issue. True, it is taken for granted that the world of the Mishnah expresses the sanctified being of Israel in general. So the Mishnah speaks about the generality of Israel, the people. But to whom, within Israel, the Mishnah addresses itself, and what groups are expected to want to know what the Mishnah has to say, are matters that never come to full expression.

Yet there can be no doubt of the answer to the question. The building block of Mishnaic discourse (the circumstance addressed whenever the issues of concrete society and material transactions are taken up) is the householder and his context. The Mishnah knows about all sorts of economic activities. But for the Mishnah, the center and focus of interest lie in the village. The village is made up of households, each a unit of production in farming. The households are constructed by, and around, the householder, father of an extended family, including his sons and their wives and children, his servants, his slaves (bondsmen), the craftsmen to whom he entrusts tasks he does not choose to do. The concerns of householders are in transactions in land. Their measurement of value is expressed in acreage of top, middle, and bottom grade. Through real estate, critical transactions are worked out. The marriage settlement depends upon real property. Civil penalties are exacted through payment of real property. The principal transactions to be taken up are those of the householder who owns beasts that do damage or suffer it who harvests his crops and must set aside and so by his own word and deed sanctify them for use by the castes scheduled from on high who uses or sells his crops and feeds his family; and who, if he is fortunate, will acquire still more land.

It is to householders that the Mishnah is addressed: the pivot of society and its bulwark, the units of which the village is composed, the corporate component of the society of Israel in the limits of the village and the Land. The householder, as I said, is the building block of the house of Israel, of its economy in the classic sense of the word in Greek, *oikos,* household, which yields our word, economics.

So, to revert to the metaphor just now introduced, the great proscenium constructed by the Mishnah now looms before us. Its arch is the canopy of heaven. Its stage is the whole Land of Israel. Its actors are the holy people of Israel. Its events are the drama of unfolding time and common transactions, appointed times and holy events. Yet in this grand design we look in vain for the three principal participants: the audience, the actors, and the playwright. So we must ask why, in preparation for the discourses we shall follow in Chapter Five, when we ask about the conception of history in such an age as this, full of historical events of long-term consequence.

The reason is not difficult to discover, when we recall that, after all, what the Mishnah really wants is for nothing to happen. The Mishnah presents a tableau, a wax museum, a diorama. It portrays a world fully perfected and so fully at rest. The one thing the Mishnah does not want to tell us is about change, how things come to be what they are. That is why there can be no sustained attention to the priesthood and its rules, the scribal profession and its constitution, the class of householders and its interests. The Mishnah's pretense is that all of these have come to rest. They compose a world in stasis, perfect and complete, made holy because it is complete and perfect. It is an economy—again in the classic sense of the word—awaiting the divine act of sanctification which, as at the creation of the world, would set the seal of holy rest upon an again-complete creation, just as in the beginning. There is no place for the actors when what is besought is no action whatsoever, but only perfection, which is unchanging. There is room only for a description of how things are: the present tense, the sequence of completed statements and static problems. All the action lies within, in how these statements are made. Once they come to full expression, with nothing left to say, there also is nothing left to do, no need for actors, whether scribes, priests, or householders.

So the components of the system at the very basis of things are the social groups to whom the system refers. These groups obviously are not comparable to one another. They are not three species of the same social genus. One is a caste; the second, a profession; the third, a class. What they have in common is, first, that they do form groups; and, second, that the groups are social in foundation and collective in expression. That is not a sizable claim. The priesthood is a social group; it coalesces. Priests see one another as part of a single caste, with whom, for example, they will want to intermarry. The scribes are a social group, because they practice a single profession, following a uniform set of rules. They coalesce in the methods by which they do their work. The householders are a social group, the basic productive unit of society, around which other economic activity is perceived to function. In an essentially agricultural economy, it is quite reasonable to regard the householder, the head of a basic unit of production, as part of a single class.

This brings us back to the point at which we began: the social vision of the Mishnah, part of the encompassing world-view that the Mishnah's authorship sets forth, in the excruciating detail of the way of life that that same authorship prescribes for the social entity, holy Israel, that the authorship addresses. The Mishnah through its six divisions sets forth a coherent world-view and comprehensive way of living for holy Israel. It is a world-view that speaks of transcendent things, a way of life in response to the supernatural meaning of what is done, a heightened and deepened perception of the sanctification of Israel in deed and in deliberation. Sanctification means two things, first, distinguishing Israel in all its dimensions from the world in all its ways; second, establishing the stability, order, regularity, predictability, and reliability of Israel at moments and in contexts of danger. Danger means instability, disorder, irregularity, uncertainty, and betrayal. Each topic of the system as a whole takes up a critical and indispensable moment or context of social being. Each orders what is disorderly and dangerous. Through what is said in regard to each of the Mishnah's principal topics, what the system as a whole wishes to declare is fully expressed. These writers are obsessed with order and compelled by a vision of a world in which all things are in their right place, each bearing its own name, awaiting the benediction that comes when, everything in order, God pronounces the benediction and brings about the sanctification of the whole. But history still happens, and that carries us to the *aggadah,* where a very different, but ultimately complementary and cogent, theory of matters is set forth.

And there, as we now see, woman, excluded from the vision of a steady-state Israel of households run by men, assumes the position of the one who defines and determines the order of things. Stability, order, land-holding, the priority of exact exchanges, the holding of things in balance —these now give way. Relationships concern other matters altogether, and the stakes prove considerably higher. The *halakhah* takes up the nitty-gritty of little things, the aggadah surpasses the petty concerns of this world and aspires to transcendence. No wonder, then, that, in the *aggadah* we turn to the governing principles that determine how small matters are sorted out, dealing with the whole, encompassing all the parts. Here the systemic statement proves different in kind, not merely in degree, since issues of time, change, circumstance intervene, and everything becomes precisely what it never is in the *halakhah:* negotiable and subject to the variables of context and history.

Part Two

The Feminine

Chapter Three

Zekhut and the Feminization of Judaism

The laws we have examined fully explain why rabbinic Judaism routinely finds itself represented as a wholly patriarchal, male religious system. Certainly, descriptions of rabbinic Judaism as a male religion, subordinating women in countless ways, adduce more than ample supporting evidence, as Chapters One and Two have shown. And yet that representation proves only partially right and therefore a distortion and so wholly wrong. For at the systemic center of this patriarchal, male religious system is a deeply feminine conception of relationships—a conception set forth in the context of stories involving women as well as men and represented as taking priority over all other systemic considerations.

I. The Systemic Center and Its Reversal

To understand what is at stake, we have to identify the systemic center of the Judaism of the dual Torah or rabbinic Judaism. No sound perspective on any detail of the system can be gained if we do not know how the system itself finds its principal point. With sound reason, people have supposed that that center is defined by the systemic symbol, Torah, and by the activity required thereby, which is, the study of the Torah. That Torah-study defines the highest good is stated in countless forms. Three will serve to establish the fact at hand.

Study of the Torah

In the first, study of the Torah is presented as the highest good:

1. A. These are things which have no [specified] measure:
   B. (1) [the quantity of produce designated as] pe'ah,
   (2) [the quantity of produce given as] firstfruits,

      (3) [the value of] the appearance offering,

      (4) [the performance of] righteous deeds,

      (5) and [time spent in] study of Torah.

    C. These are things the benefit of which a person enjoys in this world, while the principal remains for him in the world to come:

    D. (1) [deeds in] honor of father and mother,

      (2) [performance of] righteous deeds,

      (3) and [acts which] bring peace between a man and his fellow.

    E. But the study of Torah is as important as all of them together.

m. Pe'ah 1:1

The scale of values is explicit and leaves no doubt on what counts. Anyone who wishes to maintain that study of the Torah takes priority has every reason to point to this statement.

Study of the Torah as a Masculine, not a Feminine, Activity

In the second, it is alleged that study of the Torah is the purpose for which man was created (and man, specifically, since in the writings at hand, women do not study the Torah).

    8. A. Rabban Yohanan b. Zakkai received [the Torah] from Hillel and Shammai.

    B. He would say, "(1) If you have learned much Torah, (2) do not puff yourself up on that account, (3) for it was for that purpose that you were created."

m. 'Abot 2:8A-B

These statements, with countless others that say the same thing, leave no doubt about the regnant system of priorities. It goes without saying that in every passage in which the Torah and Torah-study, occur, men alone play a role; no place is accorded to women, whose contribution is to accept temporary widowhood while their husbands went go to the study-circles and centers.

Study of the Torah Takes Precedence Over Practice of Its Laws

    What is important about the third piece of evidence is that it occurs in the final document, the Talmud of Babylonia, and forms a sizable, well-argued statement that study of the Torah takes precedence even over the practice of the laws of the Torah.

2.   A. Once R. Tarfon and the elders were reclining at a banquet in the upper room of the house of Nitezeh in Lud. This question was raised for them: "Is study greater or is action greater?"

B. R. Tarfon responded: "Action is greater."

C. R. Aqiba responded: "Study is greater."

D. All responded, saying, "Study is greater, for study brings about action."

3.   A. *It has been taught on Tannaite authority:*

B. R. Yosé says, "Great is study, for it preceded the commandment to separate dough offering by forty years, the commandments governing priestly rations and tithes by fifty-four years, the commandments covering remission of debts by sixty-one years, the commandment concerning the Jubilee year by one hundred and three years." [Freedman: the Torah was given to Israel two months after the Exodus from Egypt, but liability to dough offering came into force forty years later, and so throughout.]

C. . . . one hundred and three years? *But it was a hundred and four.*

D. *He takes the view that* the Jubilee effects the release of slaves and land at the outset.

E. And just as study of the Torah came prior to the actual practice of it, so judgment on that account takes precedence over judgment concerning practice of the Torah.

F. *That accords with R. Hamnuna, for* said R. Hamnuna, "The beginning of a person's judgment comes with the issue of study of Torah, for it is said, 'The beginning of judgment concerns the letting out of water' (Prov 17:14) [and water stands for Torah]."

G. And just as judgment concerning study takes priority over judgment concerning practice, so to the reward for studying the Torah takes priority over the reward for practice: "And he gave them the lands and nations, and they took the labor of the people in possession, that they might keep his statutes and observe his laws" (Ps 105:44-45).

m. Qiddushin 1:10E-G/I.2=*b. Qiddushin* 40B

Anyone who alleges, as people commonly do, that this Judaism is best characterized as the way of the Torah, and that the way of the Torah leads to intense study of the Torah, stands on very firm ground indeed.

It follows that Torah-learning finds a central place in a classical Judaic tradition. That is because of the belief that God had revealed his will to mankind through the medium of a written revelation given to Moses at Mount Sinai, accompanied by oral traditions taught in the rabbinical schools and preserved in the Talmuds and related literature. Belief in the text was coupled with the belief that oral traditions were also revealed. In the books composed in the rabbinical academies, as much as in the Hebrew Bible itself, was contained God's will for man. The act of study, memorization, and commentary upon the sacred books is holy. The reason is that, when one studies Torah, the faithful Jew hears God's word and will. The study of sacred text therefore assumes the *central* position in the Judaism of the dual Torah.

It is the simple fact that no role whatever was assigned to women. They did not study in the schools, and the life of Torah effectively was closed to them. Their exclusion is scarcely mitigated by the praise of those mothers who would encourage their sons to study Torah. Rabina, a late fourth-century master, explained how the merit of study of the Torah applied to womenfolk: Women acquire merit not through Torah-study, which is closed to them, but solely when they arrange for their sons' education in scripture and Mishnah and when they wait for their husbands to return from the schools. Since that return was often postponed by months or even years, it was no small sacrifice. But the schools were entirely male institutions, and no equivalent religious life was available for women. That is the context in which, we shall now see, women exemplify the highest virtue of which humanity is capable. For it is the simple fact that in stories in which women figure as heroic exemplars, study of the Torah is subordinated to another class of activity altogether, one in which women, as much as men, participate, but which they, more than men, are able to exemplify.

The exclusion of women from the centers of the study of the Torah through discipleship comes to expression in numerous passages, of which the following is the locus classicus:

4.   A. She hardly has sufficed to drink it before her face turns yellow, her eyes bulge out, and her veins swell.
   B. And they say, "Take her away! Take her away!"
   C. so that the Temple court will not be made unclean [by her corpse].

D. [But if nothing happened], if she had merit, she would attribute [her good fortune] to it.

E. There is the possibility that merit suspends the curse for one year, and there is the possibility that merit suspends the curse for two years, and there is the possibility that merit suspends the curse for three years.

F. On this basis Ben Azzai says, "A man is required to teach Torah to his daughter.

G. "For if she should drink the water, she should know that [if nothing happens to her], merit is what suspends [the curse from taking effect]."

H. R. Eliezer says, "Whoever teaches Torah to his daughter is as if he teaches her sexual satisfaction."

I. R. Joshua says, "A woman wants a qab [of food] with sexual satisfaction more than nine qabs with abstinence."

m. Sota 3:4

The attitudes and policies that come to expression here leave no doubt about the regnant opinion, realized in practice: women have no role whatever in the study and transmission of the Torah, and yet the Torah defines the holy way of life and the purpose of the enduring existence of holy Israel. Any allegation that the Judaism of the documents before us in fact is androgynous must contend with these well-established and broadly recognized facts. And that is precisely what we have now to do.

The way forward is clear: we must find a systemic focus that takes precedence over the study of the Torah, and that also makes provision for women's full engagement. Not only so, but we shall have to discover a systemic point of emphasis that is accorded priority, and that is presented as the systemic center. It must be explicitly represented as more important than the study of the Torah. Failing these tests, I have no basis on which to allege that this Judaism in any way, shape, or form valued androgeny, let alone accorded a position honorable in the sight of men but also plausible and desirable in the opinion of women. Nothing I have set forth to this point meets that simple, fair criterion of plausibility and desirability. And, therefore, nothing I have said explains why, for nearly two millennia, the Judaism of the dual Torah embodied the aspirations and faith of women, as much as of men. But it did, and it remains now to explain what presently appears anomalous and unnatural.

While, as we have seen, people suppose that the Torah forms the symbolic center of this Judaism and study of the Torah the critical action, so that women (excluded from academies) find no place in rabbinic Judaism at all. In fact, when we reach the systemic center, we find that "the study of Torah" does not outweigh all else, not at all. Even the stories contained in the Talmud of the Land of Israel, ca. 400 C.E., a commentary to the Mishnah on which we shall concentrate, in which the priority and sanctity of the sage's knowledge of the Torah form the focus of discourse treat study of the Torah as contingent and merely instrumental. Time and again, knowledge of the Torah forms a way-station on a path to a more distant, more central goal: attaining *zekhut,* an untranslatable word—as is any systemically-critical word—suitably rendered as "the heritage of virtue and its consequent entitlements."[1] Torah-study is one means of attaining access to that heritage, of gaining *zekhut.* There are other equally suitable means, and, not only so, but the *zekhut* gained by Torah-study is no different from the *zekhut* gained by any and all other types of acts of supererogatory grace. And still more astonishing, a single remarkable action may produce *zekhut* of the same order as a lifetime of devotion to Torah-study, and a simple ass-driver through a noteworthy act of selfless behavior may attain the same level of *zekhut* as a learned sage.

Were such stories as these located in a document other than one so authoritative and systemically critical as a Mishnah-commentary such as the Talmud of the Land of Israel (Yerushalmi), one might find tempting the thesis that they represented an anti-rabbinic viewpoint. But rabbis told these stories, preserved them, and placed them on exhibition to expose the finest virtue they could imagine. That is why we turn for our integrating conception to that final reversal and revision of the given: just as scarce resources are made abundant, legitimate power deemed only weakness, and facts displaced by revealed truth, so the one-time moment at which *zekhut* is attained from Heaven outweighs a lifetime of Torah-learning. *Zekhut* formed the foundation for the Yerushalmi's conception

---

[1]My account of *zekhut* goes over ground covered in my *The Transformation of Judaism. From Philosophy to Religion.* (Champaign: University of Illinois Press, 1992). See also *Sources of the Transformation of Judaism: From Philosophy to Religion in the Classics of Judaism. A Reader.* (Atlanta: Scholars Press for South Florida Studies in the History of Judaism, 1992).

of political economy for the social order of Israel. It and not Torah
defined the whole, of which economics and politics comprised mere
details. It set forth and accounts for an economics and a politics that
made powerlessness into power, disinheritance into wealth. How in fact
does *zekhut* function?

Zekhut is gained for a person by an act of renunciation and self-
abnegation, such that Heaven responds with an act of grace. Works of
supererogation, which Heaven cannot compel but highly prizes, *zekhut*
defines the very opposite of coercion. *Zekhut* is an act that no one could
anticipate or demand, but an act of such remarkable selflessness that
Heaven finds itself constrained to respond. That is why the systemic
center is formed by an act, on Heaven's part, of responsive grace,
meaning grace one by definition cannot demand or compel, but only
provoke. When we make ourselves less, Heaven makes us more; but we
cannot force our will upon Heaven.

That brings us to my claim that the Judaism of the dual Torah
represents a union of traits the documents themselves portray as masculine with those the same writings associate with women. Now I maintain
that the critical role accorded to *zekhut* stands for the feminization of the
Judaism of the dual Torah for a very simple reason. It is that in the
stories that portray how *zekhut* is acquired, women figure as prominently
as men, and I shall point out, at the critical point, women in fact
exemplify the virtue at its highest. When we ask about the feminization
of Judaism, our attention rests upon this fact. We want to know what is
the point of stories that show how women acquire *zekhut* and so take
priority in the scale of Heaven's estimation above men who have studied
the Torah—an amazing fact. And these same stories, we shall see, also
portray the right relationship between Israel and God in terms that are
specific to women. And, we shall learn in Chapter Four, Israel takes the
role of woman, God the role of the man, in the supernatural relationship
that the Torah portrays. And, Chapter Five will show us, Israel in the
here and now must teach itself to feel the way the sources maintain
women feel, so that Israel's emotions will be feminine, not masculine, in
their indicative traits.

At stake, therefore, is not how stereotypes, imported from we know
not where, are introduced into the characterization of the feminine and
the masculine. It is how the documents themselves formulate their own
stereotypes, and, we shall see, the document at hand is explicit that the

virtuous attitude and relationship between the Israelite and God is one that women embody in the very stories in which that relationship is portrayed. Specifically, it is where Heaven cannot force its will upon us that *zekhut* intervenes. It is that exquisite balance between our will and Heaven's will that, in the end, brings to its perfect balance and entire fulfillment the exploration of the conflict of God's will and our will that began with Adam and Eve at their last hour in Eden, and our first hour on earth. And, in context, the fact that we may inherit a treasury of *zekhut* from our ancestors logically follows: just as we inherit the human condition of the freedom to practice rebellion against God's word, so we inherit, from former generations, the results of another dimension of the human condition: our power to give willingly what none, even God, can by right or rule compel.

Since, in the successor-system, points of integration, not differentiation, that guide us to the systemic problematic, we must therefore take seriously the contingent status, the standing of a dependent variable, accorded to Torah-study in such stories as the following:

> **IV. C.** There was a house that was about to collapse over there [in Babylonia], and Rab set one of his disciples in the house, until they had cleared out everything from the house. When the disciple left the house, the house collapsed.
>
> D. And there are those who say that it was R. Adda bar Ahwah.
>
> E. Sages sent and said to him, "What sort of good deeds are to your credit [that you have that much *zekhut*]?"
>
> F. He said to them, "In my whole life no man ever got to the synagogue in the morning before I did. I never left anybody there when I went out. I never walked four cubits without speaking words of Torah. Nor did I ever mention teachings of Torah in an inappropriate setting. I never laid out a bed and slept for a regular period of time. I never took great strides among the associates. I never called my fellow by a nickname. I never rejoiced in the embarrassment of my fellow. I never cursed my fellow when I was lying by myself in bed. I never walked over in the marketplace to someone who owed me money.
>
> G. "In my entire life I never lost my temper in my household."
>
> H. This was meant to carry out that which is stated as follows: "I will give heed to the way that is blameless. Oh when wilt thou come to me? I will walk with integrity of heart within my house" (Ps 101:2).
>
> *y. Ta'anit* **3:11.IV**

Nothing in Mishnah-tractate *Pe'ah* or in tractate *'Abot* or in tractate *Qiddushin* of the Talmud of Babylonia prepares us for such a story as this. Striking in this story is that mastery of the Torah is only one means of attaining the *zekhut* that had enabled the sage to keep the house from collapsing. And Torah-study is not the primary means of attaining *zekhut.* The question at **E** provides the key, together with its answer at **F**. For what the sage did to gain such remarkable *zekhut* is not to master such-and-so many tractates of the Mishnah. It was rather acts of courtesy, consideration, gentility, restraint: *cortesía* in the Spanish sense, *gentilezza* in the Italian. These produced *zekhut.* Now all of these acts exhibit in common the virtue of self-abnegation or the avoidance of power over others and the submission to the will and the requirement of self-esteem of others. Torah-study is simply an item on a list of actions or attitudes that generate *zekhut.*

Here, in a moral setting, we find politics replicated: the form of power that the system promises derives from the rejection of power that the world recognizes. Legitimate violence is replaced by legitimation of the absence of the power to commit violence or of the failure to commit violence. And, when we ask, whence that sort of power? the answer lies in the gaining of *zekhut* in a variety of ways, not in the acquisition of *zekhut* through the study of the Torah solely or even primarily. But, we note, the story at hand speaks of a sage in particular. That alerts us once more to the systemic reversal that takes place at the systemic center: the sage has gained *zekhut* by not acting the way sages are commonly assumed to behave, but in a humble way. In *zekhut,* a word we clearly cannot translate by an exact counterpart in American, we come to the center of a religious system in which the transformation of the individual through salvific knowledge in the end simply does not provide the compelling answer to the question of personal salvation.

Rabbinic Judaism takes shape by answering a question concerning the theory of the social order, yet we find at the heart of matters an answer addressed to individuals, one that concerns their emotions, attitudes, and sense of personal virtue. The private, the particular, the sentimental and the emotional—these are commonly portrayed as women's concerns, the public and political, those of men. Here again, the systemic-center forms a paradox: a design for an Israel for eternity yields the dimensions of conduct for an Israelite in the here and now of a single, intensely private moment. None can see, none can compel, none will ever know, what he or she performs as an act of uncompelled generosity of spirit. But God knows. And God cares. That most private moment of encounter, the one to the other, with God at hand, is transformed into the most public, the most social, the most political event.

So, we see, a different question stands at center-stage, and a different answer altogether defines the dramatic tension of the theatrical globe. At stake is a public and a national question, one concerning Israel's history and destiny, to which the individual and his salvation, while important, are distinctly subordinated. Not Torah-study, which may generate *zekhut,* but *zekhut* itself defines what is at issue, the generative problematic of the system, and only when we grasp the answer provided by *zekhut* shall we reach a definition of the question that precipitated the systemic construction and the formation of its categories, principal and contingent alike.

II. The Character of *Zekhut*

When we come to a word that is critical to the system of those who use it and also that is beyond translation by a single, exact, counterpart in some other language, we know that we have reached the systemic center, the point at which what the system wishes to say is profoundly particular to that system. *Zekhut* in fact refers to two distinct matters: first, virtue that originates with one's ancestors and that is received from them as a legacy, that is, "original virtue," but, also, power that Heaven accords to people themselves in response to uncoerced acts of grace done by those people. *Zekhut* then as scarce or common as our capacity for uncoerced action dictated, as puissant or supine as our strength to refrain from deeds of worldly power decided, accomplished the systemic integration of the successor-documents.

That protean conception formed into a cogent political economy for the social order of Israel the economics and the politics that made powerlessness into power, disinheritance into wealth. Acts of will consisting of submission, on one's own, to the will of Heaven endowed Israel with a lien and entitlement upon Heaven. What we cannot by will impose, we can by will evoke. What we cannot accomplish through coercion of Heaven, trading deed for deed, we can achieve through submission, hoping for response to our freely-given act of feeling, sentiment, emotion of self-renunciation. God will do for us what we cannot do for ourselves, when we do for God what God cannot make us do. In a wholly concrete and tangible sense, it is to love God with all the heart, the soul, the might that we have. This systemic statement justifies classifying the successor-system as religious in as profound and complete a way as the initial system had been wholly and restrictedly philosophical. Here too, we move from the relationship in which one party dominates the other to one in which each party gives what cannot be coerced, so that both parties will join freely and willingly together: one of mutuality and cooperation.

The final step in the path that began with God's profession of love for Israel, the response of the freely-given, uncoerced act of love, *zekhut* stands for the empowerment, of a supernatural character, that derives from the virtue of one's ancestry or from one's own virtuous deeds of a very particular order. No single word in English bears the same meaning, nor is there a synonym for *zekhut* in the canonical writings in the original either. The difficulty of translating a word of systemic consequence with a single word in some other language (or in the language of the system's documents themselves) tells us we deal with what is unique, beyond comparison and therefore contrast and comprehension. What is most particular to (i.e., distinctive of) the systemic structure and its functioning requires definition through circumlocution: "the heritage of virtue and its consequent entitlements."[2]

It must follow, therefore, that *zekhut,* not Torah, in a single word defines the generative myth, the critical symbol of the successor-Judaism. The signal that the gnostic Torah formed a mere component in a system

---

[2]The commonly-used single word, "merit," does not apply, since "merit" bears the sense of reward for carrying out an obligation; e.g., by doing such and such, he merited so and so. *Zekhut,* by contrast, commonly refers to acts of supererogatory free will, and therefore while such acts are meritorious in the sense of being virtuous (by definition), they are not acts that one owes, but that one gives. And the rewards that accumulate in response to such actions are always miraculous or supernatural or signs of divine grace; e.g., an unusually long life, the power to prevent a dilapidated building from collapsing. Note the fine perception of S. Levy, *Original Virtue and Other Studies,* 2-3: "Some act of obedience, constituting the Ascent of man, is the origin of virtue and the cause of reward for virtue . . . What is the conspicuous act of obedience which, in Judaism, forms the striking contrast to Adam's act of disobedience, in Christianity? The submission of Isaac in being bound on the altar . . . is regarded in Jewish theology as the historic cause of the imputation of virtue to his descendants."

that transcended Torah-study and defined its structure in some way other
than by appeal to the symbol and activity of the Torah comes from a
simple fact. Ordinary folk, not disciples of sages, have access to *zekhut*
entirely outside of study of the Torah. In stories not told about rabbis, a
single remarkable deed, exemplary for its deep humanity, sufficed to win
for an ordinary person the *zekhut*—"the heritage of virtue and its consequent entitlements"—that elicits the same marks of supernatural favor
enjoyed by some rabbis on account of their Torah-study.

Accordingly, the systemic centrality of *zekhut* in the structure—
visible in the critical importance of the heritage of virtue together with
its supernatural entitlements—emerges in a striking claim. It is framed in
extreme form—another mark of the unique place of *zekhut* within the
system. Even though a man was degraded, one action sufficed to win for
him that heavenly glory to which rabbis described in lives of Torah-study
aspired. The mark of the system's integration around *zekhut* lies in its
insistence that all Israelites, not only sages, could gain *zekhut* for themselves (and for their descendants). A single remarkable deed, exemplary
for its deep humanity, sufficed to win for an ordinary person the *zekhut*
that elicits the same supernatural favor enjoyed by some rabbis on
account of their Torah-study. The centrality of *zekhut* in the systemic
structure, therefore, emerges in this striking claim: One action sufficed
to win for a degraded man that heavenly glory to which rabbis in general
aspired. The rabbinical storyteller whose writing we shall consider assuredly identifies with this lesson, since it is the point and climax of his
story.

III. Systemic Remission:
Zekhut over Torah-Learning

The document at hand itself underlines the paradox that people attain
zekhut who are not masters of the Torah, and masters of the Torah want
to know why those people, and not the sages themselves, have attained
Heaven's favor. When we come to the way in which *zekhut* is set forth,
we find ourselves in a set of narratives of a rather special order. What is
special about them is that women play a critical role, appear as heroines,
win the attention and respect of the reader or listener. It is difficult to
locate in rabbinic literature before the Talmud of the Land of Israel—the

Mishnah, the Tosefta, Sifra, for instance—stories in which women figure at all. So to take up a whole series of stories in which women are key-players comes as a surprise. But there is more. The story-teller on the surface makes the man the hero; *he* is the center of the narrative. And yet a second glance at what is coming shows us that the woman precipitates the tale, and *her* action, not the man's, represents the gift that cannot be compelled but only given; *she* is the one who freely sacrifices, and *she* also is represented as the source of wisdom. So our systemic reversal— something above the Torah and the study of the Torah takes priority—is matched by a still-less-predictable shift in narrative quality, with women portrayed as principal actors.

In all three instances that follow and define what the individual must do to gain *zekhut,* the point is that the deeds of the heroes of the story make them worthy of having their prayers answered, which is a mark of the working of *zekhut.* It is supererogatory, uncoerced deeds, those well beyond the strict requirements of the Torah, and even the limits of the law altogether, that transform the hero into a holy man, whose holiness served just like that of a sage marked as such by knowledge of the Torah The following stories should not be understood as formulations of con-descension or a patronizing attitude, that is, the expressions of the mere sentimentality of the clerks concerning the lower orders. For these tales clearly mean to deny in favor of a single action of surpassing power the sages' own lifelong devotion to what the sages held to be the highest value, their own knowledge of the Torah gained through discipleship in wholly male academies:

I.   F. A certain man came before one of the relatives of R. Yannai. He said to him, "Rabbi, attain *zekhut* through me [by giving me charity]."

G. He said to him, "And didn't your father leave you money?"

H. He said to him, "No."

I. He said to him, "Go and collect what your father left in deposit with others."

J. He said to him, "I have heard concerning property my father deposited with others that it was gained by violence [so I don't want it]."

K. He said to him, "You are worthy of praying and having your prayers answered."

y. Ta'anit 1:4.I.

The point of **K**, of course, is self-evidently a reference to the possession of entitlement to supernatural favor, and it is gained, we see, through deeds that the law of the Torah cannot require but must favor: what one does on one's own volition, beyond the measure of the law. Here is the opposite of sin. A sin is what one has done by one's own volition beyond all limits of the law. So an act that generates *zekhut* for the individual is the counterpart and opposite: what one does by one's own volition that also is beyond all requirements of the law.

In the continuation of these stories, we should not miss an odd fact. The story tells about the *zekhut* attained by a humble, poor, ignorant man. It is narrated to underline what he has done. But what provokes the event is an act of self-abnegation far greater than that willingly performed by the male hero, which is, the woman's readiness to sell herself into prostitution to save her husband. That is not a focus of the story but the given. But nothing has compelled the woman to surrender her body to save her husband; to the contrary, the marital obligations of a woman concern only conventional deeds, which indeed the Mishnah's law maintains may be coerced; failure to do these deeds may result in financial penalties inflicted on the woman in the settlement of her marriage-contract. So the story of the uncoerced act of selflessness is told about a man, but occasioned by a woman, and both actors in the story exhibit one and the same virtue. When I characterize this Judaism as the male formulation of an androgynous Judaism, here is what I mean: men tell stories about themselves, but turn out to acknowledge, with enormous respect, the priority of women's virtues and even of their actions.

When Torah-stories are told, by contrast, the point is, a man attains *zekhut* by study of the Torah, and a woman attains *zekhut* by sending her sons and her husband off to study the Torah and sitting home alone—not exactly commensurate action. Only *zekhut*-stories represent the act of the woman as the counterpart and equivalent to the act of the man; and, in fact, even here, the fact that the woman's uncoerced gift is far greater than the man's—her body, merely his ass—should not go unnoticed. Once more, we find ourselves at the systemic center, where everything is reversed. Vast learning in the Torah produces much *zekhut*. But rabbis' *zekhut* is insufficient for them to pray and so produce rain, while in a dream, it becomes clear, an ass-driver is able to pray and produce rain. How is it that his *zekhut* is so much more puissant than that of "our sages of blessed memory"? Sages address that question to him—a reversal of an extraordinary order, since, after all, people bring their questions to sages, but sages ask their questions only to God in the Torah. And here, once more, a woman takes priority in her selfless and utterly uncoerced act over a man who does an act of the same classification but of a lesser order indeed:

> I. L. A certain ass driver appeared before the rabbis [the context requires: in a dream] and prayed, and rain came. The rabbis sent and brought him and said to him, "What is your trade?"
>
> M. He said to them, "I am an ass driver."
>
> N. They said to him, "And how do you conduct your business?"
>
> O. He said to them, "One time I rented my ass to a certain woman, and she was weeping on the way, and I said to her, 'What's with you?' and she said to me, 'The husband of that woman [me] is in prison [for debt], and I wanted to see what I can do to free him.' So I sold my ass and I gave her the proceeds, and I said to her, 'Here is your money, free your husband, but do not sin [by becoming a prostitute to raise the necessary funds].' "
>
> P. They said to him, "You are worthy of praying and having your prayers answered."
>
> *y. Ta'anit* 1:4.I.

The ass-driver clearly has a powerful lien on Heaven, so that his prayers are answered, even while those of others are not. What did he do to get that entitlement? He did what no law could demand: impoverished himself to save the woman from a "fate worse than death."

> I. Q. In a dream of R. Abbahu, Mr. Pentakaka ["Five sins"] appeared, who prayed that rain would come, and it rained. R. Abbahu sent and summoned him. He said to him, "What is your trade?"
>
> R. He said to him, "Five sins does that man [I] do every day, [for I am a pimp:] hiring whores, cleaning up the theater, bringing home their garments for washing, dancing, and performing before them."
>
> S. He said to him, "And what sort of decent thing have you ever done?"
>
> T. He said to him, "One day that man [I] was cleaning the theater, and a woman came and stood behind a pillar and cried. I said to her, 'What's with you?' And she said to me, 'That woman's [my] husband is in prison, and I wanted to see what I can do to free him,' so I sold

my bed and cover, and I gave the proceeds to her. I said to her, 'Here is your money, free your husband, but do not sin.' "

U. He said to him, "You are worthy of praying and having your prayers answered."

y. Ta'anit 1:4.I.

Q moves us still further, since the named man has done everything sinful that one can do, and, more to the point, he does it every day. So the singularity of the act of *zekhut*, which suffices if done only one time, encompasses its power to outweigh a life of sin—again, an act of *zekhut* as the mirror-image and opposite of sin. Here again, the single act of saving a woman from a "fate worse than death" has sufficed.

I.   V. A pious man from Kefar Imi appeared [in a dream] to the rabbis. He prayed for rain and it rained. The rabbis went up to him. His householders told them that he was sitting on a hill. They went out to him, saying to him, "Greetings," but he did not answer them.

W. He was sitting and eating, and he did not say to them, "You break bread too."

X. When he went back home, he made a bundle of faggots and put his cloak on top of the bundle [instead of on his shoulder].

Y. When he came home, he said to his household [wife], "These rabbis are here [because] they want me to pray for rain. If I pray and it rains, it is a disgrace for them, and if not, it is a profanation of the Name of Heaven. But come, you and I will go up [to the roof] and pray. If it rains, we shall tell them, 'We are not worthy to pray and have our prayers answered.' "

Z. They went up and prayed and it rained.

AA. They came down to them [and asked], "Why have the rabbis troubled themselves to come here today?"

BB. They said to him, "We wanted you to pray so that it would rain."

CC. He said to them, "Now do you really need my prayers? Heaven already has done its miracle."

DD. They said to him, "Why, when you were on the hill, did we say hello to you, and you did not reply?"

EE. He said to them, "I was then doing my job. Should I then interrupt my concentration [on my work]?"

FF. They said to him, "And why, when you sat down to eat, did you not say to us 'You break bread too'?"

GG. He said to them, "Because I had only my small ration of bread. Why would I have invited you to eat by way of mere flattery [when I knew I could not give you anything at all]?"

HH. They said to him, "And why when you came to go down, did you put your cloak on top of the bundle?"

II. He said to them, "Because the cloak was not mine. It was borrowed for use at prayer. I did not want to tear it."

JJ. They said to him, "And why, when you were on the hill, did your wife wear dirty clothes, but when you came down from the mountain, did she put on clean clothes?"

KK. He said to them, "When I was on the hill, she put on dirty clothes, so that no one would gaze at her. But when I came home from the hill, she put on clean clothes, so that I would not gaze on any other woman."

LL. They said to him, "It is well that you pray and have your prayers answered."

y. Ta'anit 1:4.I.

Here the woman is at least an equal player; her actions, as much as her husband's, prove exemplary and illustrate the ultimate wisdom. The pious man of V, finally, enjoys the recognition of the sages by reason of his lien upon Heaven, able as he is to pray and bring rain. What has so endowed him with *zekhut*? Acts of punctiliousness of a moral order: concentrating on his work, avoiding an act of dissimulation, integrity in the disposition of a borrowed object, his wife's concern not to attract other men and her equal concern to make herself attractive to her husband. We note that, at the systemic center, women find entire equality with men; with no role whatever in the study of the Torah and no possibility of attaining political sagacity, women find a critical place in the sequence of actions that elicit from Heaven the admiring response that *zekhut* embodies.

The stories then require us to distinguish between what the Torah can require, and what God can and does admire. God responds not to mere obedience to the Torah, but to acts that transcend the Torah and over-spread the measure of the law. These, in our language, we should call acts of grace. And, we hardly require reminding, women do them as much as men, but here, women do them at a price much greater than that paid by men. In fact, as we shall now see, *zekhut*, an act of surpassing will, finds its counterpart and opposite in sin, an act of surpassing will.

The one represents an act of will that God cannot demand but to which God must respond, so too the other; but the one represents supererogatory obedience, the other, supererogatory rebellion—a proper and perfect balance between equal opposites.

That these stories represent a male perspective need not be doubted, since the heroes in all cases are the male donors. But, a second reading of the stories shows that the hero is second to the heroine; it is the woman who, in each case, precipitates the occasion for the man's attainment of *zekhut,* and she, not he, exemplifies the highest pinnacle of selfless virtue. But that is hardly the story-teller's angle of vision; it is only ours, after the fact. That underlines my insistence that we deal with how a male-formulated system portrays women's paramount status and makes ample provision for not only the masculine but also the feminine virtues, as they themselves classify these virtues, giving priority to the feminine ones. That, as I said, clarifies what it means to speak of the feminization of Judaism.

It follows, once more, that those reversals that signal the systemic center culminate in the (for so male a system as this one) ultimate reversal: woman at the height. Just as Torah-learning is subordinated, so man is subordinated; *zekhut,* the gift that can be given but not compelled, like love, in an unerring sense must be called the female virtue that sets atop a male system and structure. It goes without saying that none of these stories refers explicitly to *zekhut*; all of them tell us about what it means to enjoy not an entitlement by inheritance alone, but a lien accomplished by one's own supererogatory acts of restraint. *Zekhut* integrates what has been differentiated. Holding together learning, virtue, and supernatural standing, by explaining how Torah-study transforms the learning man, *zekhut* further makes implausible those points of distinction between economics and politics that bore the systemic message of the initial philosophy. Hierarchical classification, with its demonstration of the upward-reaching unity of all being, gives way to a different, and more compelling proposition: the unity of all being within the heritage of *zekhut,* to be attained equally and without differentiation in all the principal parts of the social order. The definition of *zekhut* therefore carries us to the heart of the integrating and integrated religious system of Judaism.

IV. Systemic Integration

Thus far we have dealt only with *aggadah* in a Mishnah-commentary, one of the Talmuds. We turn now to the way in which other documents of narrative and exegesis portray the same matter. *Zekhut,* an entirely available idea, had been systemically tangential to the philosophical Judaism, and only now proved itself critical in the successor-structure. Showing that *zekhut* was both available and systemically inert both proves the connectedness of the two systems and also shows how the successor-system transformed the first. That is to say, the system-builders represented by the Talmud of the Land of Israel, *Genesis Rabbah,* *Leviticus Rabbah*, and *Pesiqta DeRab Kahana* made their own choices within their inheritance. Their system consequently defined its own categories and accomplished through its own medium the integration of its systemic components, the counterpart-categories.

In the earlier documents, the word *zekhut* bears a variety of meanings, as Jastrow summarizes the data,[3] and the pertinence of each possible meaning is to be determined in context: (1) acquittal, plea in favor of the defendant; (2) doing good, blessing; (3) protecting influence of good conduct, *zekhut*; (4) advantage, privilege, benefit. The first meaning pertains solely in juridical (or metaphorically-juridical) contexts; the second represents a very general and imprecise use of the word, since a variety of other words bear the same meaning. Only the third and the fourth meanings pertain, since they are particular to this word, on the one side, and also religious, on the other. The simple definition used here—the heritage of entitlements—emphasizes "heritage," because the advantages or privileges conferred by *zekhut* may be inherited and also passed on; it stresses "entitlements" because advantages or privileges always, invariably result from receiving *zekhut* from ancestors or acquiring it on one's own; and the word "virtue" refers to those supererogatory acts that demand a reward because they form matters of choice, the gift of the individual and his or her act of free will, an act that is at the same time

---

[3]Marcus Jastrow, *A Dictionary of the Targumim, The Talmud Babli and Yerushalmi, and the Midrashic Literature* (repr. N. Y.: Pardes Publishing House, Inc., 1950) 398.

(1) uncompelled, e.g., by the obligations imposed by the Torah, but (2) also valued by the Torah.

Because *zekhut* is something one may receive as an inheritance, out of the distant past, *zekhut* imposes upon the definition of the social entity, "Israel," a genealogical meaning. It furthermore imparts a distinctive character to the definitions of way of life. So the task of the political component of a theory of the social order, which is to define the social entity by appeal to empowerment, and of the economic component, which is to identify scarce resources by specification of the rationality of right management, is accomplished in a single word, which stands for a conception, a symbol, and a myth. All three components of this religious theory of the social order turn out to present specific applications, in context, for the general conception of *zekhut*. For the first source of *zekhut* derives from the definition of Israel as family; the entitlements of supernatural power deriving from virtue then care inherited from Abraham, Isaac, and Jacob. The second source is personal: the power one can gain for one's own heirs, moreover, by virtuous deeds. *Zekhut* deriving from either source is to be defined in context: what can you do if you have *zekhut*, that you cannot do if you do not have *zekhut*, and to whom can you do it. The answer to that question tells you the empowerment of *zekhut*.

Now in the nature of things, a theory of power or violence that is legitimately exercised falls into the category of a politics, and a conception of the scarce resource, defined as supernatural power that is to be rationally managed, falls into the category of an economics. That is why in the concept of *zekhut,* we find the union of economics and politics into a political economy that treats the worldly as supernatural: a theory of the whole society in its material and social relationships as expressed in institutions that permanently are given the right to impose order through real or threatened violence and in the assignment of goods and benefits, as systemically defined to be sure, through a shared rationality.

V. *Zekhut* in Documentary-Historical Context

Tracing the formation of the concept of *zekhut* in accord with the documentary-historical method draws us back to the beginnings in the Mishnah. At *m. Sanhedrin* 4:1, 5:4, 5:5, and 6:1, we find *zekhut* in the sense of "acquittal," as against conviction; at *m. Ketubot* 13:6 the sense is, "right," as in "right of ownership;" at *m. Gittin* 8:8 the sense is not "right of ownership" in a narrow sense, but "advantage," in a broader one of prerogative: "It is not within the power of the first husband to render void the right of the second." These usages of course bear no point in common with the sense of the word later on. But the evidence of the Mishnah seems to me to demonstrate that the sense of *zekhut* paramount in the successor-documents is not original to them. The following usage at *m. Qiddushin* 4:14 seems to me to invite something very like the sense that proposed here. So states *m. Qiddushin* 4:14E-I:

> R. Meir says, "A man should always teach his son a clean and easy trade. And let him pray to him to whom belong riches and possessions. For there is no trade which does not involve poverty or wealth. For poverty does not come from one's trade, nor does wealth come from one's trade. But all is in accord with a man's *zekhut*."

How to translate our key-word in this passage is not quite self-evident. The context permits a variety of possibilities. The same usage seems to me to be located at *m. Sota* 3:4, 3:5, and here there is clear indication of the presence of a conception of an entitlement deriving from some source other than one's own deed of the moment:

> **4.** E. There is the possibility that *zekhut* suspends the curse for one year, and there is the possibility that *zekhut* suspends the curse for two years, and there is the possibility that *zekhut* suspends the curse for three years.
>
> F. On this basis Ben Azzai says, "A man is required to teach Torah to his daughter.
>
> G. "For if she should drink the water, she should know that [if nothing happens to her], *zekhut* is what suspends [the curse from taking effect]."
>
> **5.** A. R. Simeon says, "*Zekhut* does not suspend the effects of the bitter water.
>
> B. "And if you say, '*Zekhut* does suspend the effects of the bitter water,' you will weaken the effect of the water for all the women who have to drink it.
>
> C. "And you give a bad name to all the women who drink it who turned out to be pure.

D. "For people will say, 'They are unclean, but *zekhut* suspended the effects of the water for them.' "

E. Rabbi says, "*Zekhut* does suspend the effects of the bitter water. But she will not bear children or continue to be pretty. And she will waste away, and in the end she will have the same [unpleasant] death."

m. Sotah 3:4-5

Now if we insert for *zekhut* at each point, "the heritage of virtue and its consequent entitlements" (thus: "For people will say, 'They are unclean, but *zekhut* suspended the effects of the water for them,' " then, "For people will say, 'They are unclean, but the heritage of virtue and its consequent entitlements suspended the effects of the water for them' "), we have a good sense of the meaning. That is to say, the woman may not suffer the penalty to which she is presumably condemnable, not because her act or condition (e.g., her innocence) has secured her acquittal or nullified the effects of the ordeal, but because she enjoys some advantage extrinsic to her own act or condition. She may be guilty, but she may also possess a benefice deriving by inheritance, hence, heritage of virtue, and so be entitled to a protection not because of her own, but because of someone else's action or condition. Once more, when it comes to *zekhut,* the canonical writings find themselves constrained to state matters in terms of woman's, not man's, virtue. No one imagines a woman can attain Heaven's favor by Torah-study but she enjoys, equally with men, the inheritance of unearned *zekhut*.

While the word bore, among its meanings, the one important later on, that word played no systemic role, in the philosophical system adumbrated by the Mishnah, commensurate with the importance accorded to the word and its sense in the religious system that took shape and came to expression in the successor-writings. The evidence of tractate *'Abot* is consistent with that of the Mishnah. The juridical sense of *zekhut* occurs at 1:6, "Judge everybody as though to be acquitted" (more comprehensibly translated, "And give everybody the benefit of the doubt"), forming a sense reasonably coherent with the usages important in Mishnah-tractate *Sanhedrin*. In *'Abot*, however, we have clear evidence for the sense of the word that seems to me demanded later on. At *m. 'Abot* 2:2 we find the following:

2. C. "And all who work with the community—let them work with them for the sake of Heaven.

D. "For the [1] *zekhut* of their fathers strengthens them, and their [fathers'] [2] righteousness stands forever.

E. "And as for you, I credit you with a great reward, as if you had done [all of the work required by the community on your own *zekhut* alone]."

Here there is no meaning possible other than that given above: "the heritage of virtue and its consequent entitlements." The reference to an advantage that one gains by reason of inheritance out of one's fathers' righteousness is demanded by the parallel between *zekhut* of clause (1) and *righteousness* of clause (2). The sense in the following is still clearer, that *zekhut* is the opposite of sin, so as there was original sin, so there is original *zekhut:*

18. A. He who causes *zekhut* to the community never causes sin.

B. And he who causes the community to sin—they never give him a sufficient chance to attain penitence.

m. 'Abot **5:18**

Here the contrast is between causing *zekhut* and causing sin, so *zekhut* is the opposite of sin. The continuation is equally clear that a person attained *zekhut* and endowed the community with *zekhut,* or sinned and made the community sin:

18. C. Moses attained *zekhut* and bestowed *zekhut* on the community.

D. So the *zekhut* of the community is assigned to his [credit],

E. as it is said, "He executed the justice of the Lord and his judgments with Israel" (Deut 33:21).

F. Jeroboam sinned and caused the community to sin.

G. So the sin of the community is assigned to his [debit],

H. as it is said, "For the sins of Jeroboam which he committed and wherewith he made Israel to sin" (1 Kgs 15:30).

m. 'Abot **5:18**

The appropriateness of interpreting the passage in the way proposed will now be shown to be self-evident. All that is required is to substitute for *zekhut* the proposed translation:

18. C. Moses attained the heritage of virtue and bestowed its consequent entitlements on the community.

D. So the heritage of virtue and its entitlements enjoyed by the community are assigned to his [credit],

m. 'Abot **5:18**

The sense then is simple. Moses through actions of his own (of an unspecified sort) acquired *zekhut,* which is the credit for such actions that accrued to him and bestowed upon him certain supernatural entitlements; and he for his part passed on as an inheritance that credit, a lien on Heaven for the performance of these same supernatural entitlements: *zekhut*, pure and simple. Original sin is then matched by original virtue, inherited with the human condition.

VI. The Household of Israel and the Heritage of *Zekhut*

In the Talmud of the Land of Israel, Israel the people emerges above all as a family, the social metaphors of people, nation, and kingdom, giving way to the one social metaphor that a feminine half of androgynous Judaism must select for itself. Coming to the Talmud of the Land of Israel and associated Midrash-compilations, we turn first to the conception of the *zekhut* that has been accumulated by the patriarchs and been passed on to Israel, their children. The reason is that the single distinctive trait of *zekhut,* as we have seen it to this point, is its transitive quality: one need not earn or *zekhut* the supernatural power and resource represented by the things you can do if you have *zekhut* but cannot do if you do not have it. One can inherit that entitlement from others, dead or living. Moses not only attains *zekhut* but he also imparts *zekhut* to the community of which he is leader, and the same is so for any Israelite.

That conception is broadened in the successor-documents into the deeply historical notion of *zekhut abot,* empowerment of a supernatural character to which Israel is entitled by reason of what the patriarchs and matriarchs in particular did long ago. It forms the foundation for the paramount sense of *zekhut* in the successor-system: the Israelite possesses a lien upon Heaven by reason of God's love for the patriarchs and matriarchs, his appreciation for certain things they did, and his response to those actions not only in favoring them but also in entitling their descendants to do or benefit from otherwise unattainable miracles. *Zekhut,* as we noted earlier, explains the present—particularly what is odd and unpredictable in the presence—by appeal to the past and hence, forms a distinctively historical conception. But that observation must underline the strange notion of "history" that is in play here: a history that has lost its passed-ness and come to form an eternal presence.

Within the historically-grounded metaphor of Israel as a family expressed by the conception of *zekhut abot,* Israel was a family, the children of Abraham, Isaac, and Jacob, or children of Israel, in a concrete and genealogical sense. Israel hence fell into the genus family, as the particular species of family generated by Abraham and Sarah. The distinguishing trait of that species was that it possessed the inheritance, or heritage, of the patriarchs and matriarchs, and that inheritance, consisting of *zekhut,* served the descendants and heirs as protection and support. It follows that the systemic position of the conception of *zekhut* to begin with lies in its power to define the social entity, and hence, *zekhut* (in the terms of the initial category-formation, the philosophical one) forms a fundamentally political conception and only secondarily an economic and philosophical one.

But *zekhut* serves, in particular, that counterpart category that speaks of not legitimate but illegitimate violence, not power but weakness. In context, time and again, we observe that *zekhut* is the power of the weak. People who through their own *zekhut* and capacity can accomplish nothing, can accomplish miracles through what others do for them in leaving a heritage of *zekhut..* And, not to miss the stunning message of the triplet of stories cited above, *zekhut* also is what the weak and excluded and despised can do that outweighs in power what the great masters of the Torah have accomplished. In the context of a system that represents Torah as supernatural, that claim of priority for *zekhut* represents a considerable transvaluation of power, as much as of value. And, by the way, *zekhut* also forms the inheritance of the disinherited: what you receive as a heritage when you have nothing in the present and have gotten nothing in the past, that scarce resource that is free and unearned but much valued. So let us dwell upon the definitive character of the transferability of *zekhut* in its formulation, *zekhut abot,* the *zekhut* handed on by the ancestors, the transitive character of the concept and its standing as a heritage of entitlements.

It is in the successor-documents that the concept of *zekhut* is joined
with *abot*; that is, the *zekhut* that has been left as Israel's family inheritance by the patriarchs or ancestors, yielding the very specific notion,
defining the systemic politics, its theory of the social entity, of Israel not
as a (mere) community (e.g., as in tractate *'Abot's* reference to Moses's
bestowing *zekhut* upon the community) but as a family, with a history
that takes the form of a genealogy, precisely as Genesis has represented
that history. Now *zekhut* was joined to the metaphor of the genealogy of
patriarchs and matriarchs and served to form the missing link, explaining
how the inheritance and heritage were transmitted from them to their
heirs. Consequently, the family, called "Israel," could draw upon the
family estate, consisting of the inherited *zekhut* of matriarchs and
patriarchs in such a way as to benefit today from the heritage of yesterday. This notion involved very concrete problems. If "Israel, the family"
sinned, it could call upon the "*zekhut*" accumulated by Abraham and
Isaac at the binding of Isaac (Gen 22) to win forgiveness for that sin.
True, "fathers will not die on account of the sin of the sons," but the
children may benefit from the *zekhut* of the forebears. That concrete
expression of the larger metaphor imparted to the metaphor a practical
consequence, moral and theological, that was not at all neglected.

A survey of *Genesis Rabbah*—other Midrash-compilations of the
same group can have yielded equally interesting results—proves indicative of the character and use of the doctrine of *zekhut*, because that
systematic reading of the book of Genesis dealt with the founders of the
family and made explicit the definition of Israel as family. *Zekhut* draws
in its wake the notion of the inheritance of an on-going (historical)
family, that of Abraham and Sarah, and *zekhut* worked itself out in the
moments of crisis of that family in its larger affairs. So the Israelites later
on enjoy enormous *zekhut* through the deeds of the patriarchs and
matriarchs. That conception comes to expression in what follows:

2. A. ". . . for with only my staff I crossed this Jordan, and now I
have become two companies":
    B. R. Judah bar Simon in the name of R. Yohanan: "In the Torah,
in the Prophets, and in the Writings we find proof that the Israelites
were able to cross the Jordan only on account of the *zekhut* achieved by
Jacob:
    C. "In the Torah: '. . . for with only my staff I crossed this Jordan,
and now I have become two companies.'

D. "In the prophets: 'Then you shall let your children know, saying, "Israel came over this Jordan on dry land" ' (Josh 4:22), meaning our father, Israel.

E. "In the Writings: 'What ails you, O you sea, that you flee? You Jordan, that you burn backward? At the presence of the God of Jacob' (Ps 114:5ff.)."

Genesis Rabbah LXXVI:V

Here is a perfect illustration of the definition of *zekhut* as an entitlement one may enjoy by reason of what someone else—an ancestor—has done; and that entitlement involves supernatural power. Jacob did not only leave *zekhut* as an estate to his heirs. The process is reciprocal and on-going. *Zekhut* deriving from the ancestors had helped Jacob himself:

3.   A. "When the man saw that he did not prevail against Jacob, [he touched the hollow of his thigh, and Jacob's thigh was put out of joint as he wrestled with him]" (Gen 32:25):

B. Said R. Hinena bar Isaac, "[God said to the angel,] 'He is coming against you with five "amulets" hung on his neck, that is, his own *zekhut,* the *zekhut* of his father and of his mother and of his grandfather and of his grandmother.

C. " 'Check yourself out, can you stand up against even his own *zekhut* [let alone the *zekhut* of his parents and grandparents].'

D. "The matter may be compared to a king who had a savage dog and a tame lion. The king would take his son and sick him against the lion, and if the dog came to have a fight with the son, he would say to the dog, 'The lion cannot have a fight with him, are you going to make out in a fight with him?'

E. "So if the nations come to have a fight with Israel, the Holy One, blessed be he, says to them, 'Your angelic prince could not stand up to Israel, and as to you, how much the more so!' "

Genesis Rabbah LXXVII:III

The collectivity of *zekhut*, not only its transferability, is illustrated here as well: what an individual does confers *zekhut* on the social entity. It is, moreover, a matter of the legitimate exercise of supernatural power. The reciprocity of the process extended in all directions. Accordingly, what we have in hand is first and foremost a matter of the exercise of legitimate violence, hence a political power. *Zekhut* might project not only backward, deriving from an ancestor and serving a descendant, but forward as well. Thus Joseph accrued so much *zekhut* that the generations that came before him were credited with his *zekhut:*

2.   A. "These are the generations of the family of Jacob. Joseph [being seventeen years old, was shepherding the flock with his brothers]" (Gen 37:2):
      B. These generations came along only on account of the *zekhut* of Joseph.
      C. Did Jacob go to Laban for any reason other than for Rachel?
      D. These generations thus waited until Joseph was born, in line with this verse: "And when Rachel had borne Joseph, Jacob said to Laban, 'Send me away' " (Gen 32:15).
      E. Who brought them down to Egypt? It was Joseph.
      F. Who supported them in Egypt? It was Joseph.
      G. The sea split open only on account of the *zekhut* of Joseph: "The waters saw you, O God" (Ps 77:17). "You have with your arm redeemed your people, the sons of Jacob and Joseph" (Ps 77:16).
      H. R. Yudan said, "Also the Jordan was divided only on account of the *zekhut* of Joseph."

Genesis Rabbah **LXXXIV:V**

The passage at hand asks why only Joseph is mentioned as the family of Jacob. The inner polemic is that the *zekhut* of Jacob and Joseph would more than suffice to overcome Esau. Not only so, but Joseph survived because of the *zekhut* of his ancestors:

1.   A. "She caught him by his garment . . . but he left his garment in her hand and fled and got out of the house. [And when she saw that he had left his garment in her hand and had fled out of the house, she called to the men of her household and said to them, 'See he has brought among us a Hebrew to insult us; he came in to me to lie with me, and I cried out with a loud voice, and when he heard that I lifted up my voice and cried, he left his garment with me and fled and got out of the house']" (Gen 39:13-15):
      B. He escaped through the *zekhut* of the fathers, in line with this verse: "And he brought him forth outside" (Gen 15:5).
      C. Simeon of Qitron said, "It was on account of bringing up the bones of Joseph that the sea was split: 'The sea saw it and fled' (Ps 114:3), on the *zekhut* of this: '. . . and fled and got out.' "

Genesis Rabbah **LXXXVII:VIII**

Zekhut, we see, is both personal and national. **B** refers to Joseph's enjoying the *zekhut* he had inherited, with **C** referring to Israel's enjoying the *zekhut* that they gained through their supererogatory loyalty to that same *zekhut*-rich personality. It specifies what later benefit to the heir, Israel the family, derived from which particular action of a patriarch or matriarch.

2.   A. "And Abram gave him a tenth of everything" (Gen 14:20):

B. R. Judah in the name of R. Nehorai: "On the strength of that blessing the three great pegs on which the world depends, Abraham, Isaac, and Jacob, derived sustenance.

C. "Abraham: 'And the Lord blessed Abraham in *all* things' (Gen 24:1) on account of the *zekhut* that 'he gave him a tenth of *all* things' (Gen 14:20).

D. "Isaac: 'And I have eaten of *all*' (Gen 27:33), on account of the *zekhut* that 'he gave him a tenth of *all* things' (Gen 14:20).

E. "Jacob: 'Because God has dealt graciously with me and because I have all' (Gen 33:11) on account of the *zekhut* that 'he gave him a tenth of *all* things' (Gen 14:20)."

3.   A. Whence did Israel gain the *zekhut* of receiving the blessing of the priests?

B. R. Judah said, "It was from Abraham: '*So* shall your seed be' (Gen 15:5), while it is written in connection with the priestly blessing: '*So* shall you bless the children of Israel' (Num 6:23)."

C. R. Nehemiah said, "It was from Isaac: 'And I and the lad will go *so* far' (Gen 22:5), therefore said the Holy One, blessed be he, '*So* shall you bless the children of Israel' (Num 6:23)."

D. And rabbis say, "It was from Jacob: 'So shall you say to the house of Jacob' (Exod 19:3) (in line with the statement), '*So* shall you bless the children of Israel' (Num 6:23)."

Genesis Rabbah **XLIII:VIII**

Number **2** links the blessing at hand with the history of Israel. Now the reference is to the word "all," which joins the tithe of Abram to the blessing of his descendants. Since the blessing of the priest is at hand, Number **3** treats the origins of the blessing. The picture is clear. "Israel" constitutes a family as a genealogical and juridical fact. It inherits the estate of the ancestors. It hands on that estate. It lives by the example of the matriarchs and patriarchs, and its history exemplifies events in their lives. *Zekhut* forms that entitlement that one generation may transmit to the next, in a way in which the heritage of sin is not to be transmitted except by reason of the deeds of the successor-generation. The good that one does lives onward, the evil is interred with the bones.

To conclude this brief survey of *zekhut* as the medium of historical existence, that is, the *zekhut* deriving from the patriarchs or *zekhut abot,* let me present a statement of the legitimate power—sufficient to achieve salvation, which, in this context, always bears a political dimension—imparted by the *zekhut* of the ancestors. That *zekhut* will enable them to accomplish the political goals of Israel: its attaining self-rule and avoiding government by gentiles. This statement appeals to the binding of Isaac as the source of the *zekhut,* deriving from the patriarchs and matriarchs, which will in the end lead to the salvation of Israel. What is important here is that the *zekhut* that is inherited joins together with the *zekhut* of one's own deeds; one inherits the *zekhut* of the past, and, moreover, if one does what the progenitors did, one not only receives an entitlement out of the past, one secures an entitlement on one's own account. So the difference between *zekhut* and sin lies in the sole issue of transmissibility:

5.   A. Said R. Isaac, "And all was on account of the *zekhut* attained by the act of prostration.

B. "Abraham returned in peace from Mount Moriah only on account of the *zekhut* owing to the act of prostration: '. . . and we will worship [through an act of prostration] and come [then, on that account] again to you' (Gen 22:5).

C. "The Israelites were redeemed only on account of the *zekhut* owing to the act of prostration: And the people believed . . . then they bowed their heads and prostrated themselves' (Exod 4:31).

D. "The Torah was given only on account of the *zekhut* owing to the act of prostration: 'And worship [prostrate themselves] you afar off' (Exod 24:1).

E. "Hannah was remembered only on account of the *zekhut* owing to the act of prostration: 'And they worshiped before the Lord' (1 Sam 1:19).

F. "The exiles will be brought back only on account of the *zekhut* owing to the act of prostration: 'And it shall come to pass in that day that a great horn shall be blown and they shall come that were lost . . . and that were dispersed . . . and they shall worship the Lord in the holy mountain at Jerusalem' (Isa 27:13).

G. "The Temple was built only on account of the *zekhut* owing to the act of prostration: 'Exalt you the Lord our God and worship at his holy hill' (Ps 99:9).

H. "The dead will live only on account of the *zekhut* owing to the act of prostration: 'Come let us worship and bend the knee, let us kneel before the Lord our maker' (Ps 95:6)."

Genesis Rabbah LVI:II

The entire history of Israel flows from its acts of worship ("prostration") beginning with that performed by Abraham at the binding of Isaac. Every sort of advantage Israel has ever gained came about through that act of worship done by Abraham and imitated thereafter. Israel constitutes a family and inherits the *zekhut* laid up as a treasure for the descendants by the ancestors. This family draws upon that *zekhut*, but, by doing the deeds they did, it also enhances its heritage of *zekhut* and leaves to the descendants greater entitlement than they would enjoy by reason of their own actions. But their own actions—here, prostration in worship—generate *zekhut* as well.

VII. Eternal Israel and Responsive Grace

Accordingly, *zekhut* may be personal or inherited. The *zekhut* deriving from the prior generations is collective and affects all Israel. But one's own deeds can generate *zekhut* for oneself, with the simple result that *zekhut* is as much personal as it is collective. Specifically, Jacob reflects on the power that Esau's own *zekhut* had gained for Esau. He had gained that *zekhut* by living in the land of Israel and also by paying honor and respect to Isaac. Jacob then feared that, because of the *zekhut* gained by Esau, he, Jacob, would not be able to overcome him. So *zekhut* worked on its own; it was a credit gained by proper action, which went to the credit of the person who had done that action. What made the action worthy of evoking Heaven's response with an act of supernatural favor is that it was an action not to be required but if done to be rewarded, an act of will that cannot be coerced but must be honored. In Esau's case, it was the simple fact that he had remained in the holy land:

2.   A. "Then Jacob was greatly afraid and distressed" (Gen 32:7): [This is Jacob's soliloquy:] "Because of all those years that Esau was living

in the Land of Israel, perhaps he may come against me with the power
of the *zekhut* he has now attained by dwelling in the Land of Israel.

B. "Because of all those years of paying honor to his father,
perhaps he may come against me with the power of the *zekhut* he
attained by honoring his father.

C. "So he said: 'Let the days of mourning for my father be at hand,
then I will slay my brother Jacob' (Gen 27:41).

D. "Now the old man is dead."

Genesis Rabbah **LXXVI:II**

The important point, then, is that *zekhut* is not only inherited as part of
a collective estate left by the patriarchs. It is also accomplished by an
individual in his or her own behalf. By extension, we recognize, the
successor-system opens a place for recognition of the individual, both
man and woman as a matter of fact, within the system of *zekhut*. As we
shall now see, what a man or a woman does may win for that person an
entitlement upon Heaven for supernatural favor of some sort. So there is
space, in the system, for a private person, and the individual is linked to
the social order through the shared possibilities of generating or inheriting
an entitlement upon Heaven.

For if we now ask, what are the sorts of deeds that generate *zekhut,*
we realize that those deeds produce a common result of gaining for their
doer, as much as for the heirs of the actor, an entitlement for Heavenly
favor and support when needed. This fact concerning gaining and bene-
fiting from *zekhut* brings us to the systemic message to the living
generation, its account of what now is to be done. This message proves
acutely contemporary, for its stress is on the power of a single action to
create sufficient *zekhut* to outweigh a life of sin. Then the contrast
between sin and *zekhut* gains greater depth still. One sin of sufficient
weight condemns, one act of *zekhut* of sufficient weight saves; the entire
issue of entitlements out of the past gives way, then, when we realize
what is actually at stake.

We recall that Torah-study is one—but only one—means for an
individual to gain access to that heritage, to get *zekhut*. There are other
equally suitable means, and, not only so, but the *zekhut* gained by Torah-
study is no different from the *zekhut* gained by acts of a supererogatory
character. If one gets *zekhut* for studying the Torah, then we must suppose there is no holy deed that does not generate its share of *zekhut*. But
when it comes to specifying the things one does to get *zekhut,* the

documents before us speak of what the Torah does not require but does recommend: not what we are commanded to do in detail, but what the right attitude, formed within the Torah, leads us to do on our own volition. What is it that Israelites as a nation do to gain a lien upon Heaven for themselves or entitlements of supernatural favor for their descendants? Here is one representative answer to that question:

1. A. "If the God of my father, the God of Abraham and the Fear of Isaac, had not been on my side, surely now you would have sent me away empty-handed. God saw my affliction and the labor of my hand and rebuked you last night" (Gen 31:41-42):

B. Zebedee b. Levi and R. Joshua b. Levi:

C. Zebedee said, "Every passage in which reference is made to 'if' tells of an appeal to the *zekhut* accrued by the patriarchs."

D. Said to him R. Joshua, "But it is written, 'Except we had lingered' (Gen 43:10) [a passage not related to the *zekhut* of the patriarchs]."

E. He said to him, "They themselves would not have come up except for the *zekhut* of the patriarchs, for it if it were not for the *zekhut* of the patriarchs, they never would have been able to go up from there in peace."

F. Said R. Tanhuma, "There are those who produce the matter in a different version." [It is given as follows:]

G. R. Joshua and Zebedee b. Levi:

H. R. Joshua said, "Every passage in which reference is made to 'if' tells of an appeal to the *zekhut* accrued by the patriarchs except for the present case."

I. He said to him, "This case too falls under the category of an appeal to the *zekhut* of the patriarchs."

Genesis Rabbah LXXIV:XII

So much for *zekhut* that is inherited from the patriarchs, a now familiar notion. But what about the deeds of Israel in the here and now?

J. R. Yohanan said, "It was on account of the *zekhut* achieved through sanctification of the divine name."

K. R. Levi said, "It was on account of the *zekhut* achieved through faith and the *zekhut* achieved through Torah."

Genesis Rabbah LXXIV:XII

Faith despite the here and now, study of the Torah—these are what Israel does in the here and now with the result that they gain an entitlement for themselves or their heirs.

> **1.** L. "The *zekhut* achieved through faith: 'If I had not believed . . .' (Ps 27:13).
> M. "The *zekhut* achieved through Torah: 'Unless your Torah had been my delight' (Ps 119:92)."
> **2.** A. "God saw my affliction and the labor of my hand and rebuked you last night" (Gen 31:41-42):
> B. Said R. Jeremiah b. Eleazar, "More beloved is hard labor than the *zekhut* achieved by the patriarchs, for the *zekhut* achieved by the patriarchs served to afford protection for property only, while the *zekhut* achieved by hard labor served to afford protection for lives.
> C. "The *zekhut* achieved by the patriarchs served to afford protection for property only: 'If the God of my father, the God of Abraham and the Fear of Isaac, had not been on my side, surely now you would have sent me away empty-handed.'
> D. "The *zekhut* achieved by hard labor served to afford protection for lives: 'God saw my affliction and the labor of my hand and rebuked you last night.' "
>
> ***Genesis Rabbah* LXXIV:XII**

Here is as good an account as any of the theology of *zekhut*. The issue of the *zekhut* of the patriarchs comes up in the reference to the God of the fathers. The conception of the *zekhut* of the patriarchs is explicit, not general. It specifies what later benefit to the heir, Israel the family, derived from which particular action of a patriarch or matriarch. But acts of faith and Torah-study form only one medium; hard labor, that is, devotion to one's calling, defines that source of *zekhut* that is going to be accessible to those many Israelites unlikely to distinguish themselves either by Torah-study and acts of faith, encompassing the sanctification of God's name, or by acts of amazing gentility and restraint.

The system here speaks to everybody, Jew and gentile, past and present and future; *zekhut* therefore defines the structure of the cosmic social order and explains how it is supposed to function. It is the encompassing quality of *zekhut*—its pertinence to past and future, high and low, rich and poor, gifted and ordinary—that marks as the systemic statement the message of *zekhut,* now fully revealed as the conception of reciprocal response between Heaven and Israel on earth to acts of devotion beyond the requirements of the Torah but defined all the same by the Torah. As scripture had said, God responds to the faith of the ancient generations by supernatural acts to which, on their own account, the moderns are not entitled, hence a heritage of entitlement. But those acts, now fully defined for us, can and ought to be done, also, by the living generation. And, as a matter of fact, no one today, at the time of the system-builders, is exempt from the systemic message and its demands: even steadfastness in accomplishing the humble work of the everyday and the here and now.

The systemic statement made by the usages of *zekhut* speaks of relationship, function, the interplay of humanity and God. One's store of *zekhut* derives from a relationship, that is, from one's forebears. That is one dimension of the relationships in which one stands. *Zekhut* also forms a measure of one's own relationship with Heaven, as the power of one person, but not another, to pray and so bring rain attests. What sort of relationship does *zekhut*, as the opposite of sin, then posit? It is not one of coercion, for Heaven cannot force us to do these types of deeds that yield *zekhut,* and this, story after story suggests, is the definition of a deed that generates *zekhut:* doing what we ought to do but do not have to do. But then, we cannot coerce Heaven to do what we want done either, for example, by carrying out the commandments. These are obligatory, but do not obligate Heaven.

Whence then the lien on Heaven? To recapitulate: it is through deeds of a supererogatory character. Heaven responds to such deeds by deeds also of a supererogatory character: supernatural favor to this one, who through deeds of ingratiation of the other or self-abnegation or restraint exhibits the attitude that in Heaven precipitates a counterpart attitude, hence generating *zekhut*, rather than to that one, who does not. The simple fact that rabbis cannot pray and bring rain, but a simple ass-driver can, tells the whole story. The relationship measured by *zekhut*— Heaven's response by an act of uncoerced favor to a person's uncoerced gift; e.g., act of gentility, restraint, or self-abnegation—contains an element of unpredictability for which appeal to the *zekhut* inherited from ancestors accounts. So while one cannot coerce heaven, he or she—for women as much as men enjoy full access to *zekhut,* though they do not to the study of the Torah—can through *zekhut* gain acts of favor from Heaven, and that is by doing what Heaven cannot require. Heaven then responds to one's attitude in carrying out his or her duties—and more than those duties. That act of pure disinterest—giving the woman one's means of livelihood—is the one that gains Heaven's deepest interest.

So *zekhut* forms the political economy of the religious system of the social order put forward by the Talmud of the Land of Israel, *Genesis Rabbah, Leviticus Rabbah*, and related writings. Here we find the power that brought about the transvaluation of value, the reversal of the meaning of power and its legitimacy. *Zekhut* expresses and accounts for the economic valuation of the scarce resource of what we should call moral authority. *Zekhut* stands for the political valorization of weakness, that which endows the weak with a power that is not only their own but their ancestors. It enables the weak to accomplish goals through not their own power, but their very incapacity to accomplish acts of violence—a transvaluation as radical as that effected in economics. *Zekhut* holds together both the economics and the politics of this Judaism: it makes the same statement twice.

VIII. The World Upside Down and Right Side Up: The Power of the Weak

Here we find the ultimate reversal, which the moves from scarcity of real estate to abundance of Torah-learning, the legitimacy of power to the legitimacy of weakness, in perspective are shown merely to adumbrate. "Make God's wishes yours, so that God will make your wishes his. . . . Anyone from whom people take pleasure, God takes pleasure" (*'Abot* 2:4). These two statements hold together the two principal elements of the conception of the relationship to God that in a single word *zekhut* conveys. Give up, please others, do not impose your will but give way to the will of the other, and Heaven will respond by giving a lien that is not coerced but evoked. By the rationality of discipline within, we have the power to form rational relationships beyond ourselves, with Heaven; and that is how the system expands the boundaries of the social order to encompass not only the natural but also the supernatural world.

Treating every deed, every gesture as capable of bringing about enchantment, the successor-system imparted to the givens of everyday life—at least in their potential—remarkable power. The conviction that, by dint of special effort, one may so conduct himself or herself as to acquire an entitlement of supernatural power turns one's commonplace

circumstance into an arena encompassing Heaven and earth. God
responds to an individual's—and holy Israel's—virtue, filling the gap—so
to speak—about oneself and about one's entire family that we leave when
we forebear, withdraw, and give up what is one's own: our space, one's
self. When one does so, then God responds; one's sacrifice then evokes
memories of Abraham's readiness to sacrifice Isaac; devotion to the other
calls up from Heaven what by demanding one cannot coerce. What
imparts critical mass to the conception of *zekhut,* that gaining of supernatural entitlements through the surrender of what is mine, is the
recasting, in the mold and model of that virtue of surrender, of the political economy of Israel in the Land of Israel. That accounts for the
definition of legitimate power in politics as only weakness, economics as
the rational increase of resources that are, but need not be, scarce, valued
things that are capable of infinite increase.

God in the successor-system [of Mishnah commentary] gains what
the philosophical God [of the Mishnah] lacks, which is personality, active
presence, pathos, and empathy. The God of the religious system breaks
the rules, accords an entitlement to this one who has done some one
remarkable deed, but not to that one who has done nothing wrong and
everything right. So a life in accord with the rules—even a life spent in
the study of the Torah—in Heaven's view is outweighed by a single
moment, a gesture that violates the norm, extending the outer limits of
the rule, for instance, of virtue. And who but a God who—like us, feels,
not only thinks—responds to impulse and sentiment can be portrayed in
such a way as this?

> "So I sold my ass and I gave her the proceeds, and I said to her,
> 'Here is your money, free your husband, but do not sin [by becoming
> a prostitute to raise the necessary funds].' "
>
> They said to him, "You are worthy of praying and having your
> prayers answered."
>
> *y. Ta'anit 1:4.I.Ob–P*

No rule exhaustively describes a world such as this. Here the law of love
is transcended, for love itself is now surpassed. Beyond love is the
willing, uncoerced sacrifice of self: love of the other more than the love
of self, love of the Other most of all. The feminine component of androgynous Judaism relates to God as lovers relate to one another: giving not
in order to receive, receiving only in order to give.

If the God of the philosophers' Judaism makes the rules, the God of the religious Judaism breaks them. The systemic difference, of course, is readily extended outward from the personality of God: the philosophers' God thinks, the God of the religious responds, and we are in God's image, after God's likeness, not only because we through right thinking penetrate the principles of creation, but through right attitude replicate the heart of the Creator. Humanity on earth incarnates God on high, the Israelite family in particular, and, in consequence, earth and Heaven join—within.

What is asked of Israel and of the Israelite individual now is truly Godly restraint, supernatural generosity of soul that is "in our image, after our likeness:" that is what sets aside all rules. And, since as a matter of simple fact, that appeal to transcend the norm defined not personal virtue but the sainthood of all Israel, living all together in the here and in the now, we must conclude that, within Israel's society, within what the Graeco-Roman world will have called its *polis*, its political and social order, the bounds of earth have now extended to Heaven. In terms of another great system composed in the same time and in response to a world-historical catastrophe of the same sort, Israel on earth dwells in the city of God. And, it must follow, God dwells with Israel, in Israel: "today, if you will it."

The Judaism set forth in the successor-documents portrayed a social order in which, while taking full account of circumstance and historical context, individuals and nation alike controlled their own destiny. The circumstance of genealogy dictated whether or not the moral entity, whether the individual or the nation, would enjoy access to entitlements of supernatural favor without regard to the *zekhut* of either one. But, whether favored by a rich heritage of supernatural empowerment as was the nation, or deprived, by reason of one's immediate ancestors, of any lien upon Heaven, in the end both the nation and the individual had in hand the power to shape the future. How was this to be done? It was not alone by keeping the Torah, studying the Torah, dressing, eating, making a living, marrying, procreating, raising a family, burying and being buried, all in accord with those rules.

That life lived in conformity with the rule, obligatory but merely conventional, did not evoke the special interest of Heaven. Why should it? The rules describe the ordinary. But (in language used only in a later document) "the All-Merciful really wants the heart," and that is not an ordinary thing. Nor was the power to bring rain or hold up a tottering house gained through a life of merely ordinary sanctity. Special favor responded to extraordinary actions, in the analogy of special disfavor, misfortune deemed to punish sin. And just as culpable sin, as distinct from mere error, requires an act of will (specifically, arrogance) so an act of extraordinary character requires an act of will. But, as mirror image of sin, the act would reveal in a concrete way an attitude of restraint, forbearance, gentility, and self-abnegation. A sinful act, provoking Heaven, was one that one did deliberately to defy Heaven. Then an act that would evoke Heaven's favor, so imposing upon Heaven a lien that Heaven freely gave, was one that, equally deliberately and concretely, displayed humility.

Zekhut as the power of the powerless, the riches of the disinherited, the valuation and valorization of the will of those who have no right to will. *Zekhut* arms Israel with the weapons of woman: the strength of weakness, the power of patience and endurance, the coercion that comes about through surviving, come what may. This feminine part of androgynous Judaism's Israel is a family,[4] its God a lover and beloved, its virtue uncoerced, its wisdom uncompelled—this Judaism served for those long centuries in which Judaism addressed a people that could not dominate, but only reason; that could not manipulate, but only hope; that could not guarantee results, but only trust in what would be.

In the context of Christian Palestine, in which the Talmud of the Land of Israel, *Genesis Rabbah*, *Leviticus Rabbah*, and related writings took shape, Jews found themselves on the defensive. Their ancestry called into question, their supernatural standing thrown into doubt, their future denied, they called themselves "Israel," and the land, "the Land of Israel." But what power did they possess, legitimately, if need be through violence, to assert their claim to form "Israel"? And, with the holy land passing into the hands of others, what scarce resource did they own and manage to take the place of that measure of value that now no longer was subjected to their rationality? Asserting a politics in which all violence was illegitimate, an economics in which nothing tangible, even

---

[4]But, I repeat, I cannot allege that selection of the metaphor of family marks a feminine perspective, since I see nothing in the stories we have surveyed to suggest that the system regards the centrality of the family as a distinctively feminine conception at all.

real property in the Holy Land, had value, the system through its counterpart-categories made a single, simple, and sufficient statement.

We now appreciate the entire systemic reversal that we find at the very heart of Rabbinic Judaism, which I now present as androgynous at its foundations. Study of the Torah, which only men could do, emerges as contingent; the life of obedience to the commandments—many more of which are incumbent on men than on women—proves necessary but not sufficient. Israel's relationship to God finds its definition not in what it must do, but in what it alone can decide to do, not commanded, not coerced, but also not so positioned as to dominate or manipulate. This Judaism values relations that are mutual and negotiated, cooperative and suggestive, not assertive, coercive, or aggressive.

The conception of *zekhut* came to the fore to integrate of the system's theory of the way of life of the social order, its economics, together with its account of the social entity of the social order, its politics. The remarkable actions—perhaps those of omission more than those of commission—that produced *zekhut* yielded an increase in the scarcest of all resources, supernatural favor, and at the same time endowed a person rich in entitlements to Heavenly intervention with that power to evoke that which vastly outweighed the this-worldly power to coerce in the accomplishment of one's purpose. It is no wonder that, at the systemic apex, woman and the virtue that is natural to her situation now sits enthroned. The right relationship to God is one of responsive grace and love freely given, one that is not subject to conditions, but that embodies perfect commitment.

So to conclude: the relationship between God and the human being in rabbinic Judaism emerges as feminine by the simple criterion that women, as much as men, exhibit the traits of virtue in relationship to *zekhut*. Since, as I have stressed, women are excluded from other meritorious actions and therefore also relationships—they cannot take a position in the chain of tradition, from disciple to master and upward to Sinai—that fact demands the high degree of importance assigned to it here. The upshot is that God at the center does not coerce humanity, but responds freely to the gift freely given; humanity at the heart of matters does not compel God or engage in acts of force or manipulation. Humanity gives freely, God responds freely. Masculine relationships are conceived in terms of dominance: God commands, man obeys; women's are portrayed in terms of mutuality and negotiation: giving what cannot be commanded, but what is profoundly necessary. The right relationship with God emerges in the dual Torah as not coerced, not assertive, not manipulative, but as one of mutuality and response, the one to the other: a transaction of responsive grace.

So much for the feminine theology that encompasses the masculine world of law and commandment. Now to the next step: from this account of how God responds to individual attitudes and actions of surpassing grace, we turn to the canon's characterization of Israel's relationship with God. To this point I have appealed for the classification of the masculine and the feminine to anything but the system's own criteria. Here we see how that relationship is explicitly represented in terms portrayed as feminine to the core—and how the system states its expectation that men will feminize themselves to love God.

P 141
perfect submissn
perfect trust

Chapter Four

Feminine Israel, Masculine God

How do we know how our sages of blessed memory classify virtues as masculine or as feminine? Identifying the point at which, at the systemic center, women as much as men gain access to Heavenly favor forms only one criterion for defining this Judaism's feminine and masculine taxa. But classifying virtues as feminine finds justification in more direct and therefore more decisive evidence than that just now set forth. Within *aggadah* we have several systematic exegeses that focus on women and thus permit us to characterize the sages' conception of women's virtues and, it will follow, the virtues they classify as feminine. The sages' reading of the scriptural books of Ruth and Esther and their treatment of Miriam the prophetess and other scriptural prophetesses allow access to their thinking on what characterizes the virtuous woman, her alone.

Among the *aggadic* expositions pertinent to this matter, however, none more reliably records the sages' conception of the feminine and the feminine's relationship to the masculine than their reading of the Song of Songs in the *Song of Songs Rabbah*, an exegetical compilation contemporary with the Talmud of Babylonia, ca. 600.[1] In reading the Song

---

[1]On *Song of Songs Rabbah*, see Moses D. Herr, "Song of Songs Rabbah," *Encyclopaedia Judaica* 15:152-54: the name of the compilation, definition, language, sources, and dating in the Land of Israel, in the middle of the sixth century; H. L. Strack and Günter Stemberger, *Introduction to the Talmud and Midrash* (Minneapolis: Fortress Press, 1992), trans. by Markus Bockmuehl, 342-44: text, translation; and my *The Midrash Compilations of the Sixth and Seventh Centuries: An Introduction to the Rhetorical Logical, and Topical Program. IV. Song of Songs Rabbah.* (Atlanta: Scholars Press for Brown Judaic Studies, 1990). The translation cited here is my own, prepared in consultation of that of Maurice Simon, *Song of Songs,* in H. Freedman and Maurice Simon, eds., *Midrash Rabbah* (London: Soncino Press, 1939) vol. IX. When I use Simon's translation verbatim, I signify in this way: [Simon, 00:]. What follows is then his translation, word-for-word or nearly so, until the opening of a new unit of thought. I also cite his notes verbatim, so indicating throughout.

of Songs as a statement of the relationship of God and Israel, *Song of Songs Rabbah* identifies Israel as the female-beloved, God as the male-lover. We need not speculate, therefore, on correct traits for women; in the document at hand, they are those explicitly assigned to feminine Israel. So we now turn to a brief survey of what is said in so many words.

Because of the critical place of *Song of Songs Rabbah* in the representation of androgynous Judaism and, in particular, the definition of the feminine component of the androgyneity, I cite specific passages at considerable length. The bulk of this chapter is made up of those abstracts, since without carefully examining what is said and how the message is stated, we cannot fully grasp the system's own formulation of its deeply feminine character. Not only so, but the presentation of matters of emotion and sentiment, which in the end frame the dominance of the feminine (on which Chapter Five focuses), derives to begin with from the passages portrayed here. Only when, in *Song of Songs Rabbah*, we understand that certain emotions are both identified with women and also assigned the highest standing of virtue for men as well as women will the final step in my argument become possible. This accounts for the decidedly anthological character of what now follows.

The first point is the most telling. The relationship of Israel to God is the same as the relationship of a wife to the husband, and this is explicit in the following:

Song 7:10: *I am my beloved's, and his desire is for me.*
1. A. "I am my beloved's, and his desire is for me":
   B. There are three yearnings:
   C. The yearning of Israel is only for their Father who is in heaven, as it is said, "I am my beloved's, and his desire is for me."
   D. The yearning of a woman is only for her husband: "And your desire shall be for your husband" (Gen 3:16).
   E. The yearning of the Evil Impulse is only for Cain and his ilk: "To you is its desire" (Gen 4:7).
   F. R. Joshua in the name of R. Aha: "The yearning of rain is only for the earth: 'You have remembered the earth and made her desired, greatly enriching her' (Ps 65:10).
   G. "If you have merit, the rains will enrich it, but if not, they will tithe it [the words for enrich and tithe differ by a single letter], for it will produce for you one part for ten of seed."

Song of Songs Rabbah XCIX.i

Here, therefore, we find that gender-relationships are explicitly characterized, and, with them, the traits associated with the genders as well. The same analogy is stated even more explicitly in the following, which reviews the principal points of the marriage liturgy in describing Israel's and God's marriage:

Song 4:10: *How sweet is your love, my sister, my bride! how much better is your love than wine, and the fragrance of your oils than any spice!*

1.   A. "How sweet is your love, my sister, my bride! how much better is your love than wine":

  B. R. Berekhiah and R. Helbo in the name of R. Samuel b. R. Nahman said, "There are ten passages in which Israel is called bride, six here [in the Song of Songs] and four in the prophets.

  C. "Six here: 'Come with me from Lebanon, my bride; come with me from Lebanon. Depart from the peak of Amana, from the peak of Senir and Hermon, from the dens of lions, from the mountains of leopards' (Song 4:8); 'You have ravished my heart, my sister, my bride, you have ravished my heart with a glance of your eyes, with one jewel of your necklace' (Song 4:9); 'How sweet is your love, my sister, my bride! how much better is your love than wine, and the fragrance of your oils than any spice!' (Song 4:10); 'Your lips distil nectar, my bride; honey and milk are under your tongue; the scent of your garments is like the scent of Lebanon' (Song 4:11); 'A garden locked is my sister, my bride, a garden locked, a fountain sealed' (Song 4:12); 'I come to my garden, my sister, my bride, I gather my myrrh with my spice, I eat my honeycomb with my honey, I drink my wine with my milk. Eat, O friends, and drink; drink deeply, O lovers!' (Song 5:1).

  D. "And four in the prophets: 'The voice of mirth and the voice of gladness, the voice of the bridegroom and the voice of the bride' (Jer 7:34); 'And as a bride adorns herself with jewels' (Isa 61:10); 'And gird yourself with them like a bride' (Isa 59:18); 'And as the bridegroom rejoices over the bride' (Isa 62:5).

  E. "And, correspondingly, the Holy One, blessed be he, puts on ten [nuptial] robes: 'The Lord reigns, he is clothed in majesty' (Ps 93:1); 'The Lord is clothed' (Ps 93:1); 'He has girded himself' (Ps 93:1); 'And he put on righteousness as a coat of mail' (Isa 59:17); 'And he put on garments of vengeance' (Isa 59:17); 'For clothing' (Isa 59:17); 'This one who is glorious in his apparel' (Isa 63:1); 'Wherefore is your apparel red' (Isa 63:2); 'You are clothed with glory and majesty' (Ps 104:1).

F. "This is so as to exact punishment from the nations of the world, who kept from the Ten Commandments the Israelites, who are [Simon] bound closely around them like the ornaments of a bride."

Song of Songs Rabbah **LIV:i**

The concluding lines alert us to a rather subtle shift, which we shall consider presently: Israel's relationship to God undergoes change, so too, its relationship to the world; and, as we shall see, Israel proves androgynous, female now, male in the age to come, female to God, male to the nations of the world. Since the entire composition (we cannot overemphasize) derives from men, the metaphor proves remarkably daring and much more nuanced than we should realize were we to conclude that Israel here is only feminine, God only masculine.

The Midrash-exegesis turns to everyday experience—the love of husband and wife—for a metaphor for God's love for Israel and Israel's love for God. Then, when Solomon's song says, "O that you would kiss me with the kisses of your mouth! For your love is better than wine," (Song 1:2), sages of blessed memory think of how God kissed Israel. Reading the Song of Songs as a metaphor, the Judaic sages as a matter of fact state in a systematic and orderly way their entire structure and system, and, along the way, permit us to identify the traits they associate with feminine Israel and masculine God, respectively. What is important here, however, is not the document's doctrinal message but its implicit and tacit affirmations. The document does not set forth a great many explicit doctrines, but it delivers its message through the description of attitudes and emotions. Our particular interest lies in identifying the system's designation of clearly-defined attitudes and emotions as feminine and masculine. The writers mean to paint word-pictures, evoke feelings, and speak empathetically, rather than only sympathetically. *Song of Songs Rabbah* tells one how to think and feel, describing the forming of sensibility in the formation of the heart at one with God. This makes a survey of the taxonomic characterization of traits all the more promising.

The sages who compiled *Song of Songs Rabbah* read the Song of Songs as a sequence of statements of urgent love between God and Israel, the holy people. How they convey the intensity of Israel's love of God forms the point of special interest in this document. For it is not in propositions that they choose to speak, but in the medium of symbols.

Sages here use language as a repertoire of opaque symbols in the form of words. They set forth sequences of words that connote meanings, elicit emotions, stand for events, and form the verbal equivalent of pictures, music, dance, or poetry. Through the repertoire of these verbal-symbols and their arrangement and rearrangement, the message the authors wish to convey emerges: not in so many words, but through words nonetheless. Sages chose for their compilation appeal to a highly restricted list of implicit meanings, calling upon some very few events or persons, repeatedly identifying these as the expressions of God's profound affection for Israel, and Israel's deep love for God. The message of the document comes not so much from stories of what happened or did not happened, assertions of truth or denials of error, but rather from the repetitious rehearsal of sets of symbols.

A brief survey of the main symbolic expressions suffices in preparation for our specific inquiry. In reading the love-songs of the Song of Songs as the story of the love affair of God and Israel, sages identify implicit meanings that are always few and invariably self-evident; no serious effort goes into demonstrating the fact that God speaks, or Israel speaks. The point of departure is the message and meaning the One or the other means to convey. To take one instance: time and again we shall be told that a certain expression of love in the poetry of the Song of Songs is God's speaking to Israel about (1) the Sea, (2) Sinai, and (3) the world to come; or (1) the first redemption, the one from Egypt; (2) the second redemption, the one from Babylonia; and (3) the third redemption, the one at the end of days. The repertoire of symbols covers Temple and schoolhouse, personal piety and public worship, and other matched pairs and sequences of coherent matters, all of them seen as embedded within the poetry. Here is Scripture's poetry read as metaphor, and the task of the reader is to know that for which each image of the poem stands. So Israel's holy life is "metaphorized" through the poetry of love and beloved, Lover and Israel. Long lists of alternative meanings or interpretations end up saying just one thing, but in different ways. The implicit meanings prove very few indeed. When in *Song of Songs Rabbah* we have a sequence of items alleged to form a taxon, that is, a set of things that share a common taxic indicator, of course what we have is a list. The list presents diverse matters that all together share, and therefore also set forth: a single fact or rule or phenomenon. That is why we can list them, in all their distinctive character and specificity, on a common catalogue of "other things" that pertain all together to one thing.

What do the compilers say through their readings of the metaphor—to take one interesting example—of the nut-tree for Israel? First, Israel prospers when it gives scarce resources for the study of the Torah or for carrying out religious duties; second, Israel sins but atones, and Torah is the medium of atonement; third, Israel is identified through carrying out its religious duties; e.g., circumcision; fourth, Israel's leaders had best watch their step; fifth, Israel may be nothing now but will be in glory in the coming age; sixth, Israel has plenty of room for outsiders but cannot afford to lose a single member. What we have is a repertoire of fundamentals dealing with Torah and Torah-study, the moral life and atonement, Israel and its holy way of life, and Israel and its coming salvation. A sustained survey of these composites shows the contradictory fact that while the several composites are heterogeneous, the components of the composites derive from a rather limited list: essentially scriptural events and personalities, on the one side, and virtues of the Torah's holy way of life, on the other. Here is a survey:

> Joseph, righteous men, Moses, and Solomon;
>
> patriarchs as against princes, offerings as against merit, and Israel as against the nations; those who love the king, proselytes, martyrs, penitents;
>
> first, Israel at Sinai; then Israel's loss of God's presence on account of the golden calf; then God's favoring Israel by treating Israel not in accord with the requirements of justice but with mercy;
>
> Dathan and Abiram, the spies, Jeroboam, Solomon's marriage to Pharaoh's daughter, Ahab, Jezebel, Zedekiah;
>
> Israel is feminine, the enemy (Egypt) masculine, but God the father saves Israel the daughter;
>
> Moses and Aaron, the Sanhedrin, the teachers of Scripture and Mishnah, the rabbis;
>
> the disciples; the relationship among disciples, public recitation of teachings of the Torah in the right order; lections of the Torah;
>
> the spoil at the Sea=the Exodus, the Torah, the Tabernacle, the ark;
>
> the patriarchs, Abraham, Isaac, Jacob, then Israel in Egypt, Israel's atonement and God's forgiveness;
>
> the Temple where God and Israel are joined, the Temple is God's resting place, the Temple is the source of Israel's fecundity;

Israel in Egypt, at the Sea, at Sinai, and subjugated by the gentile kingdoms, and how the redemption will come;

Rebecca, those who came forth from Egypt, Israel at Sinai, acts of loving kindness, the kingdoms who now rule Israel, the coming redemption;

fire above, fire below, meaning heavenly and altar fires; Torah in writing, Torah in memory; fire of Abraham, Moriah, bush, Elijah, Hananiah, Mishael, and Azariah;

the Ten Commandments, show-fringes and phylacteries, recitation of the Shema and the Prayer, the tabernacle and the cloud of the Presence of God, and the mezuzah;

the timing of redemption, the moral condition of those to be redeemed, and the past religious misdeeds of those to be redeemed;

Israel at the sea, Sinai, the Ten Commandments; then the synagogues and school houses; then the redeemer;

the Exodus, the conquest of the Land, the redemption and restoration of Israel to Zion after the destruction of the first Temple, and the final and ultimate salvation;

the Egyptians, Esau and his generals, and, finally, the four kingdoms;

Moses's redemption, the first, to the second redemption in the time of the Babylonians and Daniel;

the litter of Solomon: the priestly blessing, the priestly watches, the sanhedrin, and the Israelites coming out of Egypt;

Israel at the sea and forgiveness for sins effected through their passing through the sea; Israel at Sinai; the war with Midian; the crossing of the Jordan and entry into the Land; the house of the sanctuary; the priestly watches; the offerings in the Temple; the sanhedrin; the Day of Atonement;

God redeemed Israel without preparation; the nations of the world will be punished, after Israel is punished; the nations of the world will present Israel as gifts to the royal messiah, and here the base-verse refers to Abraham, Isaac, Jacob, Sihon, Og, Canaanites;

the return to Zion in the time of Ezra, the Exodus from Egypt in the time of Moses;

the patriarchs and with Israel in Egypt, at the Sea, and then before Sinai;

Abraham, Jacob, Moses;

Isaac, Jacob, Esau, Jacob, Joseph, the brothers, Jonathan, David, Saul, man, wife, paramour;

Abraham in the fiery furnace and Shadrach Meshach and Abed-
nego, the Exile in Babylonia, now with reference to the return to Zion

These components form not a theological system made up of well-
joined propositions and harmonious positions, nor propositions that are
demonstrated syllogistically through comparison and contrast. The point
is just the opposite: to show that many different things really do belong
on the same list. This point yields not a proposition that the list syllogistically demonstrates. The list yields only itself, but, to be sure— but then
the list invites our exegesis; the connections among these items require
exegesis (of course, that is, eisegesis). What this adds up to, then, is not
argument for proposition (i.e. comparison and contrast and rule-making
of a philosophical order), but rather a theological structure (comprising
well-defined attitudes). None of these word-symbols, we note, involves
a woman for its focus, though Rebecca makes a cameo appearance. But
the matter of femininity and masculinity is made explicit when feminine
Israel is contrasted with masculine Egypt, to which we shall return.

Our survey of the feminine and the masculine in *Song of Songs
Rabbah* begins with the clear characterization of God as masculine, Israel
as feminine:

Song 6:2: *My beloved has gone down to his garden, to the beds of
spices, to pasture his flock in the gardens, and to gather lilies.*
1.   A. "My beloved has gone down to his garden, to the beds of spices,
[to pasture his flock in the gardens, and to gather lilies]":
      B. Said R. Yosé b. R. Hanina, "As to this verse, the beginning of
it is not the same as the end, and the end not the same as the beginning.
      C. "The verse had only to say, 'My beloved has gone down to
pasture in his garden,' but you say, 'in the gardens'!
      D. "But 'my beloved' is the Holy One, blessed be he;
      E. " 'to his garden' refers to the world.
      F. " 'to the beds of spices' refers to Israel.
      G. " 'to pasture his flock in the gardens' refers to synagogues and
school-houses.
      H. " 'and to gather lilies' speaks of picking [taking away in death]
the righteous that are in Israel."
                          ***Song of Songs Rabbah* LXXVIII:i**

"My beloved" is God; the choice part of the garden, which is the world,
is Israel, its synagogues and houses of study. The nations, moreover,

concur that God is the lover, Israel the beloved, and characterize female Israel as an abandoned woman.

Song 6:1: *Whither has your beloved gone, O fairest among women? Whither has your beloved turned, that we may seek him with you?*
1. A. "Whither has your beloved gone, O fairest among women":

B. The nations of the world [here] speak to Israel, " 'Whither has your beloved gone?' From Egypt to the Sea to Sinai.

C. " 'Whither has your beloved turned?' "

D. And Israel answers the nations of the world, "How come you're asking about him, when you have no share in him?

E. "Once I had cleaved to him, can I depart from him? Once he had cleaved to me, can he depart from me? Wherever he may be, he comes to me."

Song of Songs Rabbah **LXXVII:i**

Now the speaker is the nations, the addressee is Israel, and the issue is Israel's relationship to God. It is one of love and cannot be sundered. Israel is now the faithful beloved, waiting patiently for her lover, always trusting in His faithfulness.

Song 8:6: *Set me as a seal upon your heart, as a seal upon your arm; for love is strong as death, jealousy is cruel as the grave. Its flashes are flashes of fire, a most vehement flame.*
1. A. "for love is strong as death":

B. As strong as death is the love with which the Holy One, blessed be he, loves Israel: "I have loved you says the Lord" (Mal 1:2).

C. "jealousy is cruel as the grave":

D. That is when they make him jealous with their idolatry: "They roused him to jealousy with strange gods. . . ." (Deut 32:16)
5. A. Another explanation of "for love is strong as death":

B. As strong as death is the love with which a man loves his wife: "Enjoy life with the wife whom you love" (Qoh 9:9).

C. "jealousy is cruel as the grave":

D. the jealousy that she causes in him and leads him to say to her, "Do not speak with such-and-so."

E. If she goes and speaks with that man, forthwith: "The spirit of jealousy comes upon him and he is jealous on account of his wife" (Num 5:14).

Song of Songs Rabbah **CVIII:ii**

Israel's feminine character is now well-established, and the ways in which the exegesis of the Song is worked out in response to that fact are clear. Then we have to ask ourselves, precisely what kind of relationship does feminine Israel have with the masculine God? The answer is, the relationship of a wife to a husband.

If we may now ask, what are feminine qualities as explicitly contrasted to masculine ones, the answer is clear. A woman has diminished rights of inheritance; a woman undertakes successive burdens and suffers in childbirth. A woman's status is not to be sought, but is to be accepted and respected. Any doubt of the entire masculine perspective of the system's division of feminine and masculine traits will be removed, moreover, by the following, which underlines feminine Israel's faithlessness, contrasted to the powerful, masculine God's reliability:

Song 1:9: *I compare you, my love, to a mare of Pharaoh's chariots.*
1. A. "I compare you, my love, [to a mare of Pharaoh's chariots]":
    B. Said R. Eliezer, "The matter may be compared to the case of a princess who was kidnapped, and her father was ready to redeem her.
    C. "But she gave indications to the kidnappers, saying to them, 'I am yours, I belong to you, and I am going after you.'
    D. "Said her father to her, 'What are you thinking? Is it that I do not have the power to redeem you? [Simon:] I would have you hold your peace [using the same word as 'compare you'], yes, be silent.'
    E. "So when the Israelites were encamped at the sea, 'and the Egyptians pursued after them and overtook them in camp by the sea' (Exod 14:9),
    F. "the Israelites, fearful, gave indicates to the Egyptians, saying to them, 'We are yours, we belong to you, and we are going after you.'
    G. "Said to them the Holy One, blessed be he, 'What are you thinking? Is it that I do not have the power to redeem you?'
    H. "For the word 'I have compared you' [bears consonants that yield the meaning,] 'I made you silent.'
    I. "Thus: 'The Lord will fight for you, and you will hold your peace' (Exod 14:14)."
2. A. Another explanation of the verse, "I compare you, my love, to a mare of Pharaoh's chariots":
    B. Rabbis say, "Since the Israelites were like mares and the wicked Egyptians like males in heat,
    C. "they ran after them until they sunk down in the sea."

D. Said R. Simon, "God forbid that the Israelites should be compared to mares!

E. "But the waves of the ocean appeared like mares, and the Egyptians were like stallions in heat, so they ran after them until they sunk down in the sea.

F. "The Egyptian said to his horse, 'Yesterday I tried to lead you to the Nile, and you would not follow me, but now you are drowning me in the sea.'

G. "And the horse said to its rider, 'He has thrown me in the sea' (Exod 14:10)—[the several consonants being read as individual words, altogether] meaning, see what is in the sea. An orgy [so Simon] has been made ready for you in the sea."

Song of Songs Rabbah **IX:ii**

Passages such as these, which are many in the document, simply establish the fact of Israel's this-worldly femininity and assign to Israel traits that writings of patriarchal origin commonly attribute to women.

Israel's status as God's beloved yields two important results. First, the metaphor is treated as neuter, in that, even though Israel is feminine, that fact bears no material consequence for the representation of Israel. The repertoire of word-symbols that convey the principal components of the structure of faith is set forth in terms of what is simply a useful metaphor. But the metaphor is not realized, e.g., in the formulation of traits set forth as unique to women and unique to feminine Israel by reason of its femininity. Representative of many passages, the following suffices to show how, despite the femininity of Israel, the framers are able to run through the principal elements of Israel's sacred history— Egypt, the Sea, Sinai, the subjugation to the kingdoms but the coming redemption by reason of Israel's faithfulness to the covenant:

Song 2:1: *I am a rose of Sharon, a lily of the valleys.*

1.   A. "I am a rose of Sharon, [a lily of the valleys]":

B. Said the Community of Israel, "I am the one, and I am beloved.

C. "I am the one whom the Holy One, blessed be he, loved more than the seventy nations."

2.   A. "I am a rose of Sharon":

B. "For I made for him a shade through Bezalel [the words for shade and Bezalel use the same consonants as the word for rose]: 'And Bezalel made the ark' (Exod 38:1)."

3. A. "of Sharon":

    B. "For I said before him a song [which word uses the same consonants as the word for Sharon] through Moses:

    C. " 'Then sang Moses and the children of Israel' (Exod 15:1)."

4. A. Another explanation of the phrase, "I am a rose of Sharon":

    B. Said the Community of Israel, "I am the one, and I am beloved.

    C. "I am the one who was hidden in the shadow of Egypt, but in a brief moment the Holy One, blessed be he, brought me together to Raamses, and I [Simon:] blossomed forth in good deeds like a rose, and I said before him this song: 'You shall have a song as in the night when a feast is sanctified' (Is 30:29)."

5. A. Another explanation of the phrase, "I am a rose of Sharon":

    B. Said the Community of Israel, "I am the one, and I am beloved.

    C. "I am the one who was hidden in the shadow of the sea, but in a brief moment I [Simon:] blossomed forth in good deeds like a rose, and I pointed to him with the finger [Simon:] (opposite to me): 'This is my God and I will glorify him' (Exod 15:2)."

6. A. Another explanation of the phrase, "I am a rose of Sharon":

    B. Said the Community of Israel, "I am the one, and I am beloved.

    C. "I am the one who was hidden in the shadow of Mount Sinai, but in a brief moment I [Simon:] blossomed forth in good deeds like a lily in hand and in heart, and I said before him, 'All that the Lord has said we will do and obey' (Exod 24:7)."

7. A. Another explanation of the phrase, "I am a rose of Sharon":

    B. Said the Community of Israel, "I am the one, and I am beloved.

    C. "I am the one who was hidden and downtrodden in the shadow of the kingdoms. But tomorrow, when the Holy One, blessed be he, redeems me from the shadow of the kingdoms, I shall blossom forth like a lily and say before him a new song: 'Sing to the Lord a new song, for he has done marvelous things, his right hand and his holy arm have wrought salvation for him' (Ps 98:1)."

Song of Songs Rabbah **XVIII.i**

To make the point that its author wishes to register, the foregoing passage does not require that Israel be represented as feminine. Nor do traits identified with femininity emerge. What we have is simply a review of standard high points in the sages' theology of Israel's history: Egypt, the Sea, Sinai, then the whole of the intervening history homogenized into the single, dreadful time of subjugation to the kingdoms, and, finally, redemption, to which we shall return at the end of this chapter.

To the list of virtues classified as distinctively feminine we add the attributes of superhuman restraint and total faithfulness:

Song 6:4: *You are beautiful as Tirzah, my love, comely as Jerusalem, terrible as an army with banners.*

2.   A. Another interpretation: "You are beautiful as Tirzah, my love":

B. this refers to the women of [Simon, verbatim:] the generation of the wilderness.

C. For said Rabbi, "The women of the wilderness were virtuous. They went and restrained themselves and did not contribute their jewelry to the work of making the golden calf.

D. "They said, 'If the Holy One, blessed be he, could pulverize the sturdy idols, how much the more so the flaccid ones!' "

Song of Songs Rabbah LXXX:i

The women acted with restraint: the men, with abandon. But Israel must learn the feminine virtue of heroic restraint and give up the natural, masculine virtue of abandon.

Not only so, but the women behaved with dignity and defined the correct attitude for all Israel, compared to a girl sought in betrothal, who acts with restraint and enormous self-respect, and that too is what male Israelites must adopt as their attitude and policy toward the world at large:

Song 1:2: *O that you would kiss me with the kisses of your mouth.*

9.   A. R. Yohanan interpreted the verse ["O that you would kiss me with the kisses of your mouth"] to speak of the Israelites when they went up to Mount Sinai:

B. "The matter may be compared to the case of a king who wanted to marry a woman, daughter of good parents and noble family. He sent to her a messenger to speak with her. She said, 'I am not worthy to be his serving girl. But I want to hear it from his own mouth.'

C. "When that messenger got back to the king, [Simon:] his face was full of smiles, but what he said was not grasped by the king.

D. "The king, who was astute, said, 'This one is full of smiles.' It would appear that she has agreed. But what he says is not to be understood by me. It appears that she has said, 'I want to hear it from his own mouth.'

E. "So the Israelites are the daughter of good parents. The messenger is Moses. The king is the Holy One, blessed be he.

F. "At that time: 'And Moses reported the words of the people to the Lord' (Exod 19:8)."

*Song of Songs Rabbah*II:i

This same point—feminine virtues encompass both dignity and self-respect, both perfect loyalty to father and husband alike—is made in a somewhat more complex tale, in which daughters' punctiliousness for their own and their fathers' honor is recognized and treated as exemplary:

Song 4:12: *A garden locked is my sister, my bride, a garden locked, a fountain sealed.*

[**4:13**: *Your shoots are an orchard of pomegranates with all choicest fruits, henna with nard.*]

1. A. "A garden locked is my sister, my bride, [a garden locked, a fountain sealed]":

B. R. Judah b. R. Simon in the name of R. Joshua b. Levi: "[The matter may be compared to the case of] a king who had two daughters, an older and a younger, and who did not take time out to marry them off but left them for many years and went overseas.

C. "The daughters went and [Simon, verbatim:] took the law into their own hands, and married themselves off to husbands. And each one of them took her husband's signature and his seal.

D. "After a long time the king came back from overseas and heard people maligning his daughters, saying, 'The king's daughters have already played the whore.'

E. "What did he do? He issued a proclamation and said, 'Everybody come out to the piazza,' and he came and went into session in the antechamber [holding court there].

F. "He said to them, 'My daughters, is this what you have done and have ruined yourselves?'

G. "Each one of them immediately produced her husband's signature and his seal.

H. "He called his son-in-law and asked, 'To which of them are you the husband?'

I. "He said to him, 'I am the first of your sons-in-law, married to your elder daughter.'

J. "He said to him, 'And what is this?'

K. "He said to him, 'This is my signature and my seal.'

L. "And so with the second.

M. "Then the king said, 'My daughters have been guarded from fornication, and you malign and shame them! By your lives, I shall carry out judgment against you.'

N. "So too with the nations of the world: since they taunt Israel and say, ' "And the Egyptians made the people of Israel work with rigor" (Exod 1:13), if that is what they could make them do in labor, how much the more so with their bodies and with their wives'!'

O. "Then said the Holy One, blessed be he, 'A garden locked is my sister, my bride.' "

Song of Songs Rabbah **LVI:i**

The further virtues of wives, portrayed as feminine, once more are those of loyalty and submission. This metaphor is exploited through the invocation of the wife's trust in the husband, the mark of the perfect wife. Israel follows wherever Moses, in behalf of God, leads; Israel trusts in God the way a woman who has accepted marriage trusts her husband:

10. A. R. Berekhiah in the name of R. Judah b. R. Ilai: "It is written, 'And Moses led Israel onward from the Red Sea' (Exod 15:22):

B. "He led them on from the sin committed at the sea.

C. "They said to him, 'Moses, our lord, where are you leading us?'

D. "He said to them, 'To Elim, from Elim to Alush, from Alush to Marah, from Marah to Rephidim, from Rephidim to Sinai.'

E. "They said to him, 'Indeed, wherever you go and lead us, we are with you.'

F. "The matter is comparable to the case of one who went and married a woman from a village. He said to her, 'Arise and come with me.'

G. "She said to him, 'From here to where?'

H. "He said to her, 'From here to Tiberias, from Tiberias to the Tannery, from the Tannery to the Upper Market, from the Upper Market to the Lower Market.'

I. "She said to him, 'Wherever you go and take me, I shall go with you.'

J. "So said the Israelites, 'My soul cleaves to you' (Ps 63:9)."

Israel's feminine virtue must exceed even the wife's trust in the husband's protection. Israel also must care only for God, the way a wife's entire desire is solely for her husband. Not only so, but the virtuous wife cares only for her husband, no one else; nothing matters to her but her husband's presence:

> 3.   A. The matter [of the situation of the Israelites] may be compared to the case of a noble lady, whose husband, the king, and whose sons and sons-in-law went overseas. They came and told her, "Your sons are coming home."
>
> B. She said, "What difference does it make to me? Let my daughters-in-law rejoice."
>
> C. When her sons-in-law came home, they said to her, "Your sons-in-law are coming."
>
> D. So she said, "What difference does it make to me? Let my daughters rejoice."
>
> E. When they told her, "The king, your husband, is coming," she said, "This is the occasion for whole-hearted rejoicing, waves upon waves of joy!"
>
> F. So in the age to come the prophets will come and say to Jerusalem, "Your sons come from afar" (Isa 60:4), and she will say, "What difference does that make to me?"
>
> G. And when they say, "And your daughters are borne on the side" (Isa 60:4), she will say, "What difference does that make to me?"
>
> H. But when they said to her, "Lo, your king comes to you, he is triumphant and victorious" Zech 9:9), she will say, "This is the occasion for whole-hearted rejoicing!"
>
> I. For so it is written, "Rejoice greatly, O daughter of Zion" (Zech 9:9); "Sing and rejoice, O daughter of Zion" (Zech 2:14).
>
> J. Then she will say, "I will greatly rejoice in the Lord, my soul shall be joyful in my God" (Isa 61:10).

These traits of submission, loyalty, and perfect devotion do not exhaust the feminine virtues. But, from the perspective of this document, they take priority, because they set forth the correct attitude that feminine Israel must take in regard to the masculine nations, not only in relation to the masculine God.

Song 2:7: *"I adjure you, O daughters of Jerusalem"*
Song 3:5: *"I adjure you, O daughters of Jerusalem, by the gazelles or the hinds of the field"*
Song 5:8: *"I adjure you, O daughters of Jerusalem, if you find my beloved, that you tell him I am sick with love"*

Song 8:4: *I adjure you, O daughters of Jerusalem, that you not stir up nor awaken love until it please*

1. A. R. Yosé b. R. Hanina said, "The two oaths [Song 2:7: 'I adjure you, O daughters of Jerusalem,' and Song 3:5, 'I adjure you, O daughters of Jerusalem, by the gazelles or the hinds of the field'] apply, one to Israel, the other to the nations of the world.

B. "The oath is imposed upon Israel that they not rebel against the yoke of the kingdoms.

C. "And the oath is imposed upon the kingdoms that they not make the yoke too hard for Israel.

D. "For if they make the yoke too hard on Israel, they will force the end to come before its appointed time."

4. A. R. Helbo says, "There are four oaths that are mentioned here [**Song 2:7**, *'I adjure you, O daughters of Jerusalem'*; Song 3:5, *'I adjure you, O daughters of Jerusalem, by the gazelles or the hinds of the field'*; **Song 5:8**, *'I adjure you, O daughters of Jerusalem, if you find my beloved, that you tell him I am sick with love'*; **Song 8:4**, *'I adjure you, O daughters of Jerusalem, that you not stir up nor awaken love until it please'*], specifically,

B. "he imposed an oath on Israel not to rebel against the kingdoms and not to force the end [before its time], not to reveal its mysteries to the nations of the world, and not to go up from the exile [Simon:] by force.

C. "For if so [that they go up from the exile by force], then why should the royal messiah come to gather together the exiles of Israel?"

Song of Songs Rabbah **XXIV:ii**

The point is unmistakable and critical. Israel is subject to an oath to wait patiently for God's redemption, not to rebel against the nations on its own; that is the concrete social politics meant to derive from the analogy of Israel's relationship to God with the wife's relationship to the husband: perfect submission and also perfect trust. Rebellion against the nations stands for arrogance on Israel's part, an act of lack of trust and therefore lack of faithfulness. Implicit in this representation of the right relationship, of course, is the promise that feminine Israel will evoke from the masculine God the response of commitment and intervention: God will intervene to save Israel, when Israel makes herself into the perfect wife of God.

The upshot is, Israel must fulfil the vocation of a woman, turn itself into a woman, and serve God as a wife serves a husband. The question then follows: is it possible that the Judaism that has treated the present document as canonical asks men to turn themselves into women? And the answer is, this demand is stated in so many words. Here we find a full statement of the feminization of the masculine. The two brothers, Moses and Aaron, are compared to Israel's breasts, a reversal of gender-classifications that can hardly be more extreme or dramatic:

> *Song 4:5: Your two breasts are like two fawns, twins of a gazelle, that feed among the lilies.*
> 1.   A. "Your two breasts are like two fawns":
>   B. this refers to Moses and Aaron.
>   C. Just as a woman's breasts are her glory and her ornament,
>   D. so Moses and Aaron are the glory and the ornament of Israel.
>   E. Just as a woman's breasts are her charm, so Moses and Aaron are the charm of Israel.
>   F. Just as a woman's breasts are her honor and her praise, so Moses and Aaron are the honor and praise of Israel.
>   G. Just as a woman's breasts are full of milk, so Moses and Aaron are full of Torah.
>   H. Just as whatever a woman eats the infant eats and sucks, so all the Torah that our lord, Moses, learned he taught to Aaron: "And Moses told Aaron all the words of the Lord" (Exod 4:28).
>   I. And rabbis say, "He actually revealed the Ineffable Name of God to him."
>   J. Just as one breast is not larger than the other, so Moses and Aaron were the same: "These are Moses and Aaron" (Exod 6:27), "These are Aaron and Moses" (Exod 6:26), so that in knowledge of the Torah Moses was not greater than Aaron, and Aaron was not greater than Moses.
> 6.   A. Happy are these two brothers, who were created only for the glory of Israel.
>   B. That is what Samuel said, "It is the Lord that made Moses and Aaron and brought your fathers up" (1 Sam 12:6).
> 7.   A. Thus "Your two breasts are like two fawns":
>   B. this refers to Moses and Aaron.
>
> ***Song of Songs Rabbah* XLIX:i**

Not only are Moses and Aaron represented through feminine metaphors, so too are Abraham, Isaac, and Jacob, as well as the tribal progenitors, Jacob's sons.

Song 6:9: *My dove, my perfect one, is only one, the darling of her mother, flawless to her that bore her. The maidens saw her and called her happy; the queens and concubines also, and they praised her.*

1.   A. ["There are sixty queens and eighty concubines, and maidens without number.] My dove, my perfect one, is only one, [the darling of her mother, flawless to her that bore her. The maidens saw her and called her happy; the queens and concubines also, and they praised her]":

B. "My dove, my perfect one, is only one": this is Abraham, "Abraham was one" (Ezek 33:24).

C. "the darling of her mother": this is Isaac, the only son his mother bore.

D. "flawless to her that bore her": this is Jacob, our father, who was the preferred child of the one who bore him, because he was wholly righteous.

E. "The maidens saw her and called her happy": this refers to the tribal progenitors [the sons of Jacob], "and the report was heard in Pharaoh's house saying, Joseph's brothers have come" (Gen 45:16).

***Song of Songs Rabbah* LXXXV:i**

So too, principal documents of the Torah (and the actors within the male bastion, the house of study) are set forth through the same process of metaphorical feminization, all being women.

2.   A. R. Isaac interpreted the verse to speak of components of the Torah: " 'There are sixty queens': this refers to the sixty tractates of laws [in the Mishnah].

B. " 'and eighty concubines': this refers to the lections of the book of Leviticus.

C. " 'and maidens without number': there is no end to the Supplements [*toseftaot*].

D. " 'My dove, my perfect one, is only one': They differ from one another, even though all of them derive support for their conflicting views from a single proof-text, a single law, a single argument by analogy, a single argument a fortiori."

3.   A. R. Yudan b. R. Ilai interpreted the verse to speak of the tree of life and the garden of Eden:

B. " 'There are sixty queens': this refers to the sixty fellowships of righteous persons who are in session in the Garden of Eden under the tree of life, engaged in study of the Torah."

5. A. [Continuing **3.B**:] " 'and eighty concubines': this refers to the eighty fellowships of mediocre students who are in session and study the Torah beyond the tree of life.

B. " 'and maidens without number': there is no limit to the number of disciples.

C. "Might one suppose that they dispute with one another? Scripture says, 'My dove, my perfect one, is only one': all of them derive support for their unanimous opinion from a single proof-text, a single law, a single argument by analogy, a single argument a fortiori."

6. A. Rabbis interpret the verse to speak of those who escaped from Egypt:

B. " 'There are sixty queens': this refers to the sixty myriads aged twenty and above who went forth from Egypt.

C. " 'and eighty concubines': this refers to the eighty myriads from the age of twenty and lower among the Israelites who went forth from Egypt.

D. " 'and maidens without number': there was no limit nor number to the proselytes."

Song of Songs Rabbah **LXXXV:i**

It is not surprising, therefore, that, having reviewed the main components of the faith, the framer should revert at the end to feminine Israel.

10. A. Another explanation: "My dove, my perfect one, is only one": this speaks of the community of Israel, "And who is like your people, like Israel, a nation that is singular in the earth" (2 Sam 7:23).

B. "the darling of her mother": "Attend to me, O my people, and give ear to me, O my nation" (Isa 51:4), with the word for "my nation" spelled to be read "my mother."

C. "flawless to her that bore her": R. Jacob translated in the presence of R. Isaac, "Beside her, there is no child belonging to the one who bore her."

D. "The maidens saw her and called her happy": "And all the nations shall call you happy" (Mal 3:12).

E. "the queens and concubines also, and they praised her": "And kings shall be your foster-fathers" (Isa 59:23).

Song of Songs Rabbah **LXXXV:i**

So the three points of application of our base-verse to the feminine gender of the faith's principal parts are, first, Israel vis-a-vis the nations of the world, then the genealogy of the family of Abraham, Isaac, Jacob,

then Torah, and finally, Israel. I cannot imagine a more satisfying repertoire of meanings identified with the social components of the system,
nor a clearer message than the one that is given: in the here and now,
Israel is feminine, in the age to come, it will be masculine. But femininity and its virtues—submission, loyalty, trust—are to be cherished,
because these represent the media of Israel's future salvation—and, not
at all incidentally, its return to whole masculinity.

This account of the feminization of Israel by the framers of *Song of
Songs Rabbah* fittingly comes to a close with a reprise of the point of the
foregoing chapter, which is the feminization of Judaism—which is to say,
the inclusion, within the system as a whole, of a massive and determinate
feminine component. In the following, feminine Israel is ornamented by
all of the jewelry contained in the treasure of the Torah: all of the acts
of faith are paraded as marks of the beauty of Israel in the explicit setting
of Israel's feminine relationship to the masculine God.

Song 1:15: *Behold, you are beautiful, my love; behold, you are
beautiful; your eyes are doves.*
1.   A. "Behold, you are beautiful, my love; behold, you are beautiful;
[your eyes are doves]"

B. "Behold you are beautiful" in religious deeds,

C. "Behold you are beautiful" in acts of grace,

D. "Behold you are beautiful" in carrying out religious obligations
of commission,

E. "Behold you are beautiful" in carrying out religious obligations
of omission,

F. "Behold you are beautiful" in carrying out the religious duties of
the home, in separating priestly ration and tithes,

G. "Behold you are beautiful" in carrying out the religious duties
of the field, gleanings, forgotten sheaves, the corner of the field, poor
person's tithe, and declaring the field ownerless,

H. "Behold you are beautiful" in observing the taboo against mixed
species,

I. "Behold you are beautiful" in providing a linen cloak with
woolen show-fringes,

J. "Behold you are beautiful" in [keeping the rules governing]
planting,

K. "Behold you are beautiful" in keeping the taboo on
uncircumcised produce,

L. "Behold you are beautiful" in keeping the laws on produce in the fourth year after the planting of an orchard,

M. "Behold you are beautiful" in circumcision,

N. "Behold you are beautiful" in trimming the wound,

O. "Behold you are beautiful" in reciting the Prayer,

P. "Behold you are beautiful" in reciting the *Shema*,

Q. "Behold you are beautiful" in putting a *mezuzah* on the doorpost of your house,

R. "Behold you are beautiful" in wearing phylacteries,

S. "Behold you are beautiful" in building the tabernacle for the Festival of Tabernacles,

T. "Behold you are beautiful" in taking the palm branch and *etrog* on the Festival of Tabernacles,

U. "Behold you are beautiful" in repentance,

V. "Behold you are beautiful" in good deeds,

W. "Behold you are beautiful" in this world,

X. "Behold you are beautiful" in the world to come.

Song of Songs Rabbah **XV:i**

Lest we conclude with the impression that the whole is a static tableau, we turn at the end to the daring conception that the marks of God's physical love for feminine Israel are contained in the Torah and the commandments thereof.

Song 2:6: *O that his left hand were under my head, and that his right hand embraced me!*

1. A. "O that his left hand were under my head":

B. this refers to the first tablets.

C. "and that his right hand embraced me":

D. this refers to the second tablets.

2. A. Another interpretation of the verse, "O that his left hand were under my head":

B. this refers to the show-fringes.

C. "and that his right hand embraced me":

D. this refers to the phylacteries.

3. A. Another interpretation of the verse, "O that his left hand were under my head":

B. this refers to the recitation of the *Shema*.

C. "and that his right hand embraced me":

D. this refers to the Prayer.

4. A. Another interpretation of the verse, "O that his left hand were under my head":

B. this refers to the tabernacle.

C. "and that his right hand embraced me":

D. this refers to the cloud of the Presence of God in the world to come: "The sun shall no longer be your light by day nor for brightness will the moon give light to you" (Isa 60:19). Then what gives light to you? "The Lord shall be your everlasting light" (Isa 60:20).

Song of Songs Rabbah **XXIII:i**

So much for Israel's response to God's caress—in the Torah. How about the equally-concrete representation of God's response to Israel's passion? Here the same picture is drawn.

Song 4:9: *You have ravished my heart, my sister, my bride, you have ravished my heart with a glance of your eyes, with one jewel of your necklace.*

1. A. "You have ravished my heart, my sister, my bride, you have ravished my heart":

B. Said the Holy One, blessed be he, "You had one heart in Egypt, but you gave me two hearts."

C. "you have ravished my heart with a glance of your eyes":

D. It was through the blood of the Passover offering and the blood of circumcision.

E. "with one jewel of your necklace":

F. this is Moses, who was unique, the hero of all your tribes.

2. A. Another interpretation of the verse, "You have ravished my heart, my sister, my bride, you have ravished my heart":

B. Said the Holy One, blessed be he, "You had one heart at the Sea, but you gave me two hearts."

C. "you have ravished my heart with a glance of your eyes":

D. "For you stood before me at Mount Sinai and said, 'All that the Lord has spoken we shall do and we shall obey' (Exod 24:7)."

E. "with one jewel of your necklace":

F. this is Moses, who was unique, the hero of all your tribes.

3. A. Another interpretation of the verse, "You have ravished my heart, my sister, my bride, you have ravished my heart":

B. Said the Holy One, blessed be he, "You had one heart in the wilderness, but you gave me two hearts."

C. "you have ravished my heart with a glance of your eyes":

D. this is setting up the tabernacle: "And on the day that the tabernacle was set up" (Num 9:15).

E. "with one jewel of your necklace":

F. this is Moses, who was unique, the hero of all your tribes.

G. There are those to say, "This refers to the women of the generation of the wilderness, who were virtuous. When that foul deed came around, they went and took counsel among themselves, and did not give a thing of their jewelry to the making of the calf.

H. "Further, when they heard that, in their menstrual periods, they were prohibited to them, they forthwith went and locked their doors."

4.   A. Another interpretation of the verse, "You have ravished my heart, my sister, my bride, you have ravished my heart":

B. Said the Holy One, blessed be he, "You had one heart in the matter of the spies, but you gave me two hearts."

C. [Supply: "you have ravished my heart with a glance of your eyes":]

D. this refers to Joshua and Caleb: "Except for Caleb son of Jephunneh the Kenizzite and Joshua the son of Nun" (Num 32:12).

E. "with one jewel of your necklace":

F. this is Moses, who was unique, the hero of all your tribes.

5.   A. Another interpretation of the verse, "You have ravished my heart, my sister, my bride, you have ravished my heart":

B. Said the Holy One, blessed be he, "You had one heart at Shittim, but you gave me two hearts."

C. "you have ravished my heart with a glance of your eyes":

D. this refers to Phineas: "Then arose Phineas and carried out judgment . . . and that was counted to him for righteousness" (Ps 106:30-31).

E. "with one jewel of your necklace":

F. this is Moses.

Song of Songs Rabbah **LIII:i**

So much for the feminization of the Torah and Israel and the masculinization of God. The process comes to fulfillment in the representation as feminine of all of the virtues, all of the saints and heroes, all of the acts of sanctification that God has commanded and that submissive Israel carries out. Once Israel is feminized, so too is everything else. Then the feminine virtues—submission, trust, perfect loyalty—are adopted by Israel. But that is only for now.

We should grossly err if we imagined that the whole story is that Israel is feminine, God is masculine. Far from it. The message of *Song of Songs Rabbah* is that, if Israel is feminine now, she will resume her masculinity in the world to come. That is a much more subtle and profound statement, a judgment of on the androgyneity of Israel that makes the union of traits, feminine and masculine, something other than a static portrait of a world at rest. In fact, the metaphor of the feminine Israel and the masculine God is subsumed within the more profound message of redemption and carries a critical element in that message: Israel must be patient, submissive, and deeply trusting in God now, so that, in the world to come, Israel may resume its fulfilled masculinity. In this age, Israel to God is as a wife to a husband. But in the age to come, Israel assumes masculine identity. It follows that Israel is represented as androgyne, feminine, then masculine.

4. A. R. Berekhiah in the name of R. Samuel b. R. Nahman said, "The Israelites are compared to a woman.

B. "Just as an unmarried women receives a tenth part of the property of her father and takes her leave [for her husband's house when she gets married], so the Israelites inherited the land of the seven peoples, who form a tenth part of the seventy nations of the world.

C. "And because the Israelites inherited in the status of a woman, they said a song in the feminine form of that word, as in the following: 'Then sang Moses and the children of Israel this song [given in the feminine form] unto the Lord' (Exod 15:1).

D. "But in the age to come they are destined to inherit like a man, who inherits all of the property of his father.

E. "That is in line with this verse of Scripture: 'From the east side to the west side: Judah, one portion . . . Dan one, Asher one . . . ' (Ezek 48:7), and so throughout.

F. "Then they will say a song in the masculine form of that word, as in the following: 'Sing to the Lord a new song' (Ps 96:1).

G. "The word 'song' is given not in its feminine form but in its masculine form."

5. A. R. Berekiah and R. Joshua b. Levi: "Why are the Israelites compared to a woman?

B. "Just as a woman takes up a burden and puts it down [that is, becomes pregnant and gives birth], takes up a burden and puts it down, then takes up a burden and puts it down and then takes up no further burden,

C. "so the Israelites are subjugated and then redeemed, subjugated and then redeemed, but in the end are redeemed and will never again be subjugated.

D. "In this world, since their anguish is like the anguish of a woman in childbirth, they say the song before him using the feminine form of the word for song,

E. "but in the age to come, because their anguish will no longer be the anguish of a woman in childbirth, they will say their song using the masculine form of the word for song:

F. "'In that day this song [in the masculine form of the word] will be sung' (Isa 26:1)."

Song of Songs Rabbah V:iii

So the real message lies in the femininity of Israel in this world in contrast to its masculinity in the world to come.

Not only so, but there is another qualification of considerable urgency. It is that feminine Israel is masculine in its aggressive relationship to the nations, and here, once more, we find what we may call temporal—or serial—androgyneity: feminine now, masculine in the age to come. It hardly needs repetition that the system is the work of men and states a masculine viewpoint, which makes the systemic androgyneity all the more remarkable.

Song 2:14: *O my dove, in the clefts of the rock, in the covert of the cliff, let me see your face, let me hear your voice, for your voice is sweet, and your face is comely*

1.   A. "O my dove, in the clefts of the rock, [in the covert of the cliff, let me see your face, let me hear your voice, for your voice is sweet, and your face is comely]":

B. What is the meaning of "my dove, in the clefts of the rock"?

C. Said R. Yohanan, "Said the Holy One, blessed be he, 'I call Israel a dove: "And Ephraim has become like a silly dove, without understanding" (Hos 7:11).'

D. " 'To me they are like a dove, but to the nations of the world they are like wild beasts: "Judah is a lion's whelp" (Gen 49:9); "Naphtali is a hind let loose" (Gen 49:21); "Dan shall be a serpent in the way" (Gen 49:17); "Benjamin is a wolf that ravages" (Gen 49:27).'

E. "For the nations of the world make war on Israel and say to Israel, 'What do you want with the Sabbath and with circumcision?'

F. "And the Holy One, blessed be he, strengthens Israel, and before the nations of the world they become like wild beasts so as to subdue them before the Holy One, blessed be he, and before Israel.

G. "But as to the Holy One, blessed be he, they are like a dove that is without guile, and they obey him: 'And the people believed, and when heard that the Lord had remembered' (Exod 4:31)."

Song of Songs Rabbah **XXXI:i**

The same point is made more articulately: Israel is one thing to God, another to the nations; feminine and submissive to God, masculine and aggressive to the nations of the world. That point is now fundamental in our characterization of the whole. Israel is feminized only for a time; Israel is fully masculine in the end of time. Israel is serially androgynous. The following makes this point in respect to God as well, who responds to Israel's character:

[**Song 5:9**: *What is your beloved more than another beloved, O fairest among women! What is your beloved more than another beloved, that you thus adjure us?*]

Song 5:10: *My beloved is all radiant and ruddy, distinguished among ten thousand.*

1. A. The Israelites answer them, " 'My beloved is all radiant and ruddy.' "

B. "radiant": to me in the land of Egypt,

C. "and ruddy": to the Egyptians.

D. "radiant": in the land of Egypt, "For I will go through the land of Egypt" (Exod 12:13).

E. "and ruddy": "And the Lord overthrew the Egyptians" (Exod 14:27).

F. "radiant": at the Sea: "The children of Israel walked upon dry land in the midst of the sea" (Exod 14:29).

G. "and ruddy": to the Egyptians at the Sea: "And the Lord overthrew the Egyptians in the midst of the sea" (Exod 14:27).

H. "radiant": in the world to come.

I. "and ruddy": in this world.

2. A. R. Levi b. R. Hayyata made three statements concerning the matter:

B. " 'radiant': on the Sabbath.

C. " 'and ruddy': on the other days of the week.

D. "radiant": on the New Year.

E. "and ruddy": on the other days of the year.

F. " 'radiant': in this world.

G. " 'and ruddy': in the world to come.

3.   A. "distinguished among ten thousand":

B. Said R. Abba b. R. Kahana, "A mortal king is known by his ceremonial garments, but here, he is fire and his ministers are fire: 'And he came from the myriads holy' (Deut 33:2).

C. "He is marked in the midst of 'the myriads holy.' "

Song of Songs Rabbah **LXX:i**

If we may explain how Israel is feminine at this time but masculine in the age to come, it is because Israel now is governed by others, so is deemed passive, therefore, by the patriarchal document, classified as feminine; but as we see time and again, this is not how matters will remain.

Song 6:13: *Return, return, O Shulammite, return, return that we may look upon you. Why should you look upon the Shulammite, as upon a dance before two armies?*

1.   A. "Return, return, O Shulammite, return":

B. R. Samuel b. R. Hiyya b. R. Yudan in the name of R. Hanina, "In the present passage, the word 'return' is written four times.

C. "These correspond to the four monarchies that have ruled over Israel, into the power of which, and out of the power of which, the Israelites entered and emerged whole."

Song of Songs Rabbah **LXXXIX:i**

The same passage contains further elements of special interest here. First of all, it introduces the matter of *zekhut*, accruing to feminine Israel (as the context makes clear).

7.   A. [Supply: Another explanation for the name Shulamite:]

B. R. Joshua of Sikhnin in the name of R. Levi said, "It is the nation solely on account of the *zekhut* of which all the good things in the world come about:

C. " 'So God give on your account of the dew of heaven and of the fat places of the earth' (Gen 27:28).

D. "The word for 'on your account' means, on account of your *zekhut* and on your account the matter depends.

E. "That is the usage in the following: 'The Lord will open for your sake his good treasure' (Deut 28:12),

F. "on account of your *zekhut* and on you the matter depends."

Second, feminine-Israel is represented as the medium of conciliation between the masculine God and the world at large. Feminine Israel has a distinctive role to play in perfecting the world, restoring the relationship between God and humanity:

8.   A. [Supply: Another explanation for the name Shulamite:]

B. R. Samuel b. R. Tanhum and R. Hanan, son of R. Berekhiah of Bosrah in the name of R. Jeremiah: "[God says,] 'It is the nation that made peace between me and my world.'

C. " 'For had they not accepted my Torah, I should have returned my world to formlessness and void.' "

D. For Huna said in the name of R. Aha, "It is written, 'The earth and all its inhabitants are dissolved' (Ps 75:4):

E. "if the Israelites had not stood before Mount Sinai and said, 'Whatever the Lord has spoken we shall do and obey' (Exod 24:7), the world would have by now dissolved.

F. "And who is it who founded the world? It is 'I,' thus: 'I myself establish the pillars of it, selah' (Ps 75:4), meaning, for the sake of their 'I am the Lord your God,' I have established its pillars."

Third, Israel's stubborn loyalty to God is recognized by the nations, but of course ridiculed by them now, though, in the end of days, the nations will appreciate what Israel has done for them:

9.   A. "return that we may look upon you":

B. The nations of the world say to Israel, "How long are you going to die for your God and [Simon:] devote yourselves completely to him?"

C. "For thus Scripture says, 'Therefore do they love you beyond death' (Song 1:3).

D. "And how long will you be slaughtered on his account: 'No, but for your sake we are killed all day long' (Ps 44:23)?

E. " 'How long are you going to do good deeds on his account, for him alone, while he pays you back with bad things?'

F. "Come over to us, and we shall make you governors, hyparchs, and generals,

G. " 'that we may look upon you:' and you will be [Simon:] the cynosure of the world: 'And you shall be the look out of all the people' (Exod 18:21)."

H. And the Israelites will answer, " 'Why should you look upon the Shulammite, as upon a dance before two armies':

I. "In your entire lives, have you ever heard that Abraham, Isaac, and Jacob worshiped idols, that their children should do so after them? Our fathers did not worship idols, and we shall not worship idols after them.

J. "But what can you do for us?

K. "Can it be like the dance that was made for Jacob, our father, when he went forth from the house of Laban?"

11. A. [Continuing 9.K:] "Or can you make a dance for us such as was made for our fathers at the sea? 'And the angel of God removed . . .' (Exod 14:19).

B. "Or can you make a dance for us like the one that was made for Elisha: 'And when the servant of the man of God was risen early and gone forth, behold a host with horses and chariots was round about the city. And his servant said to him, Alas, my master, what shall we do? And he answered, Do not be afraid, for they who are with us are more than those who are with them. Forthwith Elisha prayed and said, Lord, I pray you, open his eyes that he may see. And the Lord opened the eyes of the young man, and he saw, and behold, the mountain was full of horses and chariots of fire around about Elisha' (2 Kgs 6:15).

C. "Or can you make a dance for us like the one that the Holy One, blessed be he, will make for the righteous in the age to come?"

12. A. R. Berekiah and R. Helbo and Ulla of Beri and R. Eleazar in the name of R. Hanina said, "The Holy One, blessed be he, is going to serve as the lord of the dance for the righteous in the age to come:

B. " 'Mark well her ramparts' (Ps 48:14) may be read, 'her dance.'

C. "And the righteous will celebrate him with their finger: 'For this is God, our God, forever and ever. He will guide us eternally' (Ps 48:15).

D. "[The letters for the word 'eternally'] yield the meaning, 'like women,'

E. "like the dance of the righteous."

Israel is whole with God, but God and Israel cannot make peace with the nations of the world except on God's terms. The invocation of the dance, with God as the leader, Israel as the partner, at the end underscores the wholly feminine representation of Israel once more: "like women—like the dance of the righteous." Then feminine Israel plays the role of the wife who stands as mediator between her husband and the world at large; the mother who holds the family together, now the family of the nations and the master, who is God.[2]

Then how does this message reach theological formulation in terms of the doctrine of virtue that must shape Israel's personal life and social policy alike? This is the final question before us: how, exactly, has the union of feminine and masculine in Judaism produced a doctrine of concrete consequence for the definition of virtue?

---

[2]A question demanding inquiry concerns the gender-traits of the Messiah himself. That he is male is not the point. We should like to know how he is represented, as to attitudes and emotions, and whether or not he is given traits that conform to those recommended in Chapters Three and Four. So too, of equal interest, would be an examination of the gender-traits of the Messiah's mother and father (and other ancestors). I considered a study of this question, but it seems to me to require consideration in its own terms: the representation of the Messiah, not only the Messiah's gender-traits. A brief survey of *Esther Rabbah* I yielded little of interest. I found in *Ruth Rabbah* some material that seemed pertinent; e.g., Ruth had no ovaries, hence lacked distinctive female characteristics, but was given them when they were needed. I should like to have found the equivalent of the representations we have of a bearded Mary, on the one side, and an androgynous Jesus, on the other. But my focus here is too narrow, and after a superficial survey, the volume of relevant data struck me as too thin. A broader-based survey would be called for. Ideally, in an androgynous system, the Messiah should exhibit traits that are characterized as both feminine and masculine. Most of the speculation on the Messiah concerns who he may be, when he is coming, and what Israel must do to hasten the day or to make itself worthy of his coming. But for sustained accounts of the Messiah's own definitive characteristics, including gender-traits, we have to return to scripture, particularly the prophets; from there, to be sure, we might then turn to how the relevant verses of scripture are read in the compilations of Midrash-exegeses made by our sages of blessed memory; these will provide a test of the androgynous character I impute to the system as a whole. Within the limits of this modest formulation of the hypothesis of the androgeneity of Judaism, such a study is desirable but not acutely required.

Part Three

Androgynous Judaism

Chapter Five

Virtue and the Feminine Heart of Masculine Israel

The dual Torah, beginning to end, taught that the Israelite was to exhibit the moral virtues of subservience, patience, endurance, and hope. These would translate into the emotional traits of humility and forbearance. They would yield to social virtues of passivity and conciliation. The hero was one who overcame impulses, and the truly virtuous person was the one who reconciled others by giving way before the opinions of others. All of these acts of self-abnegation and self-denial, accommodation rather than rebellion, required one to begin with the right attitudes, sentiments, emotions, and impulses. The single most dominant motif of the rabbinic writings, start to finish, is its stress on the right attitude's leading to the right action, the correct intentionality's producing the besought decision, and above all, accommodating in one's heart to what could not be changed by one's action—meaning, the world as it was. Sages' prepared Israel for the long centuries of subordination and alienation by inculcating attitudes that best suited people who could govern little more than how they felt about things.

In the definitive writings of Judaism, "our sages of blessed memory," who defined the Judaism of the dual Torah of scripture and the Mishnah and explained and expanded both into the enduring religious world-view and way of life for Israel, the Jewish people, taught what Israel is supposed to feel. Classified in accord with the indicators set forth in Chapter Four, these emotions are feminine, not masculine. The feminine traits, according to *Song of Songs Rabbah*, are patience, submission, deep trusting, conciliation, and accommodation. Israel is represented as feminine, therefore accepting and enduring. What, in concrete terms, does it mean for androgynous Israel to feel the feelings of a woman—and how do we know which emotion is feminine, which masculine? Israel is to cultivate the virtues of submission, accommodation, reconciliation, and self-sacrifice—the virtues we have now seen are classified as feminine ones. But, later on, in time to come, having realized the reward for these virtues, Israel will resume the masculine virtues—again, in accord with the classification just now set forth—of aggression and domination.

But this is not the view of only a late Midrash-compilation. In fact, the repertoire of approved and disapproved feelings remains constant through the half-millennium—ca. 100–600 C.E.—of the unfolding of the canon of Judaism from the formative decades of the Mishnah through the Talmud of Babylonia. As a matter of fact, the emotions encouraged by Judaism in its formative age (such as humility, forbearance, accommodation, a spirit of conciliation) exactly correspond to the political and social requirements of the Jews' condition in that time. The reason that the same repertoire of emotions persisted with no material change through the unfolding of the writings of the sages of that formative age was the constancy of the Jews' political and social condition.

Viewed as norms, the permitted emotions occasionally come to expression in *halakhah*, but take up a position in the foreground of *aggadah*. But that fact makes matters no less definitive. Emotions lay down judgments. They derive from rational cognition. We shall now see how even *aggadah* sets forth norms, for the individual Israelite's innermost feelings, the microcosm, correspond to the public and historic condition of Israel, the macrocosm. What Judaism teaches the private person to feel links her or his heart to what Judaism states about the condition of Israel in history and of God in the cosmos. All form one reality, in supernatural world and nature, in time and in eternity wholly consubstantial (so to speak). In the innermost chambers of deepest feelings, the Israelite therefore lives out the public history and destiny of the people, Israel. The genius of Judaism, the reason for its resilience and endurance, lies in its power to teach Jews in private to feel what in public they also must think about the condition of both self and nation. The world within, the world without are so bonded that one is never alone. The individual's life always is lived with the people.

To begin with, we deal with a deep appreciation for paradox, meaning, things are not what they seem, but the very opposite. This deep-seated reading registers even in the simplest definitions of virtue, e.g., the following:

A. Ben Zoma says, "Who is a sage? He who learns from everybody,

B. "as it is said, 'From all my teachers I have gotten understanding' (Ps 119:99).

C. "Who is strong? He who overcomes his desire,

D. "as it is said, 'He who is slow to anger is better than the mighty, and he who rules his spirit than he who takes a city' (Prov 16:32).

E. "Who is rich? He who is happy in what he has,

F. "as it is said, 'When you eat the labor of your hands, happy will you be, and it will go well with you' (Ps 128:2) .

G. ("Happy will you be—in this world, and it will go well with you—in the world to come.")

H. "Who is honored? He who honors everybody,

I. "as it is said, 'For those who honor me I shall honor, and they who despise me will be treated as of no account'(1 Sam 2:30)."

m. 'Abot **4:1**

The series of opposites makes the point: sagacity is the manifestation of ignorance, strength, the control of inner feelings, wealth, satisfaction in the status quo, honor, the honoring of others. Other definitions of strength—"one who turns his enemy into an ally"—make the same point. These formulations express in terms of the private person that much more profound paradox of Israel's public life. God's chosen people and first love, Israel is vanquished and humiliated on earth, no longer even master of its own politics, disempowered and disgraced.

That matters of sexuality and gender-definition should serve for the formulation of theological truths is hardly surprising; the scriptural record prepares us for just such a development. The notion of the centrality of human feelings in the religious life of Israel presents no surprises. Scripture is explicit on both sides of the matter. The human being is commanded to love God. In the scriptural biography of God the tragic hero, God will despair, love, hope, and feel disappointment or exultation. The biblical record of God's feelings and God's will concerning the feelings of humanity—wanting human love, for example—leaves no room for doubt. Nor does the Judaism that emerges from late antiquity ignore or propose to obliterate the datum that "the merciful God wants the heart." The Judaism of the rabbis of late antiquity makes explicit that God always wants the heart. God commands that humanity love God with full heart, soul, mind, and might. That is the principal duty of humanity.

An epitome of the oral Torah's sages' treatment of emotions yields a simple result. Early, middle, and late, a single doctrine and program dictated what people had to say on how Israel should tame its heart. Israel's virtues were to be those of the woman-Israel of *Song of Songs Rabbah*. And it is not difficult to see why. In this world, Israel was a vanquished nation, possessed of a broken spirit. The sages' Judaism for a defeated people prepared the nation for a long future. The vanquished people, the broken-hearted nation that had lost its city and its temple, had, moreover, produced another nation from its midst to take over its scripture and much else. That defeated people, in its intellectuals, as represented in the rabbinic sources, found refuge in a mode of thought that trained vision to see other things otherwise than as the eyes perceived them. This general way of seeing things accounts also for the specific matter of the feminization of Israel: Israel now was to endure as a woman, so that, in the age to come, it would resume its masculine position among the nations: dominant and determinative. Among the diverse ways by which the weak and subordinated accommodate to their circumstance, the one of iron-willed pretense in life is most likely to yield the mode of thought at hand: things never are, because they cannot be, what they seem. The uniform tradition on emotions persisted intact because the social realities of Israel's life proved permanent, until, in our own time, they changed. The upshot was that rabbinic Judaism's Israel was instructed on how to tame its heart and govern its wild emotions, to accept with resignation, to endure with patience, above all, to value the attitudes and emotions that made acceptance and reconciliation into matters of honor and dignity, and, therefore, also made endurance plausible.

We turn to concrete statements on the proper emotions for the Israelite. While the Mishnah casually refers to emotions, e.g., tears of joy, tears of sorrow, where feelings matter, it always is in a public and communal context. For one important example, where there is an occasion of rejoicing, one form of joy is not to be confused with some other, or one context of sorrow with another. Accordingly, marriages are not to be held on festivals (*m. Mo'ed. Qat.* 1:7). Likewise mourning is not to take place then (*m. Mo'ed Qat.* 1:5; 3:7-9). Where emotions play a role, it is because of the affairs of the community at large, e.g., rejoicing on a festival, mourning on a fast day (*m. Sukk.* 5:1-4). Emotions are to be kept in hand, as in the case of the relatives of the executed felon (*m. Sanh.* 6:6). If one had to specify the single underlying principle affecting all forms of emotion, for the Mishnah it is that feelings must be kept under control, never fully expressed without reasoning about the appropriate context. Emotions must always lay down judgments.

In most of those cases in which emotions play a systemic, not merely a tangential, role, the basic principle is the same. We can and must so frame our feelings as to accord with the appropriate rule. In only one case does emotion play a decisive role in settling an issue, and that has to do with whether or not a farmer was happy that water came upon his produce or grain. This case underlines the conclusion just now drawn. If people feel a given sentiment, it is a matter of judgement and, therefore, invokes the law's penalties. So in this system, emotions are not treated as spontaneous, but as significant aspects of a person's judgment. It would be difficult to find a more striking example of that view than at *m. Makkot* 4:5 and related passages. The very fact that the law applies comes about because the framers judge the farmer's feelings to constitute, on their own and without associated actions or even conceptions, final and decisive judgments on what has happened.

The reason that emotions form so critical a focus of concern in rabbinic Judaism is that God and the human being share traits of attitude and emotion. They want the same thing, respond in the same way to the same events, share not only ownership of the Land but also viewpoint on the value of its produce. That judgment is expressed in *aggadah*, as we saw in our examination of the concept of *zekhut*. But it also comes to the fore in *halakhah*. For example, in the law of tithing, the produce becomes liable to tithing—that is, giving to God's surrogate God's share of the crop of the Holy Land—when the farmer deems the crop to be desirable. Why is that so? When the farmer wants the crop, so too does God. When the householder takes the view that the crop is worthwhile, God responds to the attitude of the farmer by forming the same opinion. The theological anthropology that brings God and the householder into the same continuum prepares the way for understanding what makes the entire mishnaic system work.

It is the matter of the intention and will of the human being as we move from theological to philosophical thought in the Mishnah's system. "Intention" stands for attitude, and there is no distinguishing attitude from emotion. For the discussion on intention works out several theories concerning not God and God's relationship to humanity but the nature of the human will. The human being is defined as not only sentient but also a volitional being, who can will with effect, unlike beasts and, as a matter of fact, angels (which do not, in fact, figure in the Mishnah at all). On the one side, there is no consideration or will or attitude of animals, for these are null. On the other side, will and attitude of angels, where these are represented in later documents, are totally subservient to God's wishes. Only the human being, in the person of the farmer, possesses and also exercises the power of intentionality. The power that intentionality possesses forms the central consideration. Because a human being forms an intention, consequences follow, whether or not given material expression in gesture or even in speech. The Mishnah and the law flowing from it impute extraordinary power to the will and intentionality of the human being.

How does this bear practical consequence? The attitude of the farmer toward the crop, like that of the Temple priest toward the offering that he carries out, affects the status of the crop. It classifies an otherwise-unclassified substance. It changes the standing of an already-classified beast. It shifts the status of a pile of grain, without any physical action whatsoever, from one category to another. Not only so, but as we shall now see, the attitude or will of a farmer can override the effects of the natural world, e.g., keeping in the status of what is dry and so insusceptible to cultic uncleanness a pile of grain that in fact has been rained upon and wet down. An immaterial reality, shaped and reformed by the householder's attitude and plan, overrides the material effect of a rain-storm. This example brings us to the remarkable essay on theories of the relationship between action and intention worked out in Mishnah-tractate *Makhshirin* and exemplified by the fourth chapter of that tractate.

Proceeding onward to the compilation of teachings on virtue, tractate *'Abot*, ca. 250 C.E., we find there the single most comprehensive account of religious affections. The reason is that, in that document above all, how we feel defines a critical aspect of virtue. The issue proves central, not peripheral. The doctrine emerges fully exposed. A simple catalogue of permissible feelings comprises humility, generosity, self-abnegation, love, a spirit of conciliation of the other, and eagerness to please. A list of impermissible emotions is made up of envy, ambition, jealousy, arrogance, sticking to one's opinion, self-centeredness, a grudging spirit, vengefulness, and the like. People should aim at eliciting from others acceptance and good will and should avoid confrontation, rejection, and humiliation of the other. This they do through conciliation and giving up their own claims and rights. So both catalogues form a harmonious and uniform whole, aiming at the cultivation of the humble and malleable person, one who accepts everything and resents nothing. Here are some representative sentiments:

> **2:4** A. He would say, "Make his wishes into your own wishes, so that he will make your wishes into his wishes.
>
> B. "Put aside your wishes on account of his wishes, so that he will put aside the wishes of other people in favor of your wishes."
>
> **3:10** A. He would say, "Anyone from whom people take pleasure—the Omnipresent takes pleasure.
>
> B. "And anyone from whom people do not take pleasure, the Omnipresent does not take pleasure."
>
> **4:1** A. Ben Zoma says, "Who is a sage? He who learns from everybody,
>
> B. "as it is said, From all my teachers I have gotten understanding (Ps 119:99).
>
> C. "Who is strong? He who overcomes his desire,
>
> D. "as it is said, He who is slow to anger is better than the mighty, and he who rules his spirit than he who takes a city (Prov 16:32).
>
> E. "Who is rich? He who is happy in what he has,
>
> F. "as it is said, When you eat the labor of your hands, happy will you be, and it will go well with you (Ps 128:2) .
>
> G. ("Happy will you be—in this world—and it will go well with you—in the world to come.")
>
> H. "Who is honored? He who honors everybody,
>
> I. "as it is said, 'For those who honor me I shall honor, and they who despise me will be treated as of no account (1 Sam 2:30)."
>
> **4:18** A. R. Simeon b. Eleazar says, "(1) Do not try to make amends with your fellow when he is angry,
>
> B. "or (2) comfort him when the corpse of his beloved is lying before him,
>
> C. "or (3) seek to find absolution for him at the moment at which he takes avow,
>
> D. "or (4) attempt to see him when he is humiliated."
>
> **4:19** A. Samuel the Small says, "Rejoice not when your enemy falls, and let not your heart be glad when he is overthrown, lest the Lord see it and it displease him, and he turn away his wrath from him (Prov 24:17)."
>
> **Tractate *'Abot***

True, these virtues, in this tractate as in the system as a whole, derive from knowledge of what really counts, which is what God wants. But God favors those who please others. Israel is praised in *Song of Songs Rabbah* because of its power to conciliate and please others. The virtues appreciated by human beings prove identical to the ones to which God responds as well. What single virtue of the heart encompasses the rest? Restraint, the source of self-abnegation, humility, serves as the anecdote for ambition, vengefulness, and, above all, for arrogance. It is restraint of our own interest that enables us to deal generously with others, humility about ourselves that generates a liberal spirit towards others.

So the emotions prescribed in tractate *'Abot* turn out to provide variations of a single feeling, which is the sentiment of the disciplined heart, whatever affective form it may take. And where does the heart learn its lessons, if not in relationship to God? So: "Make his wishes yours, so that he will make your wishes his" (*'Abot* 2:4). Applied to the relationships between human beings, this inner discipline of the emotional life will yield exactly those virtues of conciliation and self-abnegation, humility and generosity of spirit, that the framers of tractate *Abot* spell out in one example after another. Imputing to Heaven exactly those responses felt on earth, e.g., "Anyone from whom people take pleasure, God takes pleasure" (*'Abot* 3:10), makes the point at the most general level.

The talmud to tractate *'Abot*, the Fathers, which is *The Fathers According to Rabbi Nathan*, carries forward the doctrinal rules concerning right attitude and virtuous emotion. It spells out in concrete ways the requirement of humility and the prohibition of arrogance, as in the following:

VII:III

1.   A. Teach the members of your household humility [in receiving the poor].

   B. When a householder is humble and the members of his household are humble, when a poor man comes and stands at the door of the household and says to the people there, "Is your father here," they will say to him, "Indeed so. Come in."

   C. Before he comes in, the table will be set before him. He comes in and eats and drinks and says a blessing for the sake of Heaven and [the householder thereby] derives much pleasure.

D. But if the householder is not humble, then the members of the household will be surly. If then a poor man comes and stands at the door and says to them, "Is your father home," they will say to him, "No," and will show an angry face to him and nastily throw him out.

VII:IV

1. A. Another interpretation of the statement, Teach the members of your household humility: how so?

B. When a householder is humble and the members of his household are humble, if the householder goes overseas, he prays, "I give thanks before you, Lord my God, that my wife does not make fights with other people, and my children do not have quarrels with other people." He goes away with a steady heart and a serene mind until he comes home.

C. But when a householder is arrogant and the members of his household surly, when the householder goes overseas, he prays, "May it please you, Lord my God, that my wife will not make fights with other people, and my children will not have quarrels with other people." He goes away with an uncertain heart and a troubled mind until he comes home.

The Fathers According to Rabbi Nathan, Chapter Seven

Here we see a formulation entirely consistent with what has gone before; the feelings and responses of the poor person form the criterion for judging the value of the action. The householder who is to be praised is one who does not engage in contention with others, but who conciliates others; and the poor person who leaves with a troubled heart is one for which the virtuous householder should not wish to bear responsibility.

When the authors or compilers of the Tosefta finished their labor of amplification and complement for the Mishnah, ca. 300 C.E., they had succeeded in adding only a few fresh and important developments of established themes. What is striking is, first the stress upon the communal stake in an individual's emotional life. Still more striking is the Tosefta's authors' explicit effort to invoke an exact correspondence between public and private feelings. In both realms emotions are to be tamed, kept in hand and within accepted proportions. Public sanctions for inappropriate, or disproportionate, emotions entail emotions, for instance, such as shame. It need hardly be added that feeling shame for improper feelings once again underlines the social, judgmental character of those feelings. For shame is public, guilt private. People are responsible for how they feel, as much as for how, in word or deed, they express feeling. Hence an appropriate penalty derives from the same aspect of social life, that is, the affective live.

There is no more stunning tribute to the power of feeling than the allegation, surfacing in the Tosefta, that the Temple was destroyed because of vain hatred. That sort of hatred, self-serving and arrogant, stands against the feelings of love that characterize God's relationship to Israel. Accordingly, it was improper affections that destroyed the relationship embodied in the Temple cult of old. Given the critical importance accorded to the Temple cult, sages could not have made more vivid their view that how a private person feels shapes the public destiny of the entire nation. So the issues came to expression in high stakes. But the basic position of the authors of the Mishnah, inclusive of their first apologists in *'Abot*, seems entirely consistent. What Tosefta's authors accomplished is precisely what they claimed, which was to amplify, supplement, and complement established principles and positions.

What is most interesting in the Talmud of the Land of Israel, ca. 400 C.E., is the recognition that there are rules descriptive of feelings, as much as of other facts of life. These rules tells us how to dispose of cases in which feelings make a difference. The fact is, therefore, that the effects of emotions, as much as of opinions or deeds, come within the rule of law. It must follow, in the view of sages, the affective life once more proves an aspect of society. People are assumed to frame emotions, as much as opinions, in line with common and shared judgments. In no way do emotions form a special classification, one expressive of what is private, spontaneous, individual, and beyond the law and reason.

Among the emotions forbidden by the Yerushalmi is ambition, so *y. Shabbat* 14:1.VI.K: "R. Huna . . . [said], 'And the Lord will take away from you all illness' (Deut 7:15)—this refers to ambition." And in the same passage, the counterpart to ambition is the impulse to do evil.

The Talmud of Babylonia [the Bavli], ca. 600 C.E., carried forward with little change the now traditional program of emotions, listing the same ones catalogued earlier and no new ones. The authors said about those feelings what had been said earlier. A leader must be someone acceptable to the community. God then accepts him, too. People should be ready to give up quarrels and forgive. The correspondence of social and personal virtues reaches explicit statement. How so? The community must forebear, the individual must forgive. Communal tolerance for

causeless hatred destroyed the Temple; individual vendettas yield mis-
carriages. The two coincide. In both cases, people nurture feelings that
express arrogance. Arrogance is what permits the individual to express
emotions without discipline, and arrogance is what leads the community
to undertake what it cannot accomplish.

A fresh emphasis portrayed in the Bavli favored mourning and disapproved of rejoicing. We can hardly maintain that that view came to
expression only in the latest stages in the formation of the canon. The
contrary is the case. The point remains consistent throughout. Excessive
levity marks arrogance, deep mourning characterizes humility. So many
things come down to one thing. The nurture of an attitude of mourning
should mark both the individual and the community, both in mourning
for the Temple, but also mourning for the condition of nature, including
the human condition, signified in the Temple's destruction. The correct
virtue is the one recommended at the outset: a conciliatory attitude, a
willingness to settle quarrels. So we find in the following:

> A. "And Moses rose up and went to Dathan and Abiram" (Num
> 16:25):
> B. Said R. Simeon b. Laqish, "On the basis of this verse we learn
> that one should not hold on to a quarrel [but should be eager to end it,
> in the model of Moses, who modestly went out to the other side to seek
> a resolution]."
> C. For Rab said, "Whoever holds on to a quarrel [and does not seek
> to end it] violates a negative commandment, for it is said, 'And let him
> not be as Korah and as his company' (Num 17:5)."
> D. R. Ashi said, "He is worthy of being smitten with *saraat*.
> E. "Here it is written, 'As the Lord said to him by the hand of
> Moses' (Num 17:5), and elsewhere it is written, 'And the Lord said to
> him, Put your hand into your bosom [and when he took it out, behold,
> his hand was leprous as snow' (Exod 4:6)."
>
> *b. Sanhedrin* 110A

The passage is important only because it is representative of well-
established attitudes. One further example suffices, in which arrogance
is a sin, humility a virtue, and God the model for the right attitude and
emotion:

XVIII.

A. hence [in Scripture] do we derive an admonition against the arrogant?

B. Said Raba said Zeiri, " 'Listen and give ear, do not be proud' (Jer 13:15)."

C. R. Nahman bar Isaac said, "From the following: 'Your heart will be lifted up, and you will forget the Lord your God' (Deut 8:14).

D. "And it is written, 'Beware, lest you forget the Lord your God' (Deut 8:11)."

E. And that accords with what R. Abin said R. Ilaa said.

F. For R. Abin said R. Ilaa said, "In every place in which it is said, 'Beware lest . . . that you not. . . ,' the meaning is only to lay down a negative commandment [so that one who does such a thing violates a negative admonition]."

XIX.

A. R. Avira expounded, sometimes in the name of R. Assi and sometimes in the name of R. Ammi, "Whoever is arrogant in the end will be diminished,

B. "as it is said, 'They are exalted, there will be a diminution' (Job 24:24).

C. "And lest you maintain that they continue in the world [alive], Scripture states, 'And they are gone' (Job 24:24).

D. "But if [the arrogant] repents, he will be gathered up [in death] at the time allotted to him [and not before],

E. "as was the case with our father, Abraham,

F. "as it is said, 'But when they are lowly, they are gathered in like all' (Job 24:24)—like Abraham, Isaac, and Jacob, concerning whom 'all' is written [at Gen 24:1, 27:33, 33:11].

G. "And if not: 'They are cut off as the tops of the ears of corn' (Job 24:24)."

XX.

A. "With him also who is of a contrite and humble spirit" (Isa 57:15).

B. R. Huna and R. Hisda:

C. One said, "I [God] am with the contrite."

D. The other said, "I [God] am the contrite."

E. Logic favors the view of him who has said, "I [God] am with the contrite," for lo, the Holy One, blessed be he, neglected all mountains and heights and brought his Presence to rest on Mount Sinai,

F. and he did not raise Mount Sinai upward [to himself].

G. R. Joseph said, "A person should always learn from the attitude of his Creator, for lo, the Holy One, blessed be he, neglected all mountains and heights and brought his Presence to rest on Mount Sinai,

H. "and he neglected all valuable trees and brought his Presence to rest in the bush."

XXI.

A. Said R. Eleazar, "Whoever is arrogant is worthy of being cut down like an *asherah* [a tree that is worshipped].

B. Here it is written, 'The high ones of stature shall be cut down' (Isa 10:33),

C. "and elsewhere it is written, 'And you shall hew down their Asherim' (Deut 7:5)."

D. And R. Eleazar said, "Whoever is arrogant—his dust will not be stirred up [in the resurrection of the dead].

E. "For it is said, 'Awake and sing, you that dwell in the dust' (Isa 26:19).

F. "It is stated not 'you who lie in the dust' but 'you who dwell in the dust,' meaning, one who has become a neighbor to the dust [by constant humility] even in his lifetime."

G. And R. Eleazar said, "For whoever is arrogant the Presence of God laments,

H. "as it is said, 'But the haughty he knows from afar' (Ps 138:6)."

XXII.

A. R. Avira expounded, and some say it was R. Eleazar, "Come and take note of the fact that not like the trait of the Holy One, blessed be he, is the trait of flesh and blood.

B. "The trait of flesh and blood is that those who are high take note of those who are high, but the one who is high does not take note of the one who is low.

C. "But the trait of the Holy One, blessed be he, is not that way. He is high, but he takes note of the low,

D. "as it is said, 'For though the Lord is high, yet he takes note of the low' (Ps 138:6)."

XXIII.

A. Said R. Hisda, and some say it was Mar Uqba, "Concerning whoever is arrogant said the Holy One, blessed be he, he and I cannot live in the same world,

B. "as it is said, 'Whoever slanders his neighbor in secret—him will I destroy; him who has a haughty look and a proud heart I will not endure' (Ps 101:5).

C. "Do not read, 'him [I cannot endure]' but '*with* him [I cannot endure].'"

D. There are those who apply the foregoing teaching to those who slander, as it is said, "Whoever slanders his neighbor in secret—him will I destroy" (Ps 101:5).

XXIV.

A. Said R. Alexandri, "Whoever is arrogant—even the slightest breeze shakes him,

B. as it is said, 'But the wicked are like the troubled sea' (Isa 57:20).

C. "Now if the sea, which is so vast [lit.: which has so many quarter-*logs* (of water)]—the slightest breeze shakes it, a man, who is not so vast—all the more so [that the slightest breeze would shake him]."

b. Sotah 5A–B

The picture now is complete. Israel must be like God: as God is humble, long-suffering and patient, so Israel must be humble and avoid arrogance. This counsel, joined to the results of Chapter Four, leaves no doubt that the doctrine of emotions, feminine in classification by the documents' own characterization, encompasses man as much as woman, God as much as Israel. The upshot is clear: Israel must be like God, and the way in which it must imitate God finds definition in virtue. The definition of virtue comes to feminine Israel from its relationship with God. In the definition of a religious system, whole and entire, it would be difficult to identify a more complete, a more closed circle; androgynous Judaism encompasses God, the Torah, and Israel, all together and all at once.

A brief survey of the main points in the Talmud of Babylonia concludes this account of the femininity of virtue, the androgyneity of Judaism. A mark of humility is humble acceptance of suffering. This carried forward the commonplace view that suffering now produces joy later on. The ruin of the Temple, for example, served as a guarantee that just as the prophetic warnings came to realization, so too would prophetic promises of restoration and redemption. In the realm of feelings, the union of opposites came about through the same mode of thought. Hence

God's love comes to fulfillment in human suffering, and the person who joyfully accepts humiliation or suffering will enjoy the appropriate divine response of love.

Another point at which the authors of the Bavli introduce a statement developing a familiar view derives from the interpretation of how to love one's neighbor: by imposing upon one's neighbor the norms of the community, that is, rebuking the other for violating accepted practice. In this way, the emotion of love takes on concrete social value in re-enforcing the norms of the community. Since the verse at hand invites exactly that interpretation, we can hardly regard as innovative the Bavli's paragraph on the subject. Stories about sages range the changes on the themes of humility, resignation, restraint, and perpetual good will. A boastful sage loses his wisdom. A humble one retains it. Since it is wisdom about which a sage boasts, the matching of opposites conforms to the familiar mode of thought.

The strikingly fresh medium for traditional doctrines in the Bavli takes the form of prayers composed by sages. Here the values of the system came to eloquent expression. Sages prayed that their souls may be as dust for everyone to tread upon. They asked for humility in spirit, congenial colleagues, good will, good impulses. They asked God to take cognizance of their humiliation, to spare them from disgrace. The familiar affective virtues and sins, self-abnegation as against arrogance, made their appearance in liturgical form as well. Another noteworthy type of material, also not new, in which the pages of the Bavli prove rich, portrayed the deaths of sages. One dominant motif is uncertainty in face of death, a sign of humility and self-abnegation.

The basic motif—theological as much as affective—encompassing all materials is simple. Israel is estranged from God, and therefore, should exhibit the traits of humility and uncertainty, acceptance and conciliation. When God recognizes in Israel's heart, as much as in the nation's deeds and deliberation, the proper feelings, God will respond by ending that estrangement that marks the present age. So the single word encompassing the entire affective doctrine of the canon of Judaism is alienation. No contemporary, surviving the Holocaust, can miss the psychological depth of the system, which joins the human condition to the fate of the nation and the world and links the whole to the broken heart of God.

We therefore find ourselves where we started, in those sayings that say that if one wants something, he or she should aspire to its opposite.

Things are never what they seem. To be rich, accept what you have. To be powerful, conciliate your enemy. To be endowed with public recognition in which to take pride, express humility. So too the doctrine of the emotional life expressed in law, scriptural interpretation, and tales of sages alike turns out to be uniform and simple. Emotions well up uncontrolled and spontaneous. Anger, vengeance, pride, arrogance—these people feel by nature. So feelings as much as affirmations and actions must become what by nature they are not. If one wants riches, seek the opposite. If one wants honor, pursue the opposite. But how do you seek the opposite of wealth? It is by accepting what you have. How pursue humility, if not by doing nothing to aggrandize oneself?

So the life of the emotions, in conformity to the life of reflection and of concrete deed, will consist in the transformation of what things *seem* into what they *ought* to be. No contemporary psychologists or philosophers can fail to miss the point. Here we have an example of the view—whether validated by the facts of nature or not—that emotions constitute constructs, and feelings lay down judgments. So the heart belongs, together with the mind, to the human being's power to form reasoned viewpoints. Coming from sages, intellectuals to their core, such an opinion surely coheres with the context and circumstance of those who hold it.

What we see is an application of a large-scale, encompassing exercise in analogical thinking—something is like something else, stands for, evokes, or symbolizes that which is quite outside itself. It may be the opposite of something else, in which case it conforms to the exact opposite of the rules that govern that something else. The reasoning is analogical or it is contrastive, and the fundamental logic is taxonomic. The taxonomy rests on those comparisons and contrasts we should call parabolic. In this case, what lies on the surface misleads. What lies beneath or beyond the surface—there is the true reality. People who see things this way constitute the opposite of ones who call a thing as it is. Self-evidently, they have become accustomed to perceiving more—or less—than is at hand. Perhaps that is a natural mode of thought for the Jews of this period (and not then alone), so long used to calling themselves God's first love, yet now seeing others with greater worldly reason claiming that same advantaged relationship.

Not in mind only, but still more, in the politics of the world, the people that remembered its origins along with the very creation of the world and founding of humanity, that recalled how it alone served, and serves, the one and only God, for hundreds of years had confronted a quite difference existence. The radical disjuncture between the way things were and the way Scripture said things were supposed to be, and in actuality would some day become, surely imposed an unbearable tension. It was one thing for the slave born to slavery to endure. It was another for the free man sold into slavery to accept that same condition.

Accounting for the effort to see matters in a way other than what they seem to be is not difficult. The radical disjuncture between the way things were and the way scripture said things were supposed to be surely imposed on Jews an unbearable tension. It was one thing for the slave born to slavery to endure. It was another for the free man sold into slavery to accept that same condition. The vanquished people, the broken-hearted nation that had in 586 B.C.E. and again in 70 C.E. lost its city and its temple, that had, moreover, in the fourth century C.E. produced another nation from its midst to take over its Scripture and much else, could not bear too much reality. That defeated people, in its intellectuals, as represented in the sources we have surveyed, then found refuge in a mode of thought that trained vision to see things otherwise than as the eyes perceived them.

Among the diverse ways by which the weak and subordinated accommodate to their circumstance, the one of iron-willed pretense in life is most likely to yield the mode of thought at hand: things never are, because they cannot be, what they seem. The uniform tradition on emotions persisted intact because the social realities of Israel's life proved permanent, until, in our own time, they changed. The affective program of the canon, early, middle, and late, fits tightly in every detail with this doctrine of an ontological teleology in eschatological disguise. Israel is to tame its heart so that it will feel that same humility, within, that Israel's world view and way of living demand in life, at large. Submit, accept, conciliate, stay cool in emotion as much as in attitude, inside and outside—and the Messiah will come.

Why sages counseled a different kind of courage we need hardly ask. Given the situation of Israel, vanquished on the battlefield, broken in the turning of history's wheel, we need hardly wonder why wise men advised conciliation and acceptance. Exalting humility made sense, there being little choice. Whether or not these virtues found advocates in other contexts for other reasons, in the circumstance of the vanquished nation, for the people of broken heart, the policy of forbearance proved instrumental, entirely appropriate to both the politics and social condition at hand. If Israel had produced a battlefield hero, the nation could not give him an army. If Jewry cultivated the strong-minded individual, it sentenced such a person to a useless life of ineffective protest. The nation required not strong-minded leadership but consensus. But in the context of their own scripture and oral Torah, these same sages had to confront the received, and in context commonplace, definition of masculinity and of femininity. In the explicit terms of *Song of Songs Rabbah*, they viewed Israel in the status of a woman and at the same time they had to formulate for themselves an ample rationale for that status.

The problem derived from politics, but given the world as they saw it, we cannot find surprising their translation of the dilemma into theological categories, on the one side, and a revision and reversal of gender—definitions, on the other. The nations have wealth; Israel is richer, being satisfied with what it has. The nations have strong armies; Israel is stronger, valuing the capacity to conciliate the other. Not only so, but Israel with joy could accept its weakness, knowing that to God it was now a woman, but to man, in due course, it would be a mighty man indeed. Vanquished Israel, therefore, would nurture not merely policies of subordination and acceptance of diminished status among nations. Israel also would develop, in its own heart, the requisite emotional structure. The composition of individuals' hearts would then comprise the counterpart virtues. A policy of acceptance of the rule of others dictated affections of conciliation to the will of others. A defeated people meant to endure defeat would have to get along by going along. How to persuade each Jew to accept what all Jews had to do to endure? Persuade the heart, not only the mind. Then, each one privately would feel what everyone publicly had in any case to think.

This accounts for the persistence of sages' wise teachings on temper, their sagacious counsel on conciliating others and seeking the approval of the group. Society, in the canonical writings, set the style for the self's deepest sentiments. So the approved feelings retained approval for so long because emotions, in the thought of the sages of the canon at hand, followed rules. Feelings laid down judgments. Affections therefore constituted not mindless effusions but deliberate constructions. Whether or not the facts then conformed to the sages' view (or now with the mind of psychology, philosophy, and anthropology) we do not know. But the sages' view did penetrate deeply into what had to be. And that is so, whether or not what had to be ever would correspond with what was.

The human condition of Israel defined a different heroism, one filled with patience, humiliation, self-abnegation: the heroism of the woman. To turn survival into endurance, pariah-status into an exercise in Godly living, the sages' affective program served full well. Israel's hero saw power in submission, wealth in the gift to be grateful, wisdom in the confession of ignorance. Like the cross, ultimate degradation was made to stand for ultimate power. As Jesus on the cross, so Israel in exile served God through suffering. True, the cross would represent a scandal to the nations and foolishness to some Jews. But Israel's own version of the doctrine at hand endured and defined the nation's singular and astonishing resilience.

If, then, as a matter of public policy, the nurture of the personality of Israelite as a person of forbearance and self-abnegation proved right, within the community, too, the rabbis were not wrong. The Jewish people rarely enjoyed instruments of civil coercion capable of preserving social order and coherence. Governments at best afforded Jews limited rights over their own affairs. When, at the start of the fifth century, the Christian Roman government ended the existence of the patriarchate of the Jews of the Land of Israel, people can well have recognized the parlous condition of whatever Jewish authorities might ever run things. A government in charge of itself and its subjects, a territorial community able routinely to force individuals to pay taxes and otherwise conform where necessary—these political facts of normality rarely marked the condition of Israel between 429 and 1948. What was left was another kind of power, civil obedience generated by force from within. The stress on pleasing others and conforming to the will of the group, so characteristic of sayings of sages, the emphasis that God likes people whom people like—these substitute for the civil power of political coercion imparted to the community of Israel a different power of authority.

Both sources of power, the one in relationship to the public world beyond, the other in respect to the social world within, in the sages' rules gained force through the primal energy of emotion. Enough has been said to require little explication of that fact. A system that made humility a mark of strength and a mode of gaining God's approval, a social policy that imputed ultimate virtue to feelings of conciliation, restraint, and conformity to social norms had no need of the armies and police it did not have. The heart would serve as the best defense, inner affections as the police who are always there when needed. The remarkable inner discipline of Israel through its exacting condition in history from the beginnings of the sages' system to today began in those feelings that laid down judgments, that construction of affections, coherent with beliefs and behavior, that met the match of misery with grandeur of soul. So the vanquished nation every day would overcome the one-time victors. Israel's victory would come through the triumph of the broken heart, now mended with the remedy of moderated emotion. That union of private feeling and public policy imparted to the Judaic system of the dual Torah its power, its status of self-evidence, for the long centuries during which Israel's condition persisted in the definition imparted by the events of the third crisis in the formation of Judaism.

In the view of the sages of the dual Torah, attitudes or virtues of the heart, e.g., emotions, fit together with the encompassing patterns of society and culture, theology and the religious life. The affective rules formed an integral part of the way of life and world view put forward to make sense of the existence of the social group. This simple fact accounts for the long-term world-creating power of Judaism in Israel, the Jewish people. How Jews were supposed to feel in ethos matched what they were expected to think. In this way, the individual linked the deepest personal emotions to the cosmic fate and transcendent faith of that social group of which he or she formed a part. Emotions laid down judgments. They derived from rational cognition. The individual Israelite's innermost feelings, the microcosm, correspond to the public and historic condition of Israel, the macrocosm.

Androgyneity found its counterpart in the union of the individual and the community. What the dual Torah taught the private person to feel linked the individual's heart to what Judaism stated about the condition of Israel in history and of God in the cosmos. All formed one reality, in supernatural world and nature, in time and in eternity wholly consubstantial (so to speak). In the innermost chambers of deepest feelings, the Israelite therefore lived out the public history and destiny of the people, Israel. The emotions encouraged by Judaism in its formative age, such as humility, forbearance, accommodation, a spirit of conciliation, exactly correspond to the political and social requirements of the Jews' condition in that time.

How are the masculine and feminine reconciled and made one? The answer is simple and now predictable. Through the feminization of Israel in virtue, attitude, and emotion, Israel will attain that *zekhut t*o which God will respond by the sending of the Messiah. Keeping the commandments as a mark of submission, loyalty, and humility before God is the rabbinic system of salvation. So Israel does not "save itself." Israel never controls its own destiny, either on earth or in heaven. The only choice is whether to cast one's fate into the hands of cruel, deceitful men, or to trust in the living God of mercy and love. The stress that Israel's arrogance alienates God, Israel's humility and submission win God's favor, cannot surprise us; this is the very point of the doctrine of emotions that defines rabbinic Judaism's ethics.

Masculine emotions—arrogance, impatience—produce disaster; feminine ones, redemption. This is spelled out in so many words. The failed messiah of the second century, Bar Kokhba, above all, exemplifies arrogance against God. He lost the war because of that arrogance. His emotions, attitudes, sentiments, and feelings form the model of how the virtuous Israelite is not to conceive of matters. In particular, he ignored the authority of sages:

[X J] Said R. Yohanan, "Upon orders of Caesar Hadrian, they killed eight hundred thousand in Betar."

[K] Said R. Yohanan, "There were eighty thousand pairs of trumpeters surrounding Betar. Each one was in charge of a number of troops. Ben Kozeba was there and he had two hundred thousand troops who, as a sign of loyalty, had cut off their little fingers.

[L] "Sages sent word to him, 'How long are you going to turn Israel into a maimed people.'

[M] "He said to them, 'How otherwise is it possible to test them?'

[N] "They replied to him, 'Whoever cannot uproot a cedar of Lebanon while riding on his horse will not be inscribed on your military rolls.'

[O] "So there were two hundred thousand who qualified in one way, and another two hundred thousand who qualified in another way."

[P] When he would go forth to battle, he would say, "Lord of the world! Do not help and do not hinder us! 'Hast thou not rejected us, O God? Thou dost not go forth, O God, with our armies' " [Ps 60:10].

[Q] Three and a half years did Hadrian besiege Betar.

[R] R. Eleazar of Modiin would sit on sackcloth and ashes and pray every day, saying "Lord of the ages! Do not judge in accord with strict judgment this day! Do not judge in accord with strict judgment this day!"

[S] Hadrian wanted to go to him. A Samaritan said to him, "Do not go to him until I see what he is doing, and so hand over the city [of Betar] to you. [Make peace . . . for you.]"

[T] He got into the city through a drain pipe. He went and found R. Eleazar of Modiin standing and praying. He pretended to whisper something in his ear.

[U] the townspeople say [the Samaritan] do this and brought him to Ben Kozeba. They told him, "We saw this man having dealings with your friend."

[V] [Bar Kokhba] said to him, "What did you say to him, and what did he say to you?"

[W] He said to [the Samaritan], "If I tell you, then the king will kill me, and if I do not tell you, then you will kill me. It is better that the king kill me, and not you.

[X] "[Eleazar] said to me, 'I should hand over my city.' ['I shall make peace. . . .']"

[Y] He turned to R. Eleazar of Modiin. He said to him, "What did this Samaritan say to you?"

[Z] He replied, "Nothing."

[AA] He said to him, "What did you say to him?"

[BB] He said to him, "Nothing."

[CC] [Ben Kozeba] gave [Eleazar] one good kick and killed him.

[DD] Forthwith an echo came forth and proclaimed the following verse:

[EE] "Woe to my worthless shepherd, who deserts the flock! May the sword smite his arm and his right eye! Let his arm be wholly withered, his right eye utterly blinded! [Zech 11:17].

[FF] "You have murdered R. Eleazar of Modiin, the right arm of all Israel, and their right eye. Therefore may the right arm of that man wither, may his right eye be utterly blinded!"

[GG] Forthwith Betar was taken, and Ben Kozeba was killed.

y. Ta'anit 4:5

That kick—an act of temper, a demonstration of untamed emotions—tells the whole story. We notice two complementary themes. First, Bar Kokhba treats heaven with arrogance, asking God merely to keep out of the way. Second, he treats an especially revered sage with a parallel arrogance. The sage had the power to preserve Israel. Bar Kokhba destroyed Israel's one protection. The result was inevitable. The Messiah, the centerpiece of salvation history and hero of the tale, emerged as a critical figure. The historical theory of this passage is stated very simply. In their view, Israel had to choose between wars, either the war fought by Bar Kokhba or the "war for Torah." "Why had they been punished? It was because of the weight of the war, for they had not wanted to engage in the struggles over the meaning of the Torah" (*y. Ta'an.* 3:9 XVI.I). Those struggles, which were ritual arguments about ritual matters, promised the only victory worth winning. Then Israel's history would be written in terms of wars over the meaning of the Torah and the decision of the law.

The discredited messiah figure (whether Bar Kokhba actually was represented as such in his own day need not detain us) finds no apologists in the later rabbinical canon. What is striking in what follows, moreover, is that we really have two stories. At **G** Aqiba is said to have believed that Bar Kokhba was a disappointment. At **H–I**, he is said to have identified Bar Kokhba with the King-Messiah. Both cannot be true, so what we have is simply two separate opinions of Aqiba's judgment of Bar Kokhba/Bar Kozebah.

[X] [G] R. Simeon b. Yohai taught, "Aqiba, my master, would interpret the following verse: 'A star (*kokhab*) shall come forth out of Jacob' [Num 24:17] 'A disappointment (*Kozeba*) shall come forth out of Jacob.' "

[H] R. Aqiba, when he saw Bar Kozeba, said, "This is the King Messiah."

[I] R. Yohanan ben Toreta said to him, "Aqiba! Grass will grow on your cheeks before the Messiah will come!"

y. Ta'anit 4:5

The important point is not only that Aqiba had been proved wrong. It is that the very verse of Scripture adduced in behalf of his viewpoint could be treated more generally and made to refer to righteous people in general, not to the Messiah in particular. This leads us to the issue of the age, as sages' had to face it: what makes a messiah a false messiah? The answer, we recall, is arrogance.

The Talmud of Babylonia, at the end, carried forward the innovations we have seen in the Talmud of the Land of Israel. In the view expressed here, the principal result of Israel's loyal adherence to the Torah and its religious duties will be Israel's humble acceptance of God's rule. The humility, under all conditions, makes God love Israel.

> "It was not because you were greater than any people that the Lord set his love upon you and chose you" [Deut 7:7]. The Holy One, blessed be he, said to Israel, "I love you because even when I bestow greatness upon you, you humble yourselves before me. I bestowed greatness upon Abraham, yet he said to me, 'I am but dust and ashes' [Gen 18:27]; upon Moses and Aaron, yet they said, 'But I am a worm and no man' [Ps 22:7]. But with the heathens it is not so. I bestowed greatness upon Nimrod, and he said, 'Come, let us build us a city' [Gen. 11:4]; upon Pharaoh, and he said, 'Who are they among all the gods of the counties?' [2 Kgs 18:35]; upon Nebuchadnezzar, and he said, 'I will ascend above the heights of the clouds' [Isa 14:14]; upon Hiram, king of Tyre, and he said, 'I sit in the seat of God, in the heart of the seas' [Ezek 28:2]."
>
> *b. Hullin* **89a**

The heart of the matter then is Israel's subservience to God's will, as expressed in the Torah and embodied in the teachings and lives of the great sages. When Israel fully accepts God's rule, then the Messiah will come. Until Israel subjects itself to God's rule, the Jews will be subjugated to pagan domination. Since the condition of Israel governs, Israel itself holds the key to its own redemption. But this it can achieve only by throwing away the key! The feminization of Israel forms the condition of its redemption.

What we have in the doctrine of virtue, inclusive of emotions, is a very concrete way of formulating the relationship that yields *zekhut:* negotiation, conciliation, not dominance, not assertiveness. The paradox must be crystal clear: Israel acts to redeem itself through the opposite of self-determination, namely, by subjugating itself to God. Israel's power lies in its negation of power. Its destiny lies in giving up all pretense at deciding its own destiny. So weakness is the ultimate strength, forbearance the final act of self-assertion, passive resignation the sure step toward liberation. Israel's freedom is engraved on the tablets of the commandments of God: to be free is freely to obey. This is not the meaning associated with these words in the minds of others who, like the sages of the rabbinical canon, declared their view of what Israel must do to secure the coming of the Messiah. The passage, praising Israel for its humility, completes the circle begun with the description of Bar Kokhba as arrogant and boastful. Gentile kings are boastful; Israelite kings are humble.

Then what is Israel to do to hasten the coming of the Messiah, and how is Israel to contribute at all to its own redemption? The following story answers the question: Israel is to *do* nothing. Israel is to *be* obedient. The difference between doing and being matches the difference between the masculine and the feminine in *Song of Songs Rabbah*.

X.   J. "The oracle concerning Dumah. One is calling to me from Seir, 'Watchman, what of the night? Watchman, what of the night?' (Isa 21:11)."

K. The Israelites said to Isaiah, "O our Rabbi, Isaiah, What will come for us out of this night?"

L. He said to them, "Wait for me, until I can present the question."

M. Once he had asked the question, he came back to them.

N. They said to him, "Watchman, what of the night? What did the Guardian of the ages tell you?"

O. He said to them, "The watchman says 'Morning comes; and also the night. If you will inquire, inquire; come back again' (Isa 21:12)."

P. They said to him, "Also the night?"

Q. He said to them, "It is not what you are thinking. But there will be morning for the righteous, and night for the wicked, morning for Israel, and night for idolaters."

R. They said to him, "When?"

S. He said to them, "Whenever you want, He too wants [it to be]—if you want it, he wants it."

T. They said to him, "What is standing in the way?"

U. He said to them, "Repentance: 'Come back again' (Isa 21:12)."

V. R. Aha in the name of R. Tanhum b. R. Hiyya, "If Israel repents for one day, forthwith the son of David will come.

W. "What is the scriptural basis? 'O that today you would hearken to his voice!' (Ps 95:7)."

X. Said R. Levi, "If Israel would keep a single Sabbath in the proper way, forthwith the son of David will come.

Y. "What is the scriptural basis for this view? 'Moses said, Eat it today, for today is a Sabbath to the Lord; today you will not find it in the field' (Exod 16:25).

Z. "And it says, 'For thus said the Lord God, the Holy One of Israel, "In returning and rest you shall be saved; in quietness and in trust shall be your strength." And you would not' (Isa 30:15)."

y. Ta'anit 1:1

A discussion of the power of repentance would hardly have surprised a Mishnah sage. What is new is at **V–Z**, the explicit linkage of keeping the law which achieving the end of time and the coming of the Messiah. That motif stands separate from the notions of righteousness and repentance, which surely did not require it. We must not lose sight of the importance of this passage, with its emphasis on repentance, on the one side, and the power of Israel to reform itself, on the other. The Messiah will come any day that Israel makes it possible. Let me underline the most important statement of this large conception: *If all Israel will keep a single Sabbath in the proper (rabbinic) way, the Messiah will come. If all Israel will repent for one day, the Messiah will come. "Whenever you want. . . ," the Messiah will come.*

Now, two things are happening here. First, the system of religious observance, including study of Torah, is explicitly invoked as having salvific power. Second, the persistent hope of the people for the coming of the Messiah is linked to the system of rabbinic observance and belief. In this way, the austere program of the Mishnah develops in a different direction, with no trace of a promise that the Messiah will come if and when the system is fully realized. Here a teleology lacking all eschatological dimension gives way to an explicitly messianic statement that the purpose of the law is to attain Israel's salvation: "If you want it, God wants it too." The one thing Israel commands is its own heart; the power it yet exercises is the power to repent. These suffice.

Reconciliation with a circumstance of weakness bears within itself enormous strength; power lies in turning the enemy into a friend; power lies in overcoming one's own natural impulses. But then, the entire history of humanity will respond to Israel's will, to what happens in Israel's heart and soul. With the Temple in ruins, repentance can take place only within the heart and mind. Self-abnegation, forbearance, and the other feminine virtues turn out to define the condition for the redemption of Israel. Israel can free itself of control by other nations only by humbly agreeing to accept God's rule. The nations—Rome, in the present instance—rest on one side of the balance, while God rests on the other. Israel must then choose between them. There is no such thing for

Israel as freedom from both God and the nations, total autonomy and independence. There is only a choice of masters, a ruler on earth or a ruler in heaven.

Judaism taught an enduring doctrine of the virtues of the heart that did more than make Israel's situation acceptable. That same doctrine so shaped the inner life of Israel as to define virtue in the very terms imposed by politics. Israel within recreated, in age succeeding age, that exact condition of acceptance of humility and accommodation that the people's political circumstance imposed from without. So the enduring doctrine of virtue not only made it possible for Israel to accept its condition. It recreated in the psychological structure of Israel's inner life that same condition, so bringing into exact correspondence political facts and psychological fantasies.

Clearly, by "androgynous Judaism," we can mean only the feminization of an originally masculine system, the legal system put forth in the Mishnah. It was the feminization of rabbinic Judaism that accounts for its success: that is, its holding in the balance deeply masculine and profoundly feminine traits, while affirming the feminine ones as dominant for the here and now. Persuading Jews to remain "Israel" in its definition thereof, this serially-androgynous Judaism triumphed in Christendom and Islam because of its power to bring into union both heart and mind, inner life and outer circumstance, psychology and politics. The Judaism of the dual Torah not only matched the situation of Israel the conquered, but (ordinarily) tolerated people. That Judaism created, within the psychological heritage of Israel, that same condition, that is to say, the condition of acceptance of a subordinated, but tolerated position, while awaiting the superior one.

This Judaic system explicitly held that humility and forbearance were feminine virtues and at the same time articulately declared its social entity, its "Israel," to be feminine in relationship to God. This Israel dominated among the Jews, so that from late antiquity to our own day, the feminine virtues were normative; even in the academies, or especially there, robustness gave way to refinement, gentile masculinity to Israelite masculinity. So let us not at the end lose sight of the remarkable power of this religion of humility, for, after all, it is a religion that endures not in long-ago books of a far-away time and place, but in the lives of nearly everybody who today practices a Judaism. It is a religion of mind and heart, but also family and community, one that asks entire devotion to

God, not only the parts of life God can command, the life of the people together in community, but especially the secret places of existence not subject to God's will but only one's own. For the whole of their history from the formation of this Judaism to the present moment, wherever they lived, whatever their circumstances, the people, Israel, drew nourishment from these ideas and found in this system the power to endure.

Now the world did not make life easy, affording to the faith of Israel no honor, and to the Israelite no respect by reason of loyalty to that vocation. But both Islam and Christianity through conversion, which is to say, apostasy, offered Israel easy access to an honored place. At the sacrifice of home and property, even at the price of life itself, Israel resisted them and reaffirmed its eternal calling. For whatever the choice of private persons, that social order formed by Israel endured, against it all, despite it all, through all time and change. And, in the lifetime of many who read these very pages, even beyond the gates of hell, the surviving remnants determined to be Israel. They chose once more to form, in a precise sense to embody, the social order of that one whole Torah that God taught to Our Rabbi, Moses, at Sinai, that publicly-revealed Torah that rests on the private, personal, and—as the documents themselves portray it—the profoundly, deeply feminine and intimate virtue of *zekhut.*

Whether in Poland or Algeria, whether in Morocco or Iraq and Iran, whether in the land called the Land of Israel or in distant corners of the exile, north, south, west or east, Israel kept the faith, abided by the covenant, lived in stout hope and perfect trust in God. This fact defines the power of this Judaism, this dual Torah. The act of defiance of fate in the certainty of faith in God's ultimate act of grace is the one thing God cannot have commanded at Sinai. God can have said, and did say, "Serve me," but God could only beseech, "And trust me too." For even God cannot coerce trust. Only Israel could give what God could only ask, but not compel: the gifts of the heart, love and trust, for which the loving God yearns, which only the much-loved Israel can yield freely, of its own volition. And that is what Israel, in response to Sinai, willingly gave, and by its loyal persistence in its life as Israel, whether in the Land or in the patient exile, freely gives today.

In successfully joining psychology and politics, inner attitudes and public policy, the sages discovered the source of power that would sustain their system. The reason that Judaism enjoyed the standing of self-evident truth for so long as it did, in both Islam and Christendom, derives not from the cogency of its doctrines, but principally from the fusion of heart and mind, emotion and intellect, attitude and doctrine— and the joining of the whole in the fundamental and enduring politics of the nation, wherever it located itself. In my view, what accounts for the amazing power of this Judaism to sustain its Israel is its androgyneity: the perfect union of the masculine and the feminine, the holding of the two in balance—above all, the insistence that the community as a whole adopt the virtues it deemed feminine.

For quite practical reasons, public policy concerning matters of gender and emotion obviously conformed to necessity. In Christendom and Islam, Israel could survive—but only on the sufferance of others. But those others ordinarily accorded to Israel the right of survival. Judaism endured in Christendom because the later fourth century legislators distinguished Judaism from paganism. Judaism lasted in Islam because the Muslim law accorded to Judaism tolerated status. Israel therefore would nurture not merely policies of subordination and acceptance of diminished status among nations. Israel also would develop, in its own heart, the requisite emotional structure. The composition of individuals' hearts would then comprise the counterpart virtues. A policy of acceptance of the rule of others dictated affections of conciliation to the will of others. A defeated people meant to endure defeat would have to get along by going along. But there is more to it than that.

What sages accomplished in formulating an androgynous system was to conciliate two distinct constituencies to a single policy concerning gender relationships. On the one side, women had not only to accept but to affirm and embody for the coming generations the legal position of subordination that the law prescribed for them. On the other, men had to find virtue in the political status of inferiority that history accorded to them as their lot. The solution to these distinct problems lay in the explicit androgyneity we have considered. Men must feel like women, women must act like (true, authentic, Israelite) men. But they can act like men, because the authentic Israelite man exhibits virtues that, for women, come quite naturally. What was asked of the women was no more than the men themselves accepted at the hand of the nations. What was demanded of the men was no more than the relationship that their wives endured with them, which was identical to that relationship Israel affirmed with God. The circle then is closed: God is to Israel as the nations are to Israel as man is to woman—for now. But, of course, as we have seen, that is only now; then matters will right themselves. By its femininity now, Israel will regain its masculinity.

Why did the system succeed so remarkably as it did? It was because the patriarchal gender doctrine of androgyneity, the dual Torah's unique formulation of *halakhah* and *aggadah*, succeeded to persuade each Jew to accept what all Jews had to do to endure. Necessity defined virtue. Persuade the heart, not only the mind. Then each one privately would feel what everyone publicly had in any case to think. This accounts not for the mere persistence of sages' wise teachings but for their mythopoeic power. Sages' views on temper, their sagacious counsel on conciliating others and seeking the approval of the group—these not only made life tolerable, they in fact defined what life would mean for Israel. Society, in the canonical writings, set the style for the self's deepest sentiments. So the approved feelings retained approval for so long because emotions, in the thought of the sages of the canon at hand, followed rules. Feelings laid down judgments. Affections therefore constituted not mindless effusions but deliberate constructions. Whether or not the facts then conformed to the sages' view we do not know. But the sages' view did penetrate deeply into what had to be. And that is so, whether or not what had to be ever would correspond with what was.

In the Mishnah, when women marry, they go into exile, leaving their father's house and going to their husband's, thereby leaving their own family and joining some other. This is why the *halakhah* has to guarantee the woman's right to return home at specified intervals and to maintain her relationships with her own home(land). This is what happened to Israel, too. Life in "exile," viewed as living in other peoples' countries and not in their own land, meant life as a woman, not as a man. This meant for Israel, as Judaism conceived Israel, a long span of endurance, a test of patience to end only with the end of time. This required Israel to live in accord with the will of others. Under such circumstances, the virtues of the independent citizen, sharing command of affairs of state, the gifts of innovation, initiative, independence of mind, proved beside the point. From the end of the Second Revolt against Rome in 135 C.E., to the creation of the State of Israel in 1948, Israel, the Jewish people, faced a different task. The human condition of Israel therefore defined a different heroism, one filled with patience, humiliation, self-abnegation. Israel's heroes would exhibit the feminine virtues.

Index to Biblical, Rabbinical, and Extracanonical Jewish Literature

DEAD SEA SCROLLS

Zadokite Document

Temple Scroll

General Index